U1068648

OPTIONS FOR REFORMINGS SHANDONG'S FISCAL SYSTEM

Roy Bahl   Chor-Ching Goh and Baoyun Qiao

Chinese Translation by Lezheng Liu

China Financial & Economic Publishing House

CONTENTS

ACKNOWLEDGEMENT

The idea of doing this book came after we did a background paper for the World Bank which became part of the Bank' s preparatory work for a larger Fiscal Policy Analysis Program and lending operations in China. We started the work in early 2015 as Shandong has been debating options to modernize its fiscal system. We would like to give our special thanks to Yu Guoan Head of the Shandong Finance Bureau and Wang Jin, Deputy Director General of the Shandong Finance Bureau for dedicating their knowledgeable and diligent staffs to work with us. This book benefited from many discussions with officials from the Local Tax Bureau, Reform and Development Commission, Health and Family Planning Bureau, Education bureau, Human Resource and Social Security Bureau and National Taxation Office.

We also learnt a great deal from the latest work of Shandong Research Institute of Fiscal Science, led by Director Cui Zongtao. Lastly, our field visits to Jinan's Shanghe county and Shizhong District informed the work. All these valuable contributions were made possible by the hospitality and dedication of the Shandong Finance Bureau staffs.

We finalized this book with valuable contributions from a Roundtable Forum with high level officials on June 6, 2015. Our Shandong partners traveled to Beijing to join us for a half-day discussion of the book's findings with other agencies and provincial governments. Insightful suggestions by the following officials are gratefully acknowledged.

- Yang, Yuanwei, Director General, Revenue Planning Department, State Administration of Taxation

- Wang, Daoshu, Director General, Tax Management Department, State Administration of Taxation
- Hu, Hebo, Director General, Budget Division, Hunan Finance Bureau
- Liang, Changxin, Director General of Legal and Institutional Reform Department, National Energy Administration
- Wang, Chaocai, Deputy Director General, Fiscal Research Department, Ministry of Finance
- Yang, Yuangen, Director, Internal Affairs and Administration, Ministry of Finance
- Huang, Ran, Deputy Mayor of Tongling in Anhui Province
- Li, Chenglin, Deputy Director of Finance Department, Ministry of Commerce

We would also like to thank the helpful comments from the following participants at the Roundtable Forum: Dean Yang Yunjie, Professor Sun Dianming, Professor Zheng Xinye, Deputy Dean Liu Lezheng, Ma Nianyi (Nanning State Taxation Bureau), Zhang Hongzhan (Shenyang State Taxation Bureau), Wang Yongchao (Nanning Transportation Bureau), Hu, Yungui (Hunan Finance Bureau), Ma, Hao (Hunan Finance Bureau), Cong Peide (Shandong Finance Bureau), Zhao, Hui (Shandong Finance Bureau) and Liang, Hongbo (Shandong Finance Bureau).

Finally, there were theose who did a wonderful job in helping us bring this manuscript to a final form. Li Zhao of China Financial and Economic Publishing House provided professional guidance and made the publication possible. Wenrui Li provided able research assistance.

AUTHORS

Roy Bahl is Regents Professor of Economics, emeritus at the Andrew Young School of Policy Studies at Georgia State University in Atlanta Georgia, USA. He has advised countries on public finances all over the world. He is the author of numerous books and scholarly papers.

Chor-Ching Goh is the lead economist for China, Mongolia, and South Korea at the World Bank. Before moving to Beijing, she was the lead economist for Ethiopia, Sudan and South Sudan. Prior to joining the Africa region, she was the senior economist for Russia, and also worked on the former Soviet Republics, and new European Union member states. Chor-Ching was the deputy director of the *2009 World Development Report* on Economic Geography. Between 2000 and 2007, as an economist in the East Asia and Pacific Regional Office, she worked on poverty, equity, and labor market issues in the region, leading policy reports and dialogue in Cambodia, Mongolia and the Philippines. She graduated from Yale University, *summa cum laude*, with simultaneous BA and MA degrees, and from Harvard University, a Ph. D. in Economics.

Baoyun Qiao, Professor of Economics and Dean, China Academy of Public Finance and Policy, Central University of Finance and Economics. He published numerous books and scholarly papers. He has advised many countries on public finance, local governance, and economic development. Baoyun graduated from Georgia State University, U. S., where he earned his Ph. D. in economics.

The translator, **Lezheng Liu,** is Assistant Professor of Economics, China Academy of Public Finance and Policy, Central University of Finance and Economics. He published several books on public finance and taxation in China, and worked with the SAT and MoF in several research projects. Lezheng earned his Ph. D. in economics at Western Michigan University, U. S.

PREFACE

The National Peoples' Congress has called on regional governments to adopt more modern and efficient financial and debt management practices, to pull back on direct subsidies and tax preferences for the competitive sector, and to rethink their intergovernmental fiscal systems. In 2014, the State Council issued regulations to lead this reform effort. The remaining subjects on the Congress agenda—provincial and local government taxation and expenditure assignments—will come later.

Shandong province has moved forward with a reform program. It follows the State Council regulations but adapts these to its own setting. In doing this it tailors the reform to address the flaws in its financial management and tax administration practices. In addition, it offers some other policy and management proposals that respond to the State Council's call to build equity into the intergovernmental system and to "create new ways of using fiscal funding to support industry development". The Shandong Proposal could grow into a kind of model for other provinces.

In this book the Shandong proposal is studied and analyzed to add information about the potential role of provincial and local governments in implementing new reforms, and to understand how regional governments might respond to some of the more far-reaching fiscal reforms that have been suggested by the Congress.

Shandong's Population and Economic Base

With a population of nearly 100 million, Shandong is China's second largest province. The urbanization rate in Shandong doubled between 2000 and 2013 to its present level of 54 percent. This has placed significant pressure on the budgets that support urban public services and urban infrastructure needs. Other changes in the structure of the population will pose important changes for the budgets, particularly the changing age distribution which implies a shrinking labor force and more spending for pensions and health care, and the need to address environmental concerns.

Shandong accounts for 9 percent of national output. In terms of per capita GDP, it ranks 10th highest in China. The average income in urban areas is about 34 percent higher than that in counties. The level of per capita income in the counties ranges widely, with most clustered at less than 30 thousand RMB, but with 12 counties having incomes above the urban district average. This inequality in the average well-being of residents, and by implication in the average taxable capacity of local governments, suggests the need for a program of fiscal equalization.

The governance and service delivery system is decentralized in that the 140 counties and 17 prefecture levels dominate. In fact, the Provincial Government accounts for only about 10 percent of government expenditures, the lowest share in any province in China. Counties, seen by many as the bedrock of local government in China, make 66 percent of public expenditures and this is one of the highest proportions in China.

Tax and nontax revenues in the public finance budget account for 8.46 percent of GDP by comparison with 11.92 percent in the rest of China. Relative to GDP, the emphasis on land lease revenues, and on debt is also less in Shandong than in other provinces.

Government services in Shandong are financed about 80 percent from shared taxes and local government collected taxes, and 20 percent from central grants. Almost all revenues are collected at the county and prefecture level. The province and prefectures share in this revenue and decide on how much will be transferred into the budgets of deficit counties (districts). The transfers are worked out by a combination of an expert judgement approach, a formula approach, and some negotiation.

Problems and Concerns

Though the consolidated financial position of Shandong province would appear to be in balance, there are problems and concerns that suggest some vulnerability.

(1) The rate of provincial and local government expenditures in Shandong is low. Shandong ranks 10th in China in terms of per capita GDP, but in terms of per capita public finance budget expenditures, it ranks 28th. The reasons for this are a low tax effort, and a relatively low level of grants received from the central government.

(2) The average amount spent per person for public services is about nine times greater in the highest spending county than in the lowest. The gap between the highest and lowest spending prefectures also is about nine to one. The public policy question to raise is whether these disparities in per capita expenditures are too large to be acceptable.

(3) The infrastructure needs generated by urbanization in Shandong, together with an aging population will put pressure on the budget to finance infrastructure and current services.

(4) With land lease revenues falling, it is not clear how infrastructure will be financed. Shandong's debt level is low enough to provide space for borrowing, but it is not clear how the loans would be repaid.

(5) There is a direct relationship between government and the competitive sector. A significant amount of enterprises are still owned (or belong) to governments at different levels, and there is still a variety of channels through which governments can directly or indirectly encroach into private sector activities through their SOEs. In addition,

tax preferences and tax rebates to certain businesses may be imposing a significant cost on the budget and interfering with market decisions.

(6) Perverse incentives are built into the system. These include some disincentive for revenue mobilization, a disincentive to invest in public services vs. economic development, an incentive to overuse land leases, and decentralization itself can cause efficiency losses if counties are assigned responsibility for functions that are characterized by spillover effects and/or economies of scale.

(7) The allocation of public resourcesis less rule-based than it could be, and this complicates the system. Three issues illustrate the nature of the complication. First, revenues and expenditures for each provincial-local government are reported in four separate budgets. Three of the four contain current and capital expenditures, and there are transfers among these accounts at each level of government, and also between levels of government. Second, complication comes from intergovernmental transfers among the province-prefecture-county/district levels being partly negotiated and partly based on expert judgement, and because of conditionality in the transfer system. Third the past practice of using land leases to secure loans for infrastructure investment has created confusion about the responsibilities of local governments for repayment.

The Shandong Proposal

The provincial government has done a good job with developing an implementation plan for the State Council regulations and objectives. One might think of the Proposal as having three legs. The first is modernizing the financial management system and putting in safeguards against inefficient spending practices, over borrowing, and corruption. The second is using the tax system to take an important step in the direction of separating the roles of the government and competitive sectors. The third is rationalizing the system of intergovernmental transfers to provide an appropriate degree of equalization. If implementation problems do not arise, the Shandong fiscal reform could improve the efficiency of government spending, increase revenue mobilization and fairness in taxation, and enhance equity and rule-based management in the intergovernmental fiscal system.

Financial management

The implementation of the budget law is a crucially important financial management proposal. By requiring full coverage of all fiscal activities of governments in the province, it eliminates the possibility of extrabudgetary spending or revenues. Moreover, it makes provision for more transparency by integrating the four budgets of subnational governments. It generally shifts the focus of the budget from a control document to a planning document, and introduces multi-year budgets. By eliminating earmarks, it increases the flexibility in expenditure planning.

The provisions of the new budget law are complemented by the expected completion of the treasury management system by 2017. This will enable better control of spending. Moreover, the new regulations will phase out most special funds and will eliminate the practice of creating new budget lines, and calls for the creation of a budget stabilization fund to smooth out short term deficits and surpluses.

The creation of a debt management framework will bring borrowing under control. All borrowing will be approved by the Provincial Government, and no borrowing will occur off-budget. The practice of using a financial platform will be eliminated and existing (illegal) debt will be "cleaned up".

The new approach will lead to freeing up some expenditures from low priority uses and redirecting these to the provision of essential services. If this happens, there will be an indirect "revenue effect".

But, as in the case of most proposals, there are questions. There is no call for a current and capital budget. The proposal to allow budget deficits and bailouts on a one year basis can be made effective and supported by a budget stabilization fund. But care must be taken to limit deficits to short term cash flow problems in order to avoid opening the door for a soft budget constraint. On the debt management reforms, it is not clear how new debt will be repaid by local governments. The county/district governments have no independent revenue sources (other than land leases). One possibility is that new debt will be serviced by intergovernmental transfers, but this would blur the line between a loan and a grant.

Finally, there is need for an implementation strategy, i. e. , for a careful sequencing plan to introduce these many changes. In particular, there is the difficult problem of putting these improvements in place in 140 counties that range from relatively sophisticated on financing matters to rural counties with a limited resource base and limited capacity.

Tax reform

The second set of reforms are focused on rationalizing the relationship between the public sector and the competitive sector. The Shandong proposal argues for developing a fully integrated taxpayer information system to assist in improving collection rates, lowering collection costs, and lowering compliance costs. More important, the practice of giving subsidies and tax preferences to enterprises will end unless these awards are approved by the State Council. The gains from this tax reform could be significant, though no estimates of revenue mobilization are given in the proposal document. However, Shandong's collection rate against GDP is a full 3 percentage points below the national average. This suggests a significant revenue potential from the removal of tax preferences.

There will be difficulties in implementing this program. Tax preferences can be well entrenched and hard to pull back, and they may have a constituency within the government. Moreover, reductions in what many see as effective economic development subsidies are especially hard to eliminate when the growth rate in the economy has slowed. In this regard, note the recent State Council regulation that seems to call for a less aggressive approach to eliminating tax preferences.

Intergovernmental fiscal relations

The three concerns in Shandong are: (a) the assignment of expenditure and administrative responsibilities may not be clear or may not be correct, (b) the distribution of revenues among the local governments may not be adequately equalizing, and (c) the framework for administering the intergovernmental transfer system is flawed. The proposal addresses all three of these issues in a way that follows good international practice. The proposed reforms in the intergovernmental transfer system are not yet developed in any detail.

First, the existing assignment of responsibility for all expenditure functions will be reviewed with the possibility that expenditure responsibilities among province, prefecture and county may change. The reform plan calls for drawing up these new assignments, and putting them into practice in 2015, on a trial basis, for education, health and transportation.

The second major issue to be dealt with is the large fiscal disparities among the local governments within the province. The specific revenue sharing plan is not yet worked out, but the reform proposal seems to be calling for a more rule-based approach to making the distribution among local governments.

Third, the proposal calls for changes in the structure of provincial-local grants toward a reduction in earmarked grants in favor of unconditional grants, and an end to matching provisions.

Recapturing The Lost Business Tax Revenues

An important question to be addressed in Shandong is filling the revenue gap that will come from elimination of the business tax as a revenue source. Part of this gap can be filled by the implementation of reforms in this proposal, namely, the reduction in tax preferences, and the cost savings and expenditure redirection that will come from more efficient financial management. No estimates of revenue impacts have been reported in the Shandong proposal. However, if tax preferences to enterprises are equivalent to as much as one percent of GDP, nearly half of lost business tax revenues could be recovered.

Some of this revenue loss could also be compensated by new revenue sources that must be defined by the central government. But for now, these must be thought of only as future possibilities.

The Way Forward

Shandong has made a good effort on its fiscal reform program. It lays out a plan that can significantly improve expenditure efficiency and revenue mobilization, while reducing waste and addressing some facets of corruption. It adopts good international practices, follows the State Council regulations very closely, and could become a model for other provinces to follow. But for the Proposal to achieve its potential as planning and guidance tool, it should be deepened in terms of providing hard evidence about what it intends to achieve, updated to track its progress against these targets, and lay out an implementation strategy and timetable. Also, If the proposal is to be used as a plan for upgrading the fiscal system, it should be revised on a regular basis. A "one-off" study will not have a long life in guiding public finances in Shandong. The present version of the proposal contains little by way of metrics. For example, there is no estimate of the amount of tax preferences that are now given, or of subsidy that is given to enterprises for economic development support, or of equalization that is achieved by the system of provincial-local transfers.

The major concern about the Shandong Proposal is whether it can be effectively implemented in a timely manner. Here there are important concerns. One is finding a way for some entrenched but counterproductive practices to be removed so that the reforms can be introduced. The separation of the private from the public sector will be no easy matter. The government has favored the competitive sector with subsidies and tax preferences of various kinds. It is not clear how easy it will be for subnational government officials to back away from these direct relations with the competitive sectors, or how long the transition to a separation of government and private sector activities will take.

The other, and an equally difficult area is upgrading the capability of local government staff. In one sense, the new budget law calls for far-reaching changes in how financial management is done. This suggests a considerable investment in training and supervision. Even without the complication of a new law, there is a knowledge gap of staff, especially in the more rural counties. To move forward with implementation, it will be important to establish a strategy for upgrading staff capabilities. This may turn out to be a major constraint to moving forward with the reforms.

CHAPTER ONE INTRODUCTION

China has outgrown its public finance system. The regime of taxes, public expenditures, central-local fiscal relations, and the approach to financial management, is no longer compatible with the government's expanded responsibilities to its citizens. And, the setting has also changed. China is now facing slower GDP growth, an aging population, major environmental concerns, and the problems associated with catching the infrastructure up to rapid urbanization.

The Peoples' Congress has recognized this problem and has emphasized the need for fiscal reform. The State Council has begun the process with new regulations and with discussion of longer run goals for changing the fiscal structure. The new budget law and the new regulations are a significant step in the direction of modernizing the Chinese tax system of financial management.

There are more public finance reforms to come in the areas of restructuring the revenue side of subnational government budgets, reassigning expenditure responsibilities, and reforming the system of intergovernmental transfers. These bigger reforms have been discussed in general terms but no concrete regulations have yet been laid down. It is likely, however, that the reform program will involve both institutional changes, and changes in the basic ideas about the role of the local state in China. The central theme could continue to be movement toward a fiscal system that more clearly separates the traditional functions of government (delivering quality public services in an equitable and efficient way) from the investment and production functions of the competitive sectors.

This kind of fiscal reform in China is going to take time. The issues are complicated and some of the offending institutional practices are well entrenched. The approach is more likely to be gradual than to be a big bang reform. New capacities will need to be built. Even the first step in reforming the public finances, the financial management reforms that are the central focus of this book, will not be implemented quickly. In principle, implementation of the State Council recommendations could begin immediately, but the slowing growth of the Chinese economy may delay the pace of these reforms.

Objectives of This Study

In recent years there has been important research and new thinking about the public finance question in China[1]. However, almost all of the work on reforming provincial finances and intergovernmental fiscal relations in China has taken a top down approach, i. e. , the questions asked are about the central government policy reforms and regulatory changes necessary to achieve the goals that the government has set (Bahl, Goh and Qiao, 2014; World Bank and DRC, 2014; Qiao and Liu, 2013). This is in keeping with the Chinese tradition of top-down reform of government financial structure and institutions (Bahl, 1999; Wong, Heady and Woo, 1995). Typically, the subnational governments implement central government reforms, and only rarely do they initiate a reform program.

Relatively little effort has been invested in a bottom-up approach, i. e. , in an investigation of the ways in which provincial and subprovincial governments might play a role in fiscal reform. But some provincial governments have begun to ask exactly this question, i. e. , how can they move forward with their own adaptations of centrally-led fiscal reform programs to improve expenditure efficiency and to mobilize additional revenues. The Shandong fiscal reform proposal, which is the focus of this

1 Lou, 2013; Li, Qiao and Liu, 2014; Wong, 2013; Chen and Zhang 2008.

analysis, is a case in point.

The goal here is to use the Shandong proposal to add information, first, about the role of provincial and local governments in implementing new reforms, and second, about how these governments might respond to some of the more far-reaching reforms that have been suggested by the Congress. We raise two general questions. The first is what provincial and local governments in China can do to improve their fiscal performance, even if no further changes in central legislation are enacted? The focus in this discussion will be on the three areas of fiscal autonomy that have been given to subnational governments under the present regime (a) financial management, (b) provincial-local revenue sharing and expenditure assignment, and (c) financing activity related to the government fund budget and the social security budget. The Shandong proposal is focused on the first two of these three areas, and in particular on adapting the State Council regulations to the economic and governance environment of the province.

The second question is more about revenue mobilization in Shandong. One issue is the extent to which the reforms in the present set of proposals can address the loss in business tax revenues that will soon come. There also is the question as to whether and how Shandong province can accommodate structural reforms in the national system of public finances, such as increased revenue autonomy and a revision of the revenue sharing regime. Both the Peoples' Congress and the Minister of Finance have discussed the possibilities for increases subnational government taxation. Though such changes do not appear to be in the immediate future for China, they continue to be prominently discussed. This analysis could be useful in two ways. It would allow a rechecking of the match between the policy direction being proposed and discussed by the central government, and the fiscal problems that now confront the provinces. And, it can help central planners continue their investigation of provincial and local policy and management, and institutional changes that are necessary to support the next round of central reforms.

Study Approach

Shandong Province makes a good case study for both of these questions. With respect to the first, it has developed a fiscal reform package that addresses budget management, and the financing of subprovincial governments. The results of this work are presented in *Research on the Establishment of Modern Fiscal System in Shandong*. This work follows the State Council regulations, but does so in a context of Shandong's particular governance and intergovernmental finance structure.

We do not speculate about the extent to which Shandong is "representative" of Chinese provinces. On the one hand, it does fall under the same fiscal rules as other provinces, follows many of the practices that have been adopted by other Chinese provinces and is undergoing the same aging and urbanization transformation as is much of China. In that sense, the findings and recommendations of the Shandong work might be transferrable to other provinces.

On the other hand, Shandong is relatively rich, has the second largest population of the provinces, is supported by a stronger industrial base than most provinces, and has made some choices about government finance that differ from those made by other provincial and local governments. In that sense, some of the strength and weakness of the Shandong program might not fit other provinces.

Before one could generalize from this case study, he/she will need to retrace this analysis in some other provinces that have different characteristics.

The remainder of this book has two parts. In the first part, we study the Shandong context: population, economy, governance, finance structure, fiscal performance, and the public finance issues and concerns. We then review and comment on the proposed reform package that the Shandong provincial leadership has put forward. The Shandong proposal follows the change in direction for the public finance system that was offered by the Third Plenary Session of the 18th Central Committee of the Communist Party. More specifically, it is an implementation strategy for the comprehensive reforms in financial management that are described in the new regulations of the State Council.

In the second part of this book, we consider how the central government might further liberalize the intergovernmental fiscal system. To date, this longer term central program for fiscal reform has taken three forms. Partly it is an identification and discussion of general policy directions to be taken, partly it is new regulations that have been approved and are now ready for implementation, and partly it is an ongoing discussion about the kind of new fiscal system that might emerge. China's intergovernmental fiscal reforms are a work in progress, but evaluation of the reform options in a single province are important and can help strengthen the proposals.

We start this second part of the study with a discussion of the revenue problem that will come with the elimination of the business tax. The remainder of this section, which addresses revenue mobilization, is illustrative , but the fiscal package considered is something like the greater liberalization of the intergovernmental fiscal reform that some have called for. Most of these reform options have been discussed by the Chinese Ministry of Finance, international agencies, and scholars. The package includes some combination of new local government taxing powers, and a restructured system of intergovernmental transfers. What we find, interestingly, is that some of these reforms would not map easily into the existing provincial-local government structure in Shandong and would require adjustments at the provincial level.

CHAPTER TWO SHANDONG PROVINCE

Shandong Province is in the early stage of implementing a significant fiscal reform. The instruments and changes proposed are consistent with present central government policies and regulations. It is important to understand how this reform program is shaped by the structure of the provincial population and economy, by the structure of governance and finance that is in place, and by the performance of the present fiscal system. We begin the discussion with this.

Population Characteristics and Economic Structure

With a population of nearly 100 million, Shandong is China's second largest province (Table 1). About 54 percent of the population now lives in urban areas, putting Shandong on a parallel with Jilin province (54 percent) and Hainan province (53 percent) in terms of the rate of urbanization. Shandong has experienced the same kind of rapid in-migration to urban areas as many other provinces in China. The urbanization rate in Shandong doubled between 2000 and 2013. To put this in perspective, the urban population in Shandong increased by about 24 million persons between 2000 and 2013. This has placed significant pressure on the budgets that support urban public services and urban infrastructure needs (Bahl. Goh and Qiao, 2014; and World Bank and Development research Center, 2013). It has also led to an emptying out of some parts of the rural population.

Other changes in the structure of the population will pose important changes for the budgets. One is the changing age distribution which implies more spending for pensions and health care, and a shrinking labor force. As maybe seen in Table 2, about 11 percent of the provincial population is over age 65 by comparison with a national average which is about one percent lower.

Shandong is an important contributor to the national economy, accounting for 9 percent of national output. Over the last 15 years, provincial GDP has grown at about the same rate as in the rest of the country. A generally accepted measure of the level of economic development is per capita GDP. By this measure, Shandong might be considered a relatively well-developed province, ranking 10th highest in China (Table 3). Per capita GDP, at 56,323RMB (9,091 USD) in 2013 is about 23 percent higher than the average in China which is 43,320 RMB. Another perspective is that the per capita GDP level in Shandong (in US $) is roughly equivalent to the East Asia Pacific country average (9,116 USD), Romania (9,490 USD) and Mauritius (9,477 USD).

As would be the case in all provinces, this income is not distributed equally within Shandong province. The average income in urban areas is about 34 percent higher than that in counties. Note from the frequency distribution presented in Figure 1 that the level of per capita income in the counties ranges widely, with most clustered at less than 30 thousand RMB, but with 12 counties having incomes above the urban district average. This inequality in the average well-being of residents, and by implication in the average taxable capacity, suggests that there will be an important problem of providing for an equalization of service levels between urban and rural areas and among the counties.

The economic base in Shandong is more heavily concentrated in the industrial sector than is the case in the rest of China, but at the expense of a much smaller share in the tertiary sector (Table 4). Shandong has maintained its comparative advantage in manufacturing, where productivity is usually higher than in the service sector (The World Bank and Development Research Center of China, 2013).

Governance

The three levels of governance in Shandong—the provincial government, 17 prefectures, and 140 county-level governments—are described in Figure 2. Note that of the 140 counties, 20 are directly under the control of the province, as part of a pilot project. The remainder are under the control of the 17 prefectures. Of special importance to the fiscal structure, as we discuss below, are the 48 urban counties (districts) in the prefecture-controlled group. These districts raise much of the revenues in the province and their residents enjoy a higher level of public services than do those in rural areas.

The governance and service delivery system appears to be decentralized in that the county and prefecture levels dominate. Provinces have little direct service delivery responsibility and act mostly as a regulator of local government finance, a distributor of transfers and a post office for earmarked grants from the central government. In fact, as we can see in Table 5, the Provincial Government accounts for only 10 percent of government expenditures, the lowest share in any province in China. Counties, seen by many as the bedrock of local government in China, make 66 percent of public expenditures in Shandong and this is one of the highest proportions in China.

Prefectures play a larger role than provinces in direct service delivery, particularly in the urban areas where they have responsibility for delivering some area-wide services such as bus services and water. Working under the leadership of the provincial government, prefectures are also responsible for designing the redistribution of revenues among designated "surplus" and "deficit" districts. As discussed below, the provincial government changed its approach to equalization in 2013, and this has become an important component of their restructuring.

From these data and observation about institutional arrangements, we might conclude that governance and government finance in Shandong is more decentralized than that in most of China.

Comparative Service Levels and Fiscal Outcomes

We present a comparative of Shandong with other provinces in terms of indicators of public sector workloads or performance (Table 2) . Hopefully, this will give some rough idea of how well Shandong's governments perform relative to those in the rest of China. The picture we get from this comparative is mixed. With respect to some services (e. g. , numbers of health professionals), the public service levels look relatively strong, as might be expected in a higher income province. In other areas, such as environmental quality and the reach of the education system, Shandong trails the national average.

However, analysis of broad indicators such as is presented in Table 2, give only a partial picture of the relative level of services in Shandong. For example, we can observe strong numbers describing the health service infrastructure (e. g. , beds and professionals), but in its more in depth discussion in The Proposal (2014), it is noted that there are wide differences in the quality of services availability of services between the urban and rural areas.

In terms of budget comparisons, however, the picture is clearer. The fiscal outcomes in the province describe a smaller sized government than the comparison of service levels would seem to suggest. The fiscal profile described in Table 7 shows Shandong to be a low spending province by comparison with the rest of China. This is true for per capita expenditure and for expenditure as a share of GDP, and it is true for the public finance budget and for the consolidated budget. Further, per capita debt outstanding is at a relatively low level by comparison with other provinces.

Financing Public Services

Revenues in the public finance budget (not including central grants to the province) account for 8.46 percent of GDP. In the rest of China, the share is 11.92 percent (Table 6). Relative to GDP, the emphasis on government fund revenues and on revenues raised from land leases, is also less in Shandong than in other provinces.

The mix of revenues in the public finance budget is described in Table 7. There is a heavy reliance on tax revenues (79 percent of total tax and nontax revenues).[1] The largest tax revenue source is the business tax (28.6 percent). There is a heavy dependence on central grants (including repayment revenue, conditional transfers and earmarked transfers), which in total finance about 25 percent of the public finance budget. This dependence on central grants is a very important feature of the Shandong provincial financing scheme, and of great significance in understanding the budget balance that the province has maintained.

Almost all revenues are collected at the county and prefecture level. The provincial government accounts for only about 3 percent of total tax collections. But because the taxable capacity of counties and districts varies so widely, a system of horizontal equalization is used to bring about a better balance between expenditure needs and revenues. Prior to 2014, the province and prefectures decided how much revenue would be retained in each surplus county (district) budget, and how much will be transferred

1 There is sometimes confusion about the designation "local tax". In China, this refers to the entitlement to the revenues, e.g. 25 percent of VAT collections or 100 percent of business tax collections are retained by the local government. But, local governments have no power to adjust the rate or base, or to initiate a new tax in China. In most western industrial countries, a "local tax" is one where the local government has the power to set the tax rate or define the tax base. So by western definition, local taxes and shared taxes as defined in china would be intergovernmental transfers. In the remainder of this paper, we will follow the Chinese definition. For more discussion, see Bahl and Bird (2008) and Ebel and Tallercio (2008).

into the budgets of deficit counties (districts). In 2014, Shandong moved to a more traditional approach where the provincial government was allocated a share of incremental tax revenues to be used for equalization purposes. The transfers to recipient local governments are worked out by a combination of an ad hoc approach and a formula approach. With respect to the former, a "standard expenditure needs" is developed for each county and the revenue shortfall needed to cover this spending level is allocated.

The arithmetic of this system might be illustrated with a comparison of the public finance budget account for 2014 for a rich district and a poor county (see Table 8). The following example describes the 2013 horizontal sharing arrangement. The richer district (Shizhong) raises significantly more revenues (8,200 million RMB), is given an expenditure allocation of 3,207 million RMB, and transfers 4,993 million RMB to the prefecture/province for reallocation. In this case, the transfer out to other districts and counties is equivalent to about 65 percent of the revenues raised. The poor county (Shanghe) is allocated a spending amount of 2,102 million RMB, and finances 32 percent of this with own source revenues and 68 percent from transfers into its budget. Based only on observing these two counties, we can say that the system is equalizing, but not fully equalizing. The richer district spends 6,286 RMB per person and the poorer county spends a much smaller 3,681 RMB per person.

Budgetary Performance

The consolidated financial position of Shandong province would appear to be in balance. The fiscal position for each of the four budgets is summarized in Table 9. The public finance budget is brought into a surplus position by central government unconditional and earmarked transfers. Otherwise, the total of local tax bureau collections and shared tax collections would not be adequate to cover expenditures in the public finance budget. Both the government fund budget and the SOE operation budget are able to cover current costs with recurrent annual revenues. Most of the revenues of the government fund budget are from the sale of land leases.

The current expenditures in the social security budget are covered 82 percent by contributions, 18 percent by financial subsidies provided from the general budget, and a small amount from accumulated balances. In 2014, the social security fund had a balance of 241,778 million RMB, equivalent in amount to about 112 percent of total social security budget expenditures in 2014.

CHAPTER THREE PUBLIC FINANCE ISSUES AND CONCERNS

Shandong is not presently facing a fiscal crisis. The motivation for reform appears to be the need for modernization of practices, separation of public and private sector involvement in the economy, increased transparency and fitting the new State Council regulations into the Shandong context. If properly implemented, the reforms will strengthen provincial and local government finances, but they are not prompted primarily by a financing gap.

The economic base is strong and capable of generating more revenue. It is growing at about the same rate as that in the rest of China. The reform program in fiscal management and tax administration could produce efficiency gains, expenditure savings, and increased revenues. But fiscal needs are considerable. The rate of urbanization has increased significantly, placing some strain on the existing stock of urban infrastructure, and there are large disparities in public service levels among the 140 counties. The social security budget receives a financial subsidy at present, and will come under more pressure as the population continues to age and the labor force shrinks.

While the tax base is potentially strong, there is vulnerability because of the pending phase-out of the business tax. The financial reform program will generate some revenue gains from the reductions in preferential tax treatments, and could generate expenditure postponing the impact on revenues.

A revenue gap for Shandong may lie ahead for Shandong. In addition, there are other, structural problems to be dealt with. Many of these problems can be addressed with the new budget law and the financial management reform program that has been initiated. In other cases, the solutions might need to wait for the next round of fiscal reforms at the central government level. In this discussion, we focus on the following questions:

(1) Are provincial and local government expenditures in Shandong too low? Is there adequate fiscal space for the provincial and local governments to finance higher levels of public services, public infrastructure and social security?

(2) By how much should fiscal disparities among local governments within the province be reduced? What fiscal instruments should be used to reduce these disparities?

(3) Are provincial and local governments too directly involved with the competitive sector? Is the public sector in Shandong too complicated to manage efficiently?

(4) Are there perverse (unwanted) incentives in the Shandong fiscal system?

Are Government Expenditures High Enough?

Do governments in Shandong spend enough? This is no easy question to answer because there always will be unmet needs in public services. Spending more might be a good strategy or it might not be a good strategy. It depends on the quality of services now being delivered, and it depends on how efficiently public services are delivered, i. e. , province A might be able to deliver the same quality of services as province B, but at a lower cost. So, we cannot offer a definitive answer to the question of whether Shandong spends at the "right" level.

Still, we might examine the question in two other ways. The first is to survey the indicators of public service levels by comparison with other provinces. The second is to compare the level of spending with that in other provinces.

Rough measures of public service inputs and outcomes are some indication of the extent to which public service needs are being satisfied. The comparison of service levels, outcomes, inputs and provincial characteristics does not give a clear picture of Shandong as being an outlier in terms of service provision (Table 2). Environmental conditions are not at a high level, perhaps due to the concentration of industry in the economic base, nor is the literacy rate comparatively high. On the other hand, health service inputs do appear to be high and education standards are in the normal range. This indirect evidence does not allow us to support the argument that public service levels are too low. But data are limited and public service levels are difficult to measure, so this is a weak test.

The other approach is to compare the provincial and local government spending level in Shandong with that in other provinces. Here we find a curious result, at least for the public finance budget. The rate of provincial and local government expenditures in Shandong is low. Shandong ranks 10th in China in terms of per capita GDP, but in terms of per capita public finance budget expenditures, it ranks 28th, which is near the lowest of the provinces (Table 10). Per capita expenditure in Shandong in 2013 was 6, 872 RMB, equivalent to about 12 percent of per capita GDP in 2013. Meanwhile the average for all other provinces in China is 8, 836 RMB, equivalent of about 19 percent of GDP. This of course is not a sufficient reason to argue that Shandong provincial and local governments should spend at a higher rate. But it is an important observation. Policy makers in Shandong might benefit from an analysis of how their spending patterns differ from those in the rest of China, and from an explanation of why this might be the case.

Higher rates of subnational government spending usually are related to higher levels of development, and to the greater expenditure demands for public services that come with this development. In China, the revenues to fund these demands are fixed by the central government in the form of shared taxes and grants, and by authorized tax collections at the local level. There are no subnational government taxing powers as such. Still, as pointed out above, some provinces spend more than others on a per capita basis. This might come about because of a greater demand for government services, or because of heavy expenditures on an industrial policy, or because of efficiency/inefficiency in government spending. But as a practical matter, a higher level of spending happens because of what goes on with the revenue side of the budget, i. e. , some combination of different capacities to raise revenues, different levels of collection effort, different preferential tax policies, and different levels of grants received from the central government.

To make a better estimate of the size of the underspending in Shandong, we have studied the relationship between per capita subnational government expenditures and per capita GDP in Chinese provinces. The results of the analysis show that if a province has a 10 percent higher level of per capita GDP, it would be expected to spend about 5. 9 percent more on a per capita basis (See Appendix 2 Regression C). In other words, there is an equalizing pattern in the Chinese intergovernmental fiscal system. But the system is not fully equalizing because some richer provinces end up spending considerably more than the poorer ones. This comes about largely because of differences in natural endowments, and because the distribution of shared tax revenues is done on a basis of origin of collections, and because the business tax is driven by the level of economic activity. Bahl, Goh and Qiao (2014, chapter two), report that 46 percent of all transfers in 2009 were shared taxes, and that the distribution among provinces is highly correlated with the level of per capita GDP and the HDI index. Hofman and Guerra (2007, p34) show that fiscal disparities have been "persistently large" across time. Their data for the 1990s and early 2000s support the findings here, that the fiscal system in China did not have success in addressing regional equalization.

From the equation presented in Appendix 2, regression C, we can estimate that a province with Shandong's level of per capita GDP would have spent 8, 196 RMB per capita in 2013. But Shandong in fact, spent only 6, 872 RMB, which is 16 percent below the expected level. If Shandong had spent at the national (regression) average, it would have made per capita expenditures of an additional 1, 964 RMB.

What explains this result? Why does Shandong spend at a lower rate than most of the rest of the country? Three hypotheses might be offered:

1. A low level of tax effort in Shandong;

2. Shandong receives a low level of central government grants;

3. GDP for Shandong has been overestimated.

Low revenue effort

There appears to be a low revenue effort in Shandong by comparison with other provinces. A number of reasons might explain this outcome. The local and/or central tax bureau may not be as aggressive as other provinces about assessing and collecting from the full tax base, or a larger proportion of economic activity is outside the legal tax base (either by exemption or by preferential treatment). This may be a result of lax administration, or it may be a result of government officials intentionally keeping tax burdens low as a part of an industrial policy.

What we can see from Table 6 is that per capita revenues from own sources in Shandong are about 5,135 RMB by comparison with a national average of 5,546 RMB. Total revenues collected in the province (shared central taxes and collections by the local tax bureau) are equivalent to 8.46 percent of GDP. By comparison, the average for all provinces in China is 11.92 percent of GDP.

Average levels of effective tax rates are not a full proof indicator of tax effort, because they do not consider other factors that contribute to fiscal capacity (e. g. , the rate of urbanization, the share of the economy in the industrial and tertiary sectors, and per capita GDP). These factors suggest a larger tax base that is easier to reach. When we measure tax effort, we are interested in the relationship between what the Province actually collects and what we might expect them to collect at a normal effort.

We have taken these factors into account and report the results of a regression analysis in Appendix 2 to this report, regression A. [1] The results of this study show that Shandong has a capacity to raise shared and local taxes equivalent to 11. 2 percent of provincial GDP in 2011, but in fact, they raised only 8 percent. In other words, Shandong's tax effort (the ratio of actual tax collected to taxable capacity) was 27 percent below the national level. In fact, by this analysis, Shandong has had a long history of being a low taxing province (Table A-2). Suppose that Shandong raised taxes at the national average rate, i. e. , the province raised taxes equivalent to 11. 2 percent of GDP. In this case, per capita expenditures could have been 1, 833 RMB higher in 2011, and Shandong's per capita expenditure rank would have risen from 28th to 19th.

Low level of grants received

A second explanation for the lower rate of spending in Shandong is that the provincial share of central government general and earmarked grants is low compared to other provinces. As we can see in Table 10, Shandong's per capita grant allocation in 2012 is one of the lowest in China. The province receives an amount equivalent to about 4 percent of total provincial GDP, which is well below the national average. As noted above, Shandong's expenditure shortfall is 1,324 RMB per capita. Of this, 859 RMB or 65 percent might be attributed to its below average receipt of general and

---

1 The regression method of measuring tax effort is developed more fully in Lotz and Morss (1967) and Bahl (1971).

earmarked transfers.

We might look a little more deeply to explain the low allocation of earmarked and unconditional grants to Shandong. The analysis, presented in Appendix 2, regression C, shows that for all provinces in China, a 10 percent higher level of per capita GDP is associated with a 6 percent lower level of grants. In making this estimate, we have accounted for population density and the number of population per subnational government employees. As expected, the distribution of central government grants is made on an equalizing basis. But Shandong's level of grants is even lower than expected for a province with its characteristics. For a province with Shandong's level of per capita GDP, the expected level of grants is 2,888 RMB per capita, but in fact, Shandong receives only 2,029 RMB in per capita terms.

Putting these two analyses together, we can say that Shandong's per capita expenditures are 1,833 RMB lower because of its low tax effort, and 859 RMB lower because of equalization in the grant system. At an (regression) average tax effort and an (regression) average level of grants, governments in Shandong would have been able to spend 9,564 RMB per capita and would have ranked 15th in per capita spending, rather than 28th.

GDP is overestimated

A third explanation for Shandong's low level of spending is that provincial GDP is overestimated. The implications of this are interesting. If Shandong overestimated GDP by 22 percent in 2013, then its true ratio of expenditures to GDP would have been equivalent to about the national average. The true ratio of taxes to GDP would then have been 10.3 percent and Shandong would have ranked 22nd in tax effort instead of 28th. An overestimated GDP also would have contributed to a lower level of intergovernmental grants. [1]

Are Fiscal Disparities Too Large?

The equalization system used in Shandong may not adequately reduce fiscal disparities among local governments. The disparities in the level of economic development and in the level of per capita expenditures varies widely among the counties, as is shown in Table 11. Per capita GDP ranges from 116 thousand RMB to 9 thousand RMB, and per capita expenditures from 9 thousand RMB to 1 thousand RMB. In other words, the average amount spent per person for public services is about nine times greater in the highest spending county than in the lowest. The gap between the highest and lowest spending prefectures also is about nine to one. The public policy question to raise is whether these disparities in per capita expenditures are too large to be acceptable.

If government decides that the variations in spending for public services are too large, the provincial government might address these disparities with a program of equalization transfers. The idea of equalization in a system is that low income counties would receive more transfers in per capita terms, than would high income counties, so as to offset some of the greater revenue raising capacity of higher income counties. This general approach has been followed in Shandong. In 2013, 52 counties with financial difficulties received transfers of about 37 billion RMB from the provincial/prefecture level. The approach taken in making this allocation seems to be more ad hoc than formula-based. Provincial/prefecture officials, armed with good information about each county, depend heavily on expert judgement in estimating the fiscal gap.

We can estimate the extent to which this ad hoc allocation reduced the

1 Bahl, Goh and Qiao (2014) found a negative and significant correlation between per capita GDP and each of per capita conditional, earmarked and equalization grants to provinces.

spending advantage of the richer vs. poorer counties. For example, if the dispersion in per capita expenditures (which reflects the post-tax—post-transfer outcome) is less than the dispersion in per capita GDP, there will have been some equalization. If the dispersion in per capita expenditures is greater than that in per capita GDP, the system actually led to a widening of the disparities, i. e., the system would have been counter-equalizing.

A cross section analysis of 90 counties in Shandong for which we have data, shows that a one percent higher level of per capita GDP is associated with a 0.70 percent higher level of per capita expenditures (Appendix 2, regression D). This suggests that there is some equalization in the system, i. e., the spending gap is narrowed by the distribution of local surpluses to deficit counties by prefectures and the provincial government. The question is whether this is enough equalization to meet the goals of the provincial government. Should there be more equalization in the Shandong intergovernmental transfer system? The reasons for arguing that provincial grants should be more equalizing is that spending disparities are still very large, and that most of the revenue allocations in the Chinese system favor higher income places. For example, shared taxes (which account for more than 60 percent of all tax revenues in Shandong) are distributed on a derivation basis, and this favors places with a higher taxable capacity. The same is true of the collection of other "local" taxes.

Finally, it is worth noting that the elimination of the business tax will also have an equalization effect, in that this tax provides much of the surplus used to make grant distributions to poorer counties. This equalization pool is equivalent to about one-third of business tax collections. Not replacing the business tax with another revenue source, or not mobilizing additional revenues to compensate for the loss could harm the equalization objectives of the government.

Urban Public Service Needs Will Pressure Budgets

In the urban areas of Shandong, there are unmet expenditure needs. This is partly the result of the movement of 28 million people to urban areas in a 15 year period. Moreover, there will be more pressure to expand urban infrastructure and services as urbanization continues, even if it continues at a slower pace. At present in Shandong, about 45 million people live outside the urban areas. Over the past two decades, about 30 percent of the rural population in China moved to cities, some as temporary migrant workers and some as new residents. Some migrants came from rural areas within provinces and some came from other provinces. For purposes of illustration, we can note that if 30 percent of Shandong's rural population moved to its cities, the number of new urban residents would be about 13 million over the next 20 years. However, we might also note that a lower rate of GDP growth could discourage in-migration. Still, in-migration plus the natural growth in population cannot be absorbed without significant new infrastructure investment and increased operating budget expenditures.

The question remains as to whether the revenues needed will materialize to cover the increased demand for expenditures? Revenues in China probably will grow more slowly, at least in the medium term. The expected rate of GDP growth in the next few years is about 7 percent, down from 7.4 percent in 2014, and well down from the annual average of 10 percent for the 1990 – 2012 period. We can illustrate the implications of this slower growth. With a revenue-income elasticity of unity, the 2015 – 2020 period would yield new revenues of 20 billion RMB at a 12 percent GDP growth rate, but would yield 17 billion RMB at a 7.5 percent growth rate. The implied financing gap of 4 trillion RMB might call for a retrenchment in spending or an increase in revenues (World Bank and Development Research Center, 2013).

Declining Land Revenues and Infrastructure Finance

To the extent China has successfully addressed the problem of financing new infrastructure for its first wave on urbanization, it did so with the sale of land leases. The volumes and sizes in terms of percentage of GDP of land lease revenues in China are shown in Table 12. In 2014, land lease revenues were equivalent to 6.7 percent of GDP. The size of this revenue source was astounding. It was equivalent to 56 percent of total subnational governments' public finance budgets, and it accounted for 85 percent of subnational government fund budget revenues. [1] The revenue growth was fueled by a significant growth in the demand for real estate.

But such heavy dependence on land leasing has brought problems. These include concerns about the amount of land-based debt that is presumably guaranteed by local governments, poor investment choices made by some local governments, over-investment in infrastructure vs. other urban services, urban sprawl and the social and equity issues related to transferring land from agricultural to urban use. [2] Perhaps the most important problem with land revenue financing was that it challenged the management of subnational government debt. Land financing carries more fiscal risks because the expectations of a continued revenue flow encourages overspending by subnational governments. Thus, subnational governments are likely to over borrow to finance infrastructure. In addition, the use of land leases could be risky when there are negative shocks to the real estate markets, and it may also fuel the bubble of land and housing markets. The situation is exacerbated further by the lack of

1 The rising real estate price is due to various reasons. On one hand, the unprecedented scale of urbanization creates the huge quantity demanded of real estate properties, appreciating property valuation and giving subnational governments a strong incentive to participate in the land market; on the other hand, the fact that subnational governments reap the benefit of land heavily also contributes to the rising cost of housing, pushing the price higher and further strengthening the wealth effects.

2 For a comprehensive analysis of the issues, see World Bank and Development Research Center (2013).

fiscal transparency and fiscal discipline.

The use of urban development investment companies (UDICs) have been the main channel for infrastructure finance and the cause of rapid growth of the debts of subnational governments. But the growth of UDIC debt came with problems, such as the discretionary operation and illegal guarantees from the government. In order to control the increasing debt risk, the State Council issued the [2010] No. 19 document on June 13, 2010, "Notice about Strengthening the Management of UDICS", requiring that different levels of government clean up the liabilities of the financing platforms to ensure credit safety. The new Debt management regime and the new budget law together were designed to head off a repeat of the UDIC experience.

Shandong Province has raised less land lease revenue than the national average, in terms of percentage of GDP, and it has a lower level of debt outstanding (Tables 12 and 13). [1] The transfer of user rights for land accounted for 77 percent of revenues in the government fund, and was equivalent to 78 percent of total taxes collected in the province in 2014. Even though the intensity with which land revenues were used was lower than in the rest of China, it was still of great significance as a financing source in Shandong. For example, in 2013. Land lease revenues covered 83 percent of government fund expenditures and were about equal to the amount raised from general taxes.

All of this leads up to the question of the possible sources of infrastructure finance in Shandong province. Though there would seem to be fiscal space for borrowing. Municipal bonds are not a source of revenue, but rather a method of arranging payment over the life of an asset. The problem is that there are limited revenue streams available for loan repayment. The growth rate in land lease revenues began declining in the fourth quarter of 2013, and turned negative in the fourth quarter of 2014 (World Bank, 2015).

---

1 No information was available on the amount of contingent liability debt outstanding.

Moreover, the use of financial platforms is now illegal. The problem is finding a method of repayment from the present revenue structure of the province. A complicating factor is the elimination of the business tax, which could reduce further the revenue pool available to support debt.

Public Sector and Private Sector Activities Are Not Fully Separated

In theory, the role of the public sector should be limited to those services and activities that private markets will not supply efficiently—either because of the difficulty of charging a price or because of joint-consumption benefits—and those with desirable redistribution value. While there has been privatization in China in some sectors, it has yet to begin in earnest in other areas of the economy. The government's expenditure responsibilities are still very wide.

The Peoples' Congress and the government have called for a different type of relationship between the subnational governments and the competitive sectors of the economy. The role of government should move toward the provision of public services. Its involvement in economic development should be less direct, i. e. government should provide an environment conducive to economic development but should not be directly involved in shaping business operations. For example, government should provide basic infrastructure necessary for production and commerce, such as transportation, ports, water and power. It can also assist the competitive sector by providing good basic amenities (schools, health care, parks, a clean environment, and the like) which will help businesses attract a quality labor force. Government should also be responsible for establishing a regulatory framework that protects the population but is fair to enterprises.

In Shandong, there is a direct relationship between government and the competitive sector. This has taken several forms. A significant amount of enterprises are still owned (or belong) to governments at different levels, and there is still a variety of channels through which governments can directly or indirectly encroach on private sector activities through their SOEs. In recent years, UDICs created a more complicated relationship between the public and private sectors.

In addition, there are subsidies to businesses in the competitive sector. The opportunity cost of these subsidies is an equal investment in general government services. Another type of involvement is the granting of tax preferences and tax rebates to certain targeted businesses. Finally, there are contingent liabilities on loans. In none of these instances have we been able to gather data to accurately measure the extent of government involvement in the competitive sector. However, based on the State Council Regulations of 2014 and the supporting discussion in the Shandong proposal to implement these, there would appear to be significant involvement of the public sector in all of these areas.

A way forward for Shandong province is to begin with the elimination of government subsidies to enterprises, and to pull back on tax preferences, rebates and the practice of not collecting full tax liability. This would free up funds for investment in public services and could help address the revenue shortfall that will come with the elimination of the local business tax. It would also "level the playing field" for enterprises and let the market function more efficiently. The State Council regulation and the Shandong proposal to control debt by requiring provincial approval and eliminating borrowing with government guarantee, also can play a good role in separating the government-business relationship.

But, continuing to separate the government from the competitive sector in Shandong will not be an easy matter, especially at a time when the rate of economic growth has slowed. In fact, the State Council has cautioned about removing tax preferences too quickly. Still, it is reported that a large number of applications for tax preferences have already been rejected for

2015.

Perverse Incentives

The Chinese intergovernmental fiscal system is harmed by the presence of (unintentional) incentives for subnational governments to behave in ways that are contrary to the objectives of national and provincial government policy. Overcoming this structural problem will be another challenge for fiscal sustainability in Shandong.

There is a disincentive in the system to concentrate budget expenditures on public service improvement vs. economic development. The primary business of provincial and local governments is to provide adequate public services to their populations and to the businesses that operate within their jurisdiction. In most western countries, this leads to holding elected provincial and local government officials accountable for the quality of services that they deliver. But in China, provincial and local government officials are graded by a higher level government. Many would argue that the grade is influenced heavily by the economic growth and investment that can be attributed to their economic leadership. This can lead to a discounting of the importance of public services provided to households relative to the importance of public services and tax preferences provided to prospective or existing businesses. [1]

The Shandong proposal notes this concern with a relative overinvestment in economic affairs by citing government investment in the competitive sectors in areas such as manufacturing, the upgrading of corporate technology, and capital loans. The proposal points out that economic affairs in China accounts for about 34 percent of all public expenditures in Shandong but the OECD average is only about 12 percent.

1 This is a complicated issue, because success with job creation can lead to an increased welfare of households in the longer run. For a general discussion of the evaluation issue, see Wong(2012).

An additional perverse incentive associated with rewarding economic development success is the possibility that the GDP statistics will show more success than actually occurred. We have no evidence that this has happened in Shandong or anywhere else in China, but certainly the incentives for this are in place.

There is a disincentive in the system for increased revenue mobilization. In Shandong, county (district) governments feature wide disparities in revenue mobilization capacity. Under the previous "rich city to poor city" horizontal revenue sharing scheme, those who raised the greatest amounts (the urban districts and a few other counties) were allowed to retain a share to meet these public services needs and the remainder was transferred to the prefecture or provincial government for their own use or for equalization purposes. At the margin, any increased revenue mobilization effort at the district level would be transferred to the prefecture. This created a powerful incentive for the district governments (and a few counties) to lower tax collections by giving preferential tax treatments to enterprises for economic development purposes. The reformed system improved the approach considerably and weakened the disincentive significantly. Still, however, if the province is able to share in some percent of incremental revenues, there is a (smaller) disincentive to increased revenue mobilization.

This arrangement for revenue sharing also can lead to a disincentive for increased revenue mobilization in the recipient (poorer) county. Under the present arrangement, the county governments that raises less revenue may expect to have their shortfall made up with a deficit-filling transfer. Why make a greater effort to raise more revenue when the financing gap will be covered by a grant? By the same reasoning, the benefits of cost savings on the expenditure side would not benefit the local government undertaking the improvements in expenditure efficiency.

This problem of revenue mobilization disincentives can be addressed by changing the method used for revenue sharing. Each (recipient) county might be given a target level of revenue mobilization, set by the Province/Prefecture. This target would be an estimate of how much the county can raise at a prescribed level of tax effort. The gap to be funded would be the difference between standard expenditure needs and the target level of revenues. Under such a scheme, counties whose revenue effort fell below the target would receive less in grants.

Another disincentive built into the system grows out of the decentralized approach taken to expenditure assignment. The heavy assignment of functions to the grass roots county level governments (140 county level governments) may lead to inefficiency in some fiscal decisions. For example, the cost of county government underspending on services that might discourage environmental degradation could spill over into neighboring jurisdictions. The way to answer this problem is to review the regime of expenditure assignment in Shandong to make sure that externalities and economies of scale have been properly accounted for.

The system of capital finance is heavily biased in the direction of leasing land. In 2014, about 78 percent of all government fund revenue in Shandong was raised from land leases. The reasons for this reliance on land leasing are clear enough. Leases are more revenue productive than local taxes, they are much less contentious than increased collection of local taxes, and they are a revenue source that local politicians can tap without waiting for central approval. However, these incentives are so lucrative that they might cause local political leaders to overstock land for development purposes, to be driven away from capital spending to support general public services, and to incur unsustainable amounts of debt. Such perverse incentives need to be guarded against.

The Fiscal System May Be Overly Complicated

The allocation of public resources in Shandong is less rule-based than it might be, and as a result, the factors leading to particular outcomes are less transparent than they might be. This is part of the reason why the new State Council regulations call for fiscal practices that are more modern and more transparent.

Whenever decisions are not rule-based but are made according to an ad hoc approach on a case-by-case basis, or by negotiation, a number of problems can arise. Some of these problems are addressed directly in the Shandong proposals for fiscal reform. But some of these problems are not addressed in the reform program because they are the result of tradeoffs that have been made in developing the provincial finance system. The four issues discussed below illustrate the nature of the complication.

First, revenues and expenditures for each provincial-local government are reported in four separate budgets: public finance budget, government fund budget, SOE operation budget and social security budget. The public finance budget, the government fund budget, and the SOE operating fund budget contain both current and capital expenditures. There are transfers among these accounts at each level of government, and also between levels of government. The complication grows out of the national level definition of the subnational government budget, requiring these four components. Consolidating these to give a full picture of local government finances is not easily done and not easily understood, and so it makes the transparency objective more difficult to achieve.

A second complication comes from the methods used to distribute intergovernmental transfers among the province-prefecture-county/district levels. For example, the method of coming to a decision about the amount to be distributed to a county is not fully transparent. This issue might be addressed by moving to a formula-based system for reallocating money from rich to poor counties, as was discussed above.

Third, special transfer payments to local government funds have been a complication in the system. Recent improvement have been made, reducing the items of provincial-level special funds from 243 to 99. Still, there is considerable room for further reduction in these transfers.

A fourth problem with complication grows out of the past practice of using land leases to secure loans for infrastructure investment. In the past some off-budget borrowing has been guaranteed by provincial and local government budgets, but the strength of these guarantees is not clear with the result of there being some confusion about the responsibilities of local governments for repayment of the loans.

CHAPTER FOUR SHANDONG FISCAL REFORM

The provincial government of Shandong has set 2020 as a target date for establishing a "modern fiscal system". More accurately, the goal is to establish a modern financial management system by the year 2020. To this end, the provincial government has carried out a comprehensive study of how it might adapt and implement the financial management reform regulations given by the State Council.

The fiscal reform program has benefitted from the vision and leadership of Governor Guo Shuqing. The project has taken on the task of "modernizing its fiscal system", and intends to be the "... first in China to build a unified, integrated, rule by law, efficient modern fiscal system". The reform paper seems to argue that Shandong's importance to the Chinese economy provides a justification for taking this mandate earlier than many other provinces. [1]

The program is ambitious but it has been carefully kept in line with the objectives of national policy for fiscal modernization. It takes best international practices in public finance as a starting point, but it is careful to place this in the Chinese setting. The proposal includes both administration and policy dimensions. It is important to note that implementation of this program does not depend on any new legislation from the central government. It also recognizes clearly the senior-junior relationship between the central and subnational governments. Changes in central and subnational government expenditure and tax assignment, and in intergovernmental transfers from the central government, are not addressed in the Shandong proposal because they are an exclusive responsibility of the

1 Shandong is the second largest province in terms of population and accounts for 9 percent of GDP.

central government.

Reform Can Build On Strength

Shandong has seen good improvement in its fiscal structure and its fiscal outcomes since 2010. The comprehensive fiscal reform envisioned by the Shandong Government for 2020 can build on these gains. For the most part, the reform is more of a deepening of the system now in place than it is a dramatic change that takes the province in the direction of a new fiscal structure. This follows the lead of the State Council, whose recommendations are focused on modernization of practices that are outmoded, on deepening practices that are basically sound but not yet fully implemented, and on continuing to break the direct link that now exists between the government and the competitive sector. But the Shandong proposal also offers some new directions for structural reform in public finance.

The provincial government sees the following as areas were there has been a major strengthening of public finances in Shandong.

(1) There has been significant growth in the amounts spent for the provision of public services. Certainly the data support this argument. Per capita expenditures by provincial and sub provincial governments in Shandong increased from 681 RMB in 2000 to 6,872 RMB in 2013. This compound annual rate of increase (18 percent) can be compared with that in per capita GDP of 13 percent over the same period (from 9,326 RMB in 2000 to 56,184 RMB in 2013).

(2) A financial guarantee program for poor county governments has been in place since 2010. By 2013, 37 billion RMB was used to help 52 counties with financial difficulties to fill their financial gap from 2010 to 2013. In 2013, the system was reformed to reduce the disincentive to revenue mobilization for the richer districts.

(3) The budget management system has improved. In recent years, all levels of government have moved closer to including all revenues and expenditures in the budget, and to adopting a uniform system of accounts.

(4) The central treasury system has been established based on a single treasury account, and this has significantly improved budget execution and management. Government consumption have been switched from cash to a card system, capital project management has been strengthened, and the system has become less complicated.

(5) The flow of intergovernmental grants to Shandong province (conditional and earmarked) has increased from 2 percent of GDP in 2000 to 4 percent in 2012. Still, however, Shandong ranks near the bottom of all provinces in grants received.

(6) Tax collections and other local source revenue in Shandong have increased from a per capita level of 1,789 RMB in 2007 to 4,685 RMB in 2013.

(7) The financial position of the province is reasonably strong, reflecting some good financial management and fiscal planning decisions. The four budgets taken together are in balance, and in 2014, total cash balances in all funds were equivalent to about 63 percent of total expenditures.

Objectives

The Shandong Program is meant to improve the overall functioning of the present system. It does not presuppose any new central government programs, beyond those contained in the new State Council regulations, hence its implementation can begin immediately. Mostly the job is to implement the recommendations of the State Council, but to do so in a

Shandong context, and to move forward independently with fiscal reforms that are within the legal discretion of the province. The Shandong program is focused on financial management, and on adopting some far-reaching changes in the present practice. It also proposes important, but as of yet unspecified, changes in the intergovernmental transfer system.

The objectives of the Shandong fiscal reform might be summarized under nine headings:

(1) A primary goal is to continue to move the fiscal system toward one that focuses on the provision of efficient and equitable public services and away from direct involvement of the investment and production functions of the competitive sector. In particular, fiscal management should move away from its present heavy involvement in economic affairs.

(2) The reform program should address the problems that are presently causing the Shandong fiscal system to operate at less than full efficiency.

(3) The results of this program should be a comprehensive financial management system that links all fiscal activities undertaken in the province. All of the budget accounts should be unified so that every expenditure and revenue is reported in one of the four budgets. There should be no extra-budgetary accounts or off-budget activities. All contingent liabilities should be fully reported and explained.

(4) The system should function according to rule of law. Taxes should be levied and collected according to the tax laws, and grants should be earmarked or unconditional, according to the law and the regulations. There should be a minimum of negotiated arrangements.

(5) The outcomes of the budgetary process (all spending and all revenue activities) should be transparent and open to the general public for evaluation. This will enable more efficient fiscal planning and will be

conducive to gaining buy-in from the general public. Budget execution should also be transparent and this can be helped by treasury management and accounting reforms.

(6) The fiscal system should be stable and sustainable. Governments are better able to plan their activities if the rules for spending and revenue raising activities are not changed frequently. Risky practices should be minimized.

(7) The provincial and local governments need to find a balance among their four general objectives: adequate public resources, economic development, economic efficiency and equity. Identifying these balances can help guide the allocation of resources.

(8) Fiscal program evaluation must take into account both the immediate impacts and the longer term impacts. A three-year rolling fiscal plan will be established. The new debt management framework will curb inefficient borrowing practices.

(9) There should be better coordination of fiscal policies and other programs that impact on economic or social development.

Shandong's Proposals For Fiscal Reform

Following the general direction laid down in the Party Plenary session, Shandong Province has proposed a far-reaching program of modernization of its fiscal system. The proposals are mostly consistent with international good practice, and directly address many of the problems with the present intergovernmental fiscal arrangements in Shandong.

Budget management reform

Significant progress in budget management has been made in recent years by most local governments in the province. Still, important improvements are needed to upgrade and standardize budget disclosure in order to move to a more efficient and a more transparent system. The reform proposal reports that government budgets do not disclose an adequate amount of information on expenditures, and that the county budgets are particularly weak in this respect. It is reported that the disclosure rates in the province and prefecture budgets are 88 percent for the government budget, 82 percent for the department budget, and 82 percent for the "three public consumptions". [1] The corresponding percent for the county budgets are 67 percent, 43 percent, and 42 percent. The changes in budget practices that are proposed involve expanding the scope of what is reported (e.g., including all special funds and all debt), providing more detail on individual budget lines, and standardizing the way in which the material is reported.

An important focus of the proposals is on the integration of the four budgets. The public finance budget, the government fund budget, the SOE budget, and the social security budget should be coordinated and all inter-budget transfers should be made clear. The reform will enable the creation of a consolidated budget with no double counting of expenditures or revenues. All special funds and debt repayment will be linked to their related budget component. These reforms can help a great deal in making the budget plan more transparent.

Several other proposals to strengthen budget management are made. These include:

(1) Instituting a multi-year budget planning process.

(2) Basing revenue collections on actual liabilities rather than on collection targets. The present practice is too focused on meeting a revenue quota with the result that the full amount of taxes due is not collected.

1 The "three public consumptions" are the number of employees who have been abroad for official trips, the number of vehicles owned by the department, and the number of official domestic receptions.

(3) Establishing a budget stabilization fund to address short term deficits. This can be a vehicle for better using revenue collections that exceed targeted amounts, carryover of cash balances that are above acceptable amounts, and certain unspent budget expenditures.

(4) Shifting the focus of expenditure planning to performance analysis.

(5) Improving the annual budget audit and control system.

The proposal to adopt medium term budgeting and planning is important. The benefits include strengthening the link between planning and budgeting, strengthening the ability of fiscal policy to address structural demographic and economic changes, and strengthening the effectiveness and efficiency of public spending programs (World Bank and Development Research Center, 2014, pp. 424 – 425). There is some evidence that medium term expenditure frameworks are associated with many of these benefits (World Bank, 2013).

Some of the budget management proposals are pointed more toward policy changes than toward administration and management changes. Mostly, these are meant to help rationalize expenditure policy, and to move away from budget rigidity and toward both flexibility in expenditure planning and enhancement of revenues to support public service provision. The Shandong reforms would do the following: (a) remove earmarks insofar as is possible, (b) stop the practice of indexing expenditures to income growth, (c) move broad-based taxes and charges from the government fund to the public finance budget, (d) increase the size of the SOE operating budget and use the funds for provision of public welfare services and (e) make provision for a budget stabilization fund for local governments to cover short term budget deficits.

Budget Management and Reform: Commentary

The budget management proposals are well-crafted and reflect good international practice. They can move the efficiency of government expenditures and government fiscal planning forward. One general idea is to make the budget a comprehensive document that includes all transactions by government in a transparent way. This will entail developing a method for consolidating the four budgets so that surpluses and deficits in each can be identified, and so that interfund transfers can be tracked.

The other general idea is to shift the focus of expenditure budgeting away from determining that all expenditures are recorded in the correct account to determining the performance of government expenditure programs. In other words, the budget document would become an important planning and evaluation tool.

Achieving these goals will require significant changes in the current practice. And it will take time.

Creating a more transparent budget structure and presentation, and including all budget transactions, borrowings and special funds are important steps toward evaluating expenditure policy in the province. Under this format, the overall budget can be consolidated, and the impact of alternative expenditure policies can be more easily and accurately tracked. Removing earmarks and removing expenditure indexing is another step in the direction of giving budget planners more flexibility in resource allocation. This will, for example, lead to moving revenue heads such as the education surcharge into the public finance budget and eliminating the expenditure requirements placed on others such as the urban construction tax. Removing earmarks on the transfer of SOE profits to the budget, frees this money for investment in public services and is another welcome reform. This is especially important because the amount of SOE profit transfers will increase to a level of 30 percent by the year 2020. The shift in the focus of expenditure management from verifying the links between spending levels and proper accounts, toward expenditure performance, is important if the benefits of this new set of fiscal discretions is to be realized.

One might raise four questions about the new budget reforms. First, they leave open the question of capital and current expenditures appearing in both the public finance budget and in the government fund budget. Moreover, transfers between these budgets are allowed. Can capital facility planning be handled adequately under such an arrangement? Could the Government Fund eventually be converted to a capital budget, and the public finance budget to a recurrent account?

A second issue relates to the use of the budget stabilization fund for management of short term deficits. Presumably, the idea is to address short term deficits (or surpluses) due to unforeseen circumstances or cash flow problems, or to the normal irregularities of public expenditures and revenues. In this case, it can become a useful tool for budget management. But the proposal may open another door when it questions the need to balance the budget every year, and makes provision for a bailout policy. The detail is not yet provided as to how the stabilization fund will be managed or what specific kind of problems will justify an annual budget deficit. For example, the combination of annual budget deficits, bailouts and continued tax preferences will not mix well with the objectives of the reform. All of these questions lead up to the more general concern about whether the budget stabilization fund could be used by a subnational government as a way to avoid a hard budget constraint.

Third, if there are to be no earmarks on the transfers to the SOE operating budget, is there any need for this budget and can it be eliminated?

Finally, it is not clear how much increased revenue will result from this reform in the budget law. It does seem clear that it could lead to significantly more efficient spending as a result of better fiscal planning. Almost certainly some expenditures will be redirected as restrictions that are presently placed on expenditure planning are removed. And, more transparency in the budgets, together with performance analysis, will free up other funds. But the reallocation of expenditures will take some time because budget practices are entrenched and training will be necessary. It seems likely that the problem of replacing the business tax will land on subnational governments in Shandong well before the expenditure efficiencies can be realized.

Treasury management reform

The provincial government wants to complete the implementation of a central treasury payment and management system in all local governments by 2017. Modernization of the monitoring mechanisms, training and automation are all part of this task.

Some components of the Treasury reform relate directly to expenditure control. Standardized treasury accounts will be introduced and no new earmarked accounts will be allowed. Those that already exist will be phased out by 2016 unless they are approved by the State Council. Borrowing for projects that are not included in the budget will no longer be allowed. Cash management practices will be improved and treasury balances will be maintained at an appropriately low level.

The proposal also calls for stricter control over the budget. The targets for the reform lie in three areas. First, adjustments in spending for budget lines will be strictly controlled and all changes must be reported to the NPC. Second, the budget lines cannot be amended without approval from the Ministry of Finance. Third, strict limits will be placed on the carry-forward of budget balances in a fiscal year (the proposed limit is 9 percent of total expenditures in that fiscal year).

To improve expenditure efficiency and to address corruption, it is proposed to adopt a new and tighter procurement policy. Finally, the government would like an accrual financial management system in place by 2017 in order to better evaluate and manage assets and liabilities. Beginning in 2014, prefecture cities will prepare consolidated financial statements, followed by all counties and districts in Shandong in 2015 and 2016.

Treasury Management Reform: Commentary

The treasury management reform is already well along and expected completion for the entire province by 2017 is an impressive objective. The new system, when completely implemented, should significantly improve control over expenditure management. The limits on new earmarks and new fund accounts reinforce the new budget management program as does the prohibition on any borrowing outside the budget. The stricter control over budgeted spending is welcome because it forces more attention on developing a realistic budget plan. If government can carry out the plan of limiting the movement of expenditures between budget lines, and limiting the creation of new budget accounts, budget planning can be significantly improved.

The limits on the carry-forward of cash balances is understandable, but raises some difficult questions. The first is whether certain, specified reasons for the carryforward of balances will justify a relaxation of the limits, e. g. , unspent balances due to capital project delays or precautionary balances related to future transfers for family security functions. Presumably, revenue collections above targeted amounts will be routed to the budget stabilization fund. Second, how will balances in excess of 9 percent be handled, and how will end-of-year misuse of prospective balances be handled?

As with the case of the budget management reform, there are questions about how much savings can be expected. Clearly there will be a positive effect because of better procurement policies, and better management of unspent balances. However, no estimates have been provided on possible cost savings or of the amount of reduction or redirection in spending that will occur.

Finally, and perhaps most difficult is the implementation of the treasury management system, particularly at the county level. Imposing a new system on existing staff in many counties implies a significant investment in training. Neither the training plan nor its cost are presented in the Shandong proposal.

Debt management reform

Shandong province proposes to follow the State Council recommendations for a clear set of principles in managing subnational government debt. The basic rules for borrowing are laid down at the central level, though provincial governments have some autonomy in the implementation of the rules. The framework for borrowing includes the limitations that only provincial governments can borrow (local government borrowing must be indirect), that all borrowing must be included in the budget, and that higher level governments must approve the debt plans of lower level governments.

It is proposed to establish a local government debt management institution at the provincial level. It would be charged with monitoring and improving the debt framework for the province. The five duties of this institution will be: (a) insuring that borrowings and repayment are included in the correct budget, e. g., general borrowing may appear only in the public finance budget, and special purpose borrowing only in the government fund budget, (b) strengthening the approval process for local government debt, (c) establishing a risk warning mechanism and monitoring progress with respect to this, (d) improving debt disclosure, and (e) establishing an accountability mechanism in connection with illegal or excessive borrowing.

The debt framework will feature clear responsibility for repayment, and the imposition of hard budget constraints on the government involved. Government debt cannot be issued by enterprises, and corporate debt cannot be paid by government. In the case of Public-Private Partnerships, the liability should be clear from the contract. Local governments can issue bonds where the repayment is from earmarked revenue sources, but these must be repaid through the government fund budget. The proposal also provides for a workout strategy should a local government find itself in danger of failing to repay.

The proposal also addresses the "cleaning up" and the reduction of existing debt. Debts that are taken by local governments should be classified as earmarked or general, and should be budgeted appropriately. Ongoing projects can continue to borrow through a transition period, but financing platforms will no longer have the authority of borrowing through local governments.

Debt management Reform: Commentary

The debt management reform is important, even though Shandong Province is not heavily indebted. It is a significant move forward in establishing who can borrow with some form of government guarantee and who cannot. Issuing all debt through the province is a welcome plan for Shandong because it is so decentralized in terms of expenditure responsibilities, and because fiscal disparities are so great. Clarity on the liability of financing platform debt is also welcome. Cleaning up any remnants of "illegal" debt will be helpful for moving forward, as will enforced penalties for unauthorized borrowing.

However, subnational government borrowing in China has been a difficult question for much of the last decade, and will not be easily sorted out, even in a province like Shandong where the level of borrowing is not high. At least three questions might be raised. First and most important, how will the bonds be repaid by the local governments? The loss of the business tax will leave the local tax bureau with relatively little in annual collections. This leaves shared taxes and grants from the provincial/prefecture government as the main sources of repayment. Will the provincial/prefecture governments make adjustments in the revenue sharing arrangements to accommodate new borrowing?

A second question arises in the case of the provincial institution evaluating a local government for its riskiness. This will be most difficult in the case of poorer counties where the less developed economic base does not give up much shared tax revenue. Here the recourse may be for the provincial government to approve the loan and then guarantee repayment through an increased transfer. But this practice will blur the line between borrowing and grants.

Third, a question of clarity arises about the consistency between the strict limits on new earmarking and new funds, and special borrowing in the Government Fund budget.

Tax reform

The Shandong tax reform program stresses the need to complete the VAT reform, which eliminates the business tax as a local government revenue source. However, this implies that provincial and local governments will need to find additional revenues to replace the loss of business tax and to finance both upgraded services and new infrastructure. This replacement strategy will be an important part of the needed reform in Shandong's fiscal system. But Shandong must wait for central government actions before it can decide on a complete course of action. Still, there are several areas where the provincial government has the authority to move toward modernization of the system of taxation and charges, and toward increased revenue mobilization. Much of this authority is given in the State Council regulations.

The Shandong proposal calls for cleaning up and regulating preferential tax treatments under the existing system. Generally these preferential treatments take the form of tax reductions, exemptions, or refunds. The Shandong proposal gives no general accounting for these tax expenditures, so there is no way to make a good estimate of how much revenue loss is incurred. There is also a more subtle version of tax preferences which relates to collecting an annual "target" level of revenues rather than collecting the total amount of tax liability. The government intends to identify all such tax preferences that are extra-legal or have not been approved by the State Council, and eliminate them. The result should be a revenue gain, and should provide for a more fair treatment of taxpayers in the province.

Another area consistent with the goal of developing a modern fiscal system is making the tax administration (for both central and local government taxes) more efficient. The Shandong proposal argues for developing a fully integrated taxpayer information system to assist in improving collection rates, lowering collection costs, and lowering compliance costs. The system would link taxpayer information, government department information and third party information to complete this data base. This could result in stimulating revenues, mostly by identifying and capturing those who evade taxes, and by increasing the willingness to pay full tax liability by reducing some of the compliance costs on existing taxpayers.

The Shandong report notes property tax reform as an important possibility for increased revenue mobilization. It suggests reform of the existing levies on real estate use and real estate transfers, and it suggests improved administration. But the adoption of a new property tax structure, as is now under discussion, will be a decision taken by the central government. The implementation of a national property tax in China may still be a few years away. As for increased revenues from the existing real estate levies, the effective rate against GDP is now about 1. 6 percent of GDP and there may be little space for a further increase. Moreover, property markets have cooled and the automatic growth in the tax base has slowed.

It also has been proposed is to clean up the present system of administrative charges. By the end of 2013, there were 125 administrative charges, of which 101 were approved by the central government and 24 were approved by the provincial government. These administrative charges were used to finance about 20 active government funds. Shandong's fiscal reform proposal takes the correct position that there is no room for this practice in a modern tax system. The goal is to eliminate most of these charges. Some will be merged into the appropriate tax category and others will become more legitimate fees or cost recovery charges. While this is a structural change that will improve the efficiency with which revenues are mobilized, and it may redirect money to higher priority uses, it is not likely to generate much new revenue.

Tax Reform: Commentary

Increased revenue mobilization at the provincial level is crucial for Shandong. The business tax will soon be eliminated and a replacement revenue has not yet been proposed, the growth in general tax revenues will likely slow with the lower rate of national economic growth, and expenditure pressures from urbanization, environmental concerns, and from the elderly population will be mounting. The Shandong Reform proposal can only go so far, because Provinces do not have the authority to enact any new taxes.

Shandong does make good proposals to address the revenue problem—improve the tax administration efficiency with a better information system, and remove discretionary tax preferences from the present system. A significant amount of Shandong's low tax effort may be due to weak administration and to tax preferences, but no estimates of the tax expenditures are made in the Shandong fiscal reform proposal. We can say that the proposals are in the right direction, but we cannot say with any degree of accuracy how much of the tax shortfall problem they can address.

However, there is both indirect and direct evidence that the Shandong proposals, if implemented successfully, can lead to a significant revenue increase. The direct evidence is the claim in the budget management reform that revenue collections are more focused on revenue targets than on tax liability, hence a great deal of taxes due might go uncollected. The indirect evidence is that Shandong makes what appears to be a relatively low tax effort. It raises tax equivalent to about 6 percent of GDP compared to a China average of 9 percent in 2013. If only half of this gap is due to the granting of preferential tax treatments, this reform can be significant in addressing the shortfall that will result from the loss of business taxes.

Finally, there might be concerns about the implementation of this program. Tax preferences can be well entrenched and hard to pull back, and they may have a constituency within the government. Moreover, reductions in what many see as effective economic development subsidies are especially hard to eliminate when the growth rate in the economy has slowed. Note also the more recent State Council regulation that seems to call for a less aggressive approach to eliminating tax preferences. The speed of this reform—reduction in special tax preferences—is not likely to be as rapid as the provincial government would like.

Subprovincial fiscal system reform

The structure of the relationship among the provincial, prefectural and county governments is not as efficient or as equitable as would be expected in a modern intergovernmental fiscal system. The three concerns in Shandong are: (a) the assignment of expenditure and administrative responsibilities may not be correct, (b) the distribution of revenues among the local governments may not be adequately equalizing, and (c) the framework for administering the intergovernmental transfer system may not be in step with the goal of implementing a rule-based system.

A modern intergovernmental fiscal system should be characterized by clarity in the assignment of responsibilities and a scientific assignment according to the characteristics of the expenditure category under consideration. The former should assure that each expenditure is delivered by the right level, and without duplication, while the latter should identify the correct level of local government to take responsibility. The reform document focuses on three underlying problems in Shandong. The first is that expenditure assignments and administrative responsibilities are unclear. This leads to duplication in the provision of services in some cases, and failure to take responsibility for service delivery in others. Second, some expenditure responsibilities are not correctly assigned, e. g. , some functions which exhibit spillover effects or economies of scale are being delivered by counties, while some functions that are better matched with grass roots governments are the responsibility of the provincial or prefectural level. The third problem is that some services are formally assigned to more than one level of government, and this leads to inefficiencies.

Shandong intends to address these concerns by reassessing the existing assignment of responsibility for all expenditure functions. By producing a list of assignments for each level, the question of clarity can be addressed. The right assignment of a function will be based on the presence of economies of scale or spillover effects, which would dictate delivery of the service by a higher level government. If a service primarily benefits the local population, it is better assigned to the county/district. Applying these rules can lead to a change in expenditure responsibilities among province, prefecture and county in Shandong. The reform plan calls for drawing up these new assignments, and putting them into practice in 2015, on a trial basis, for education, health and transportation.

The second major issue to be resolved is the distribution of revenues among the local governments within the province. Here there are a number of design issues that the provincial reform is yet to work out. The guidelines laid out by the reform document are not very specific, but seem to be led by two principles. One is that all local government tax revenues, including those shared with the central government, should be the revenue of the city and county governments. The other is that the province should administer a unified revenue sharing mechanism to reduce the disparity in fiscal capacity among local governments. The parameters might change, but this is roughly the system that is presently in place, except that the reform seems to be calling for a more rule-based approach.

Finally, the proposal raises some concerns about the present system for structuring grants to local governments. The first concern is the balance between general grants and special (earmarked) grants. There seems to be a sense that earmarked grants can be consolidated, made more standard, and perhaps the vertical share can be reduced. It is noted that the number of earmarked grants (special purpose intergovernmental transfer programs) already have been reduced from 243 to 271, but there is still room for further reduction. The second concern with the present approach is that matching provisions place too much stress on local government finances. This echoes a concern expressed in the State Council regulations. Third, there is need for a change in some of the distribution rules for transfers, such as the need to include immigrants more directly in subsidy programs and upgrading transfers for ecological purposes. Fourth, the framework is not "rational in that general transfers are smaller in amount than special (earmarked) transfers.

The provincial reform calls for addressing these problems with a number of actions, including the following:

(1) Complete a review of the intergovernmental fiscal system that spells out a better arrangement for the transfer of funds to subnational governments.

(2) Clarify the special transfer regime, reduce the number of special transfers, and make provision for a sunset on these awards.

(3) Innovate in the methods used to distribute grants by considering factors such as area management, accountability of city and county governments, and general public service demands.

(4) Establish an administration system for the regular assessment of special grants, and make continuation of grants dependent on performance.

Subprovincial Fiscal System Reform: Commentary

This leg of the fiscal reform program in Shandong is not so far along as the others. It is more focused on describing the approach it plans to take in formulating the reform. In fact, the general approach described is the modern one taken by most governments that move toward redefining their intergovernmental fiscal system. And, it follows the lead of the State Council regulations.

Shandong proposes to look first at the expenditure assignment regime to determine if the functional responsibilities are correctly placed. This is the right place for the reform to begin. To the extent they find that externalities and economies of scale have been given too little weight, they likely will move to a less decentralized fiscal system, i. e. , a system where counties have less responsibility than under the present system, and more responsibilities are shifted to the provincial level. This would be much more than a cosmetic change.

Revenue assignment follows expenditure assignment in modern intergovernmental fiscal systems, and if spending responsibilities change, so too will revenue allocations. A major question in this regard is how equalization will be treated in this realignment of functions and finance. Modernization and rule of law suggest that a movement toward a more formula-based system should at least be considered. However, the Shandong proposal is not far enough along in its development to know if that is the direction to be taken. This is a very important issue.

The proposed reforms in the intergovernmental transfer system are not yet developed, but some rough idea of the approach is given. Among the targets for reform appear to be a reduction of conditional grants in favor of an increase in general purpose grants, and the elimination of required matches by local governments. The rough outlines of the thinking about reform suggest that an equalization grant program will be considered. However, there is not yet a discussion about how it will be financed or how large it will be relative to shared taxes, or how much equalization is desired.

These intergovernmental fiscal reforms are very important. They call on the Provincial Government to address some fundamental issues. These include whether more governance decisions will be made at the higher province level rather than at the grass roots county level, and whether a trade will be made between equalization of service levels and stimulating economic growth.

Fiscal expenditure management

The Shandong proposal calls for expenditure management reform in three areas: reduce unnecessary spending, eliminate spending on competitive sector activities, and find new ways of using public funds to support economic development.

The first emphasis, focused on thrift, is to standardize policies that would reduce spending on less essential activities in favor of those that do more to improve general public services. The actions that might be followed in this respect include the introduction of a standardized fee management system which covers fees connected to government receptions, cars, travel, etc. There are many other targets of a "thrift" program that might be implemented by using standardized procedures, including procurement, over-recruiting, investment evaluation, and the like. These are outlined in the proposal.

The Shandong proposal calls on provincial and subprovincial governments to pull back on spending on activities that are competitive with the private sector. This includes various forms of subsidy that have led to overspending on economic affairs at the cost of underspending on general public services.

It asks for a shift in government expenditures toward the provision of essential public services.

Finally, there is a stated objective in the Shandong proposal to find new ways to use fiscal funding to support industry development and public services. The proposal encourages subnational governments to move away from the old model of using direct subsidies and other awards that are allocated to individual companies. The new proposal is to establish a special fund to support industrial job creation. The goals are to leverage private capital investment, and to promote industrial restructuring and upgrading. Projects would be prioritized according to emphasis on procurement of government services, Public Private Partnerships and other new models of stimulating social capital in areas which the government is promoting. The fund would be capitalized by provincial and market sources, and targeted industries would be recipients of new capital based on a committee rather than a department decision.

A second "new" approach is to look to the market to fund and even manage social welfare services such as services to the elderly. Financing and delivery might involve competition among providers, pricing, contracting, franchises, and public-private partnerships.

Fiscal Expenditure management: Commentary

The reform proposal asks for three disparate approaches to expenditure management reform. Two of the three call for generating savings in the budget by cutting non-essential spending and by pulling back on direct support to the competitive sector, and to redirect the funds to general public services.

The proposal to practice thrift is a good initiative. Targeting non-essential spending supports good financial management practice, may target corruption, and sends an important message to the population and to government servants. But this does not always lead to significantly large savings and it often requires significant administrative effort.

The fiscal reform proposal also calls for reduced direct spending to support competitive sector activities. This is consistent with the general recommendations of the CCCP and with the State Council regulations. The proposal presents some evidence that Shandong spends at a much higher rate on economic services than do industrial countries, and at a lower rate on social services. Reducing subsidies to the enterprise sector would free up funds for investment in general public services. It is reported that there have already been denials of numerous requests for subsidies by enterprises.

The State Council regulations also asks provinces to find new ways to support economic development. The response of the proposal is to offer an initiative that will support the competitive sector, by targeting preferred industries and industry support activities. Subsidies given by departments would be replaced by awards made by a committee based on an economic development strategy. Though few details are given, it appears that the Fund will be capitalized by a combination of provincial government and market sources. This proposal would be a significant improvement over the award of subsidies by departments, but still it would seem to be at odds with the goals of separating the public from the private sector, and focusing the activities of government on public service provision.

Modernize the financial management system

The financial management system is weak, in part because of structural flaws, in part because of ineffective monitoring and regulation, and in part because of limited capacity on the part of government personnel. The proposal cites issues such as theft, misappropriation, false accounting, lax asset management, and wasting special funds. The Shandong proposal calls for a significant upgrading of the performance in all areas of financial management. It suggests that a better adherence to the law, particularly the budget law, is needed.

A first action is to improve the supervision mechanism, including increased intensity of investigation of illegal actions and discipline violations. The recommendations also call for making the budget and financial accounts more available to the public so as to improve the transparency of how the financial management system operates. This should lead to the results of better execution of the budget law, more acceptance of the supervision of the NPC, and improved financial management transparency.

The second area for improvement is to upgrade the operations of financial management in local governments. In many cases, local governments do not take a scientific approach to financial management with the result of a significant loss in funds. Sometimes this is due to an inadequate implementation of the system, and sometimes it is due to unqualified staff. The results are "paying too high a price for tax relief", taking unnecessary financial risks, incurring illegal expenses, and the like. An upgrade in the quality of the financial management staff, operating within the limits of the law, and a better supervision system, are necessary to correct this problem. The Shandong proposal calls for a significant upgrading of staff through better hiring practices and more training.

Modernize the Financial Management System: Commentary

The proposal does a good job of recognizing the importance of implementation of the new regulations laid down by the State Council. It seems clear that there is a significant gap between the current practice and best practice. Achieving the objective of a more scientific approach to financial management and a more efficient delivery of this service will be constrained by three issues.

The first is that the quality of the practice likely varies greatly within the province, with the rural counties probably the weakest. But these counties have limited resources, pay their officers less, and may have a weaker talent pool from which to draw. Districts, on the other hand, also probably face a need to significantly upgrade their financial management practices, but their needs and their starting points are likely to be quite different. The proposal does not address the particular needs of different types of local government.

Second, the proposal calls for better attitudes and work effort, and a more scientific approach, but there is no concrete implementation plan for getting this done. For example, in the case of training programs, there are questions on how these might be delivered and about the resources necessary to do this.

CHAPTER FIVE NATIONAL CONTEXT: LIBERALIZING THE INTERGOVERNMENTAL FISCAL SYSTEM

In the fall of 2014, China's top leaders presented a program for fiscal reform of the nation's tax system, budgeting practices and center-local fiscal relations. The broad proposals are impressive, as is the statement of the general objective:

"Public finance is the foundation and a critical pillar for state governance. A scientifically designed fiscal and tax regime is the institution that guarantees resource allocation optimization, market unification, social equality, and long-lasting security and peace for a nation."

China has set a timetable to modernize its fiscal system. The Minister of Finance has said that the major reform tasks concerning the fiscal and tax system will be completed by 2016, and a modern system will be fully developed by 2020. On August 31th of 2014, China's legislature adopted a revision to the Budget Law. This is the first time the Budget Law has been revised since it took effect in 1995. The old Budget Law was adopted when China was more strongly influenced by planned economy concepts, leaving a great deal of room for interpretation by governments. The amendments to the Budget Law are closely interrelated with China's fiscal reform. It took an unusually long time to revise it—seven years to draft a bill for the first reading in 2011 and four readings to get it passed. Subsequently in September of 2014, the State Council followed suit with directives on deepening the reform of budget and debt management.

General Directions Recommended By the Plenary Session[1]

On November 12, 2013, the Third Plenary Session of the 18th Central Committee of the Communist Party of China adopted the "Decision of the CCCPC on Some Major Issues Concerning Comprehensively Deepening the Reform". The Decision of the CCCPC puts forth a clear set of requirements for deepening the fiscal and taxation systems. Among the key areas for reform are to improve legislation, clarify powers and responsibilities, restructure the tax system, stabilize tax burdens, produce transparent budgets, increase efficiency, and establish a modern fiscal system for both the central and local governments. In order to achieve these goals, the CCCPC proposes three major reform measures: improvement of the budget management system, improvement of the tax system, and establishment of a system of matching between administrative authority and expenditure responsibility.

Improve the budget management system

A completely standardized, open and transparent budget system will be adopted. The focus of budget review will be extended from fiscal balance and deficit size to expenditure budget analysis and fiscal policies. Most major expenditures that are presently indexed to increases in financial revenues or GDP will be delinked. This will allow a significant increase in budget flexibility. China also will establish a multi-year budget balance mechanism, a comprehensive government financial reporting system on an accrual basis, and a standardized and reasonable debt management and early warning risk mechanism for both central and local governments.

The factors determining the allocation of general transfer payments will be

1 The material presented below is based on translation by Baoyun Qiao.

improved, mostly by increasing the transfer payments to old revolutionary base areas, regions inhabited by ethnic minorities in compact communities, border areas and poverty-stricken areas. Local fiscal gaps caused by the central authority's policy of increasing spending will be filled by general transfer payments. The plan also includes integrating and regulating special transfer payments, and gradually cancelling funds that flow from local governments to the competitive sector. Special transfer payments for relief and emergency purposes, as well as the remaining special transfer payments, will be studied and if they concern local affairs, included.

Improve the taxation system

Reforms in the tax structure will be implemented, and there will be a gradual increase in the proportion of direct taxes. The ongoing reform of the VAT will continue with the folding-in of the business tax, and the tax rate structure will be simplified. The structure of consumption taxes will be upgraded and will be imposed on products that consume too much energy and cause serious pollution as well as some high-end consumer goods. Other elements of the tax reform plan include establishing an individual income tax system in which taxable income is defined in both comprehensive and categorized ways, passing new real estate tax legislation and implementing this in a timely manner, accelerating the resource tax reform, and changing the current environmental protection fee into an environmental tax.

In line with the principles of unifying the tax system, promoting equality in tax burdens and fair competition in the private market sector, the management of preferential tax policies, especially regional preferential tax policies, will be rationalized. Legislation regarding the use of preferential tax treatments will be made clear and regulations will be issued. This will enable determination of which preferential policies can be continued and which cannot. In addition, the collection and management system for provincial and local government taxes will be upgraded.

Establish correspondence between administrative authority and expenditure responsibility

The administrative authority and expenditure responsibility of the central government, including those concerning national defense, foreign affairs, national security, and unified national market rules and management will be made stronger. The administrative authority over some social security programs, and the construction and maintenance of major trans-regional projects will be shared between the central and the local governments. Regional public services will remain the responsibilities of local governments. The central government will delegate some expenditure responsibilities to local governments and finance these with transfer payments.

Comments on CCCPC decision by Minister Lou

Finance Minister Lou Jiwei commented on these CCCPC decisions by pointing out that the budget management system reform, is the foundation and should be the first step taken in the reform. [1] The reform of revenue distribution should be implemented after the substantial completion of tax system reform. Meanwhile, building a better system of matching between administrative authority and expenditure responsibility may require more time to form a consensus plan. The crucial years for the fiscal and taxation reforms are 2014 and 2015. While the reform of budget management system may make decisive progress in the short run, and reform of the taxation system may make significant progress in legislation and promotion in the short run, the reform of assignments of administrative authorities and expenditure responsibilities may only get as far as reaching a basic consensus. The major works and tasks of fiscal and taxation reforms will

1 The comments of Minister Lou, reported here, are taken from Minister Lou's Speech from http://news.xinhuanet.com/fortune/2014-03/07/c_126233438.htm.

be basically achieved by 2016 and various reforms will be put in place, but a modern fiscal system may not be established before 2020.

The next round of fiscal and taxation reforms will open some new and important areas that are in step with the decision of the CCCPC:

(1) Legislation improvement will emphasize the rule of law as applied to financial operations.

(2) The assignment of administrative authority and expenditure responsibility between the central and local governments will be clarified.

(3) The taxation system reform will include a gradual increase in the proportion of direct taxes, replacement of various administrative fees with taxes, reinforcement of the role of income tax as a main channel to collect fiscal revenue, and improvement of the tax collection and management system.

(4) The ratio of fiscal revenues to GDP should be reasonably stable, and the distribution of tax burdens should be controlled.

(5) A comprehensive and standardized budget disclosure system should be implemented. This can promote a democratic financial management system, and can help build an open government and a government that operates by the rule of law.

(6) A scientific approach to financial management and budget evaluation can lead to more efficient financing of public revenues.

Minister Lou stressed that deepening the reform of the fiscal and taxation system is a complex undertaking. The specific implementation of the reform should adhere to the following principles: balancing the relationship between the government and the market, mobilizing the initiative of both the central and local governments, taking account of both efficiency and fairness, and taking account of both long-term and immediate issues.

State Council Regulations

In order to move toward implementation of the 18th NCCPC (National Congress of Communist Party of China) and the Third Plenary Session of 18th Central Committee of the Communist Party, the State Council issued "Decision of the State Council on Deepening the Reform of Budget Management System" (No. 45 [2014]) on September 26, 2014. This document includes specific decisions on deepening the reform of the budget management system, based on China's new Budget Law that will guide the implementation of a comprehensive, standardized, open and transparent budget system.

The Decision of the State Council lists a series of problems to be addressed: an unscientific budget management and control method that results from the lack of a multi-year budget plan, local government borrowing not being under the control of the budget management system, budget constraints are weak, the structure of fiscal revenue and expenditure is not in step with government objectives, the size of fiscal carry-over of surplus funds is too large and expenditures are made in an inefficient way. All of these factors are challenges to the sustainable development of public finances in China.

The principles of the new budget management system reform include:

(1) Constructing a standardized and modern budget system and connecting it with revised and improved laws and regulations.

(2) Drawing a clear boundary between the government and the market. Preferential fiscal subsidies and tax policies shall be reviewed and where appropriate, will be dropped.

(3) Promoting open and transparent budgets.

(4) Placing emphasis on the top-level design, but also taking into consideration the external environment and constraints so that the relationship between the budget management system reform and the administrative management system reform can be coordinated.

The eight major elements of the upgraded budget management system are outlined below:

The first is to improve the overall government budget system and promote the disclosure of budgetary information. This can be done by defining the scope of the general public finance budget, government fund budget, state-owned capital operating budget, and social insurance fund budget. The regulations should provide for all government fiscal activities to be included in the budget, and for a clear and modern process of preparation, execution and review of the budget.

Second, there should be further improvements in the systems for delivering basic expenditures. The level of expenditure should be determined by the basic requirements for the operation of government offices, and improved mechanisms of personnel and capital management. Departmental budgets and government budgets and final accounts should follow a standard economic classification.

The government should promote the full disclosure of budget information. The budgets and final accounts of specific-purpose transfers may be disclosed by function, project and region. Fiscal policies will also be disclosed and the scope of disclosure of the budget will be extended to the final accounts of individual departments. In addition, more effort will be made to fully disclose detail of the "three public consumptions".

The management and control of government budgets must be improved and a multi-year budget practice must be established. The finance departments may, jointly with other departments concerned, compile the three-year rolling fiscal plan to analyze and forecast the major revenues and expenditures in the coming three years. This fiscal plan should be linked with the outline of planning for national economic and social development and with national macroeconomic policy.

Budget controls need to be tightened and refocused. Audits of the general public budgets should shift focus from budget balance and deficit size to expenditure performance and policy analysis. For reinforcing the budget constraints, governments at all levels should highlight the contents of expenditure policies when reporting the expenditure budgets to the NPC. Any increase or decrease in general budgetary expenditures should be reported to the standing committees of NPC at same level, for review and approval. The revenue budgets should shift from monitoring the binding constraint to forecasting according to the economic factors and policy changes.

For the central budgets, the general public budgets may, according to the demands of macro-control policies, show deficits which will be covered by issuing Treasury bonds. Local governments may, with the approval of the State Council, show a deficit in general public finance budgets which will be covered by issuance of the general debts. The size of local debts will be incorporated into the ceiling management. The State Council will determine and report the local debt ceilings to the NPC and its standing committees for review and approval.

The government fund budget will be prepared based on the revenues available and actual expenditure needs of government fund projects. With the approval of the State Council, the local governments may issue special debts in the government fund budgets, for the development of revenue generating public services. The size of special local debts will be brought into the ceiling management. The State Council will determine and report the ceilings of special local debts to the NPC and its standing committees for review and approval.

The state-owned capital operation budget will be based on the principle of revenue-expenditure balance, i. e. , there should be no deficit.

A multi-year budget balancing mechanism will be established. For the central budgets, the surplus in the central general public budgets will be used to offset deficits and supplement the central budget stabilization funds. Shortages will be filled by transferring funds from central budget stabilization funds, reducing expenditures or issuing debts under the ceiling for treasury bonds approved by the NPC and its standing committees. For the local budgets, the surplus in the implementation of local general public budgets will be used to retire outstanding government debt or to supplement local budget stabilization funds, while deficits will be covered by fund transfers from local budget stabilization funds, or other budgetary funds, and by expenditure reduction. If budget balance is still not realized, the provincial-level governments may increase the size of deficits and report to the Ministry of Finance after approval by the provincial-level NPC and its standing committees. The incremental deficits will be offset by annual budgets of the following year. The prefectural- and county-level governments will balance their budgets by applying for temporary bailouts from upper-level governments and repaying in the followingyear. The surplus in the government fund budgets and state-owned capital operation budgets will be carried forward to the following year, when shortages will be offset by the expenditure reduction.

Third, the management of fiscal revenue should be improved and preferential tax policies should be regulated. The goal is to strengthen tax collection and management. The taxation departments shall not violate the laws and regulations or overstep their authorities to collect the taxes over the payable limit or in advance, or reduce, exempt, or suspend the taxes payable.

Preferential policies for taxation should be regulated. Unless State Council regulations state otherwise, all government departments shall not depart from the unified national fiscal and taxation systems by stipulating preferential tax policies. This includes a prohibition on tax preferences when drafting other laws, regulations, development planning and regional policies. Regions and government departments may not, without the approval of the State Council, make tax preferential policies for enterprises. Policies with economic and social development value that have no law and regulation barriers, can be implemented nationwide as soon as possible. In principle, the implementation of policies with specific implementation time limits shall all be terminated upon expiration, and the implementation time limit shall be set for policies without one.

Several other actions are proposed to improve non-tax revenue management. Among the most important are to limit administrative fees and government funds, and abolish illegal and unreasonable charges or funds; to strengthen and improve profit-sharing mechanisms for state-owned resources and capital, and to clearly specify the profit ownership of state-owned capital; to enhance the budget classification system for non-tax revenues; and to improve the collection, payment and supervision systems.

Fourth, the structure of fiscal expenditure should be improved, some rigidities in the use of public funds should be removed, and the management of carry-over and surplus funds should be made stronger. Several steps can be taken in this regard.

(1) To optimize the productivity of government expenditures, it will be required to strictly control recurrent expenditures such as those for government buildings, fiscal-supported staff and "three public consumptions".

(2) The practice of indexing the growth of major expenditures to GDP should end.

(3) The governments should implement the tax-for-fee system reform by gradually abolishing the special-purpose funds in the city maintenance and construction tax, sewage charges, prospecting and mining rights, and mineral resources compensation fees.

(4) Budget allocations should be improved by gradually incorporating all budgetary funds into the finance departments.

Fifth, the structure of fiscal transfers will undergo reforms and restructuring, including the following:

(1) Improve the growth mechanism of general purpose transfers by increasing the size and proportion of general purpose transfers to over 60 percent of total transfers, and significantly increasing the transfers to old revolutionary base areas, ethnic minority areas, border areas and poverty-stricken areas. General-purpose transfers (unconditional grants) should be used to offset the local fiscal gaps caused by the central government policies.

(2) Reform of the regime of special-purpose transfers should be undertaken. Those special purpose transfers concerning local affairs will be put into the category of general-purpose transfers. The CCCP will screen and investigate the special-purpose transfers in competitive areas one by one, and "small, scattered, and chaotic" and ineffective ones will be abolished. The rest will be compressed in size and kept to zero growth. The allocation methods will be improved, and the use of administrative allocation will be reduced. The special-purpose transfers with similar goals will be combined. In addition, the CCCP will regulate the establishment of new special-purpose transfers, strictly control new projects, and establish and improve the regular assessments and the withdrawal mechanism for special-purpose transfers;

(3) Accelerate the revision of central-local transfer management measures to make provision for project initiation, fund allocation, use management, performance evaluation, and information disclosure. A mechanism for linkage between fiscal transfers and "citizensation" for the rural migrant population will be established. On the basis of reasonable specification of central and local expenditure responsibilities,

CCCPC will rationalize the existing matching policies. Local governments shall be not required to provide matching funds for public affairs functions. All regions shall integrate and regulate the special funds arranged by the government at its level, improve the fund management measures, and improve the effectiveness of fund use.

Sixth, there will be a strengthening of the management of carry-over and surplus funds. Governments at all levels shall

(1) Establish a mechanism for carry-over and surplus funds. The carry-over funds from previous-year budgets may be used as the expenditure for the next-year. The carry-over funds unused in two consecutive years may be managed as a balance, and may be used to supplement the budget stabilization funds. All departments and units shall manage the carry-over and surplus funds of previous-year budgets as prescribed by the Ministry of Finance;

(2) Increase the rate of use of carry-over funds. Where funds are not necessary to comply with their original, intended use purpose, they may be transferred to the areas where funds are needed to support economic and social development;

(3) Build an administrative mechanism for the management and reporting of carry-over and surplus funds

(4) Establish a mechanism for the scientific and reasonable assessment of the progress of budget implementation.

All funds required for purchasing services shall be listed in the fiscal budget. All government departments shall, according to relevant provisions, be encouraged to purchase the services to effectively reduce the costs of public services and improve the quality of public services.

Seventh, budget implementation management should be strengthened, and the performance of government expenditure should be improved. The following approach should be followed in budget implementation:

(1) Harden the budget constraints in the implementation of annual budgets. Do not introduce policies for expenditure increases during the budget year except for emergency expenditures such as disaster relief (which will be covered by drawing on budget reserves). Funds for some policies, which it is necessary to introduce, will be covered in future annual budgets. Budgets involving government procurement shall be implemented according to the relevant provisions of government procurement;

(2) General- and special-purpose transfers shall be formally issued from the central to local governments respectively, in 30 days and 90 days after the approval by the NPC. After receiving central general- and special-purpose transfers, provincial-level governments shall officially transfer them to local governments at all levels above the county in 30 days;

(3) All departments and units shall implement their budgetary expenditures according to the approved budget lines. Budgetary funds shall, if needed, be transferred for use between different budgetary items, different budget levels or different budget projects according to the requirements and procedures set down by the Ministry of Finance.

Treasury fund management will be regulated to promote efficiency in the use of revenue and in spending. Therefore, government will

(1) comprehensively review the special financial accounts. Regions shall not set up new special financial accounts. The special financial accounts will be removed in 2 years except for those reviewed by the Ministry of Finance and approved for continuation by the State Council. Local governments at all levels may not open new special financial accounts;

(2) Accrual-basis accounting will be strictly regulated. Local governments

at all levels shall not disburse from the costs and expenses based on the accrual system except from year-end balances paid by the treasury single account. The specific items calculated by the accrual system, as prescribed by the State Council, shall be reported to the standing committees of the NPC at the same level;

(3) Existing government loans and advances will be reviewed and "cleaned up". The loans and advances which should be paid through the budget should be disbursed according to the relevant provisions. Those temporary loans and advances that are in line with the regulations shall be recovered in a timely fashion, and those which do not conform to the regulations shall be taken back within a defined time period;

(4) Governments at all levels are strictly forbidden to lend or advance fiscal funds to off-budget units or projects which are not included in the annual budgets. In addition, governments at all levels shall strengthen the management and supervision on the Treasury.

The budget performance management system should be improved. The scope of performance management may be gradually extended to budget units at all levels and all financial funds, the emphases of performance evaluation will be expanded from project expenditures, and evaluation results should be taken as an important basis for further expenditure planning.

An accrual-based, comprehensive government financial reporting system will be established. When the conditions are right, a comprehensive government financial statement shall be reported to the NPC and its standing committees at the same level. This will become an important basis for assessing local government performance and budgetary position. In addition, a disclosure mechanism for comprehensive government financial reporting will be gradually established.

Eighth, the management of local debts should be regulated and a risk management program should be put in place. A first step toward this goal is establishing a standard local debt financing mechanism with a proper debt-raising authority for local governments. Provincial-level governments may, with approval by the State Council, issue debt, while the prefectural- and county-level governments may raise the debts indirectly through the provincial-level governments. The government debts shall be raised only by governments and their departments, not by enterprises and institutions. Local governments can raise debts with government bonds. Local government financing platforms shall be eliminated from the government financing function. For promoting the utilization of the Public-Private Partnership model, social capital shall be encouraged to involve in the investment and operation of profit-making public welfare undertakings, including urban infrastructure, by means of franchises and other operations.

General debts of local governments raised by issuing general bonds shall be included in the general public budget, while special debts raised by issuing special bonds shall be placed into the government fund budget.

Local governments may borrow within approved limits approved by the State Council but must seek approval from the the NPC and its standing committees at the corresponding level. Local government shall follow market principles when raising debts. In addition, a local government credit rating system may be established and this will improve the functioning of the local government bond market. The debts raised by local governments shall be used only for capital expenditure of public welfare functions and appropriate repayment of debt stock, and may not be used for recurrent expenditures.

The Ministry of Finance may assess the risks of regional debt according to indicators such as the debt ratio, the incremental debt ratio, the debt service rate, and the overdue debt ratio. For the high-risk regions, active measures will be taken to reduce the risks. After screening and incorporating the debt stock of local governments into budget management, all regions may apply for the issuance of local government bonds to substitute for the existing debt stock in order to reduce the interest burdens and optimize the maturity structure. For hardening the budget constraint and preventing the moral hazard, local governments shall bear the responsibility for repaying their debts and the central government will offer a bail-out.

Government debt will be used as an indicator in the performance assessment of governments. Provincial-level governments shall be responsible for local government debts in their jurisdiction. Local governments at all levels shall take the responsibilities for their debt management and for preventing and resolving financial risks. The person in charge of governments shall bear the primary responsibilities for putting these policies into action.

Fiscal discipline will be established by putting in place a sound assessment and supervision mechanism, an information disclosure and tip-off system, and an accountability mechanism. This might be done in three ways. One is for all regions and departments to strictly abide by various laws and regulations of finance and taxation like the budget law, the tax collection and management law, the accounting law and the government procurement law. They will exercise the administrative decision-making powers and fiscal management powers, and actively accept the supervisions from the NPC and the public. The final account auditing system will be established to further enhance the auditing supervision.

Another way to establish fiscal discipline is to better regulate the finance management behavior. The construction and operation of various systems including the budget preparation, revenue collection and management, fund allocation, treasury management, government procurement, financial supervision, performance assessment, and accountability will be improved. Third, local governments at all levels will conduct a comprehensive inspection of the implementation of the economic and financial discipline in all departments and units in their jurisdictions. The existing problems will be identified by financial departments and auditing bodies. Accountability also will be strengthened by punishment according to laws and regulations like the budget law, the irregular and illegal behaviors referring to falsely reporting, falsely claiming, retaining, misappropriating, detaining fiscal funds as well as introducing preferential tax policies that are not in conformity with the laws and regulations.

Commentary by Minister of Finance on Revenue Management[1]

Minister Lou made a special note of revenue management. He pointed out that the existing tax preferential policies, especially regional tax preferential policies, are excessive. China has currently introduced the implementation of about 50 regional tax preferential policies which cover nearly all provinces (regions and municipalities). Some local governments and departments of finance and taxation carry out "local policies" to reduce or rebate taxes in disguised form of tax returns. This results in the erosion of the tax base, the transfer of profits to enterprises, and the emergence of a tax "wasteland". These "local policies" are not conducive to making optimal use of tax revenues, or to achieving the goal of social justice. Moreover, such policies have a negative effect on fair competition and the unified market environment, and do not accord with the requirements of the establishment of the modern fiscal system.

Hereafter, local governments' drafting of laws, regulations, development planning and regional policies may not break through the unified national fiscal and taxation systems and stipulate preferential tax policies except in the case of special tax laws and regulations. Local governments, without approval of the State Council, may not make tax preferential policies for enterprises. In principle, the implementation of such policies with a specific implementation time limit shall all be terminated upon expiration. The implementation a time limit shall be set for policies without one. The Ministry of Finance will regularly review and assess the practice, and will

1 This is our interpretation of what Minister Lou said, rather than his exact words.

severely punish illegal behaviors.

The State Council issued "Notice on Reviewing and Regulating Preferential Policies for Taxation and Other Aspects (No. 62 [2014] of the State Council) (hereinafter to be referred as 'the No. 62 Notice of the SC')" on November 27, 2014. By cleaning up and regulating the tax preferential policies, the No. 62 Notice of the SC aims to prevent local protectionism and unfair competition, and make the market play a decisive role in the allocation of resources.

Facing the difficult economic situation, the State Council issued the "Notice on Issues Concerning Preferential Policies for Taxation and Other Aspects (No. 25 [2015] of the State Council). The No. 25 Notice of the SC specified that (1) unified national preferential policies may be implemented, (2) Regional and departmental preferential policies shall be implemented in accordance with the prescribed time limit. For those in the absence of prescribed time limit, local governments and relevant departments shall set up a transition period and continue to implement them during the transition period. (3) Local preferential policies that are part of contracts with enterprises shall continue to be effective. The fulfilled policies shall not be retrospective. (4) All regions and departments, in formulating new preferential policies involving taxes or centrally-approved non-tax revenues, should submit these to the State Council for approval. Expenditures arranged for those policies may not link to tax or non-tax revenues paid by enterprises. (5) Special clean-up works specified by the No. 62 Notice of the SC will be suspended until further deployments.

Commentary by Minister of Finance on tax reform[1]

The goal of tax reform is to build a fiscal and taxation system that is characterized by scientific development, social fairness and market

1 This is our interpretation of what Minister Lou said, rather than his exact words.

unification. The reforms to be implemented, now under discussion, mainly focus on 6 major categories of taxes: valued-added tax (VAT), consumption tax, resource tax, environmental protection tax, property tax and individual income tax.

The VAT reform is aimed at establishing a standardized consumption-based VAT system that is driven primarily by the neutrality principle of taxation. The next step for the "Replacing Business Tax with VAT" reform is to extend its scope to various industries including life services, construction, real estate, finance and other industries. By 2015, "Replacing Business Tax with VAT" reform will be completed as planned, with the life service industry, finance industry and real estate industry included. Minister Lou noted that the most difficult part will be to bring the real estate industry into the base. Extending the VAT reform scope to construction and real estate industries requires that the problem of real estate input tax deduction be solved.

China's economic development has entered a "new normal" period, i. e., a slower but more sustainable growth rate. The current economy is performing at an overall smooth and steady condition, but it is facing a significant downward pressure. Resisting slower growth requires the co-operative efforts of enterprises and governments. Enterprises should exert their autonomy and inventiveness to adapt to the new normal of economic development. Governments should create an environment conducive to the development of mass entrepreneurship and innovation.

On the one hand, governments may carry out policies and measures of structural tax reductions and general fee cutting that will alleviate the burdens on small and medium-sized enterprises and enhance their growth potential. On the other hand, governments may further promote policies that will appropriately stimulate the vitality of market entities.

A number of other taxes are being discussed for structural reform, but formal actions have not been taken. For the Improvement of the consumption tax system, the possible structural changes include a broadening of the coverage of the tax base and a rationalization of the rate structure.

For accelerating the reform of the coal resource tax, the government may promote a price-based reform of resource taxes and gradually extend the scope of resource taxes to natural ecological spaces like water, forests, grasslands and tidal-flat areas.

For establishing the environmental protection tax, the existing sewage charges will be replaced with the environmental protection tax. The goal would be to use the taxation as an instrument of protecting the ecological environment, according to the principles of focusing on regulation and control, and replacing various administrative fees with taxation.

For accelerating the property tax legislation and timely promoting the property tax reform, we may reinforce the investigation on tax structure issues, including property survey, and insist on the full development of legislation.

For exploring the options of gradually establishing an individual income tax system with a combination of integration and classification, the government will consider amending the "Tax Collection Law" and other relative laws and regulations.

The allocation of administrative authorities among levels of governments is an important institutional arrangement, and it must be dealt with. Maintaining the overall stability of the existing central-local finance pattern is a prerequisite to the reasonable allocation of revenue between the central and local governments. At present, the degree of fiscal concentration of China's central government is not high, compared with Britain, France, Italy, Australia and other countries of which the proportions of central fiscal revenue are over 70 percent. The USA's proportion of central fiscal revenue in total fiscal revenue also reaches about 65 percent in normal years.

For furthering the rationalization of the allocation of revenue between the central and local governments, we may make reasonable adjustments to help maintain the overall stability of the current central-local financial pattern. It is important to maintain the overall stability of the current financial pattern of the central and local governments, and further rationalize the division of revenues between them through tax reform. Taxes with a large volatility of tax incomes, a strong redistributive function, and a great mobility of tax bases will be classified as the central taxes. Taxes where local governments have a comparative advantage in information necessary for tax assessment and collection, where there is a significant influence on local resource allocation, will be assigned to local governments in a relatively large proportion. After the revenue assignments are made, the fiscal gaps of local governments will be covered by the central finance through tax sharing.

For the rational division of administrative authority and expenditure responsibility between levels of governments, it is critical to consider the objective factors that can point the way to an efficient division of responsibilities. Based on these principles, the central government may be assigned the administrative authorities of defense, foreign affairs and national security concerning unified national market rules and management. In addition, the Congress will assign the regional public services to local administrative authorities and clarify the joint administrative authorities of the central and local governments. The central government may delegate parts of administrative authorities and expenditure responsibilities to local governments through the fiscal transfer mechanism.

CHAPTER SIX TAX REFORM, FINANCIAL MANAGEMENT REFORM AND SHANDONG FINANCES

Shandong's reform program has followed the guidelines set out by the State Council in its 2014 regulations. Though the Plenary Session statement seemed to promise much more by way of fiscal reform[1], the State Council has so far moved forward only with reform of the budget management system. The slowdown in economic growth may be a reason for slowing the pace of reform.

A next round of reform may come in the next few years. We might use the Shandong case to illustrate the reasons why. First, the replacement of lost revenues from the business tax is a problem that must be addressed. In Shandong, the business tax is the most important tax revenue source of provincial and local governments. Second, there is the larger question of filling the revenue gap in Shandong that will come from the slowdown in revenues from land lease sales, the tax revenue slowdown that will accompany the slower rate of economic growth, and the increased level of spending required to upgrade public services, repay debt, and fund social security.

Certainly, the present reform package will address these problems. Part of this gap can be filled by the reduction in tax preferences, and by enactment of the tax for fee reform, and by cost savings from more efficient financial management. All of these actions are provided for by the State Council and in the Shandong proposal, but no estimates of revenue impacts have been made. Some of this revenue loss could also be compensated by new

1 See also the comments above by Minister of Finance Lou Jiwei.

revenue sources that must be defined by the central government, by chanes in the grant system, or by expenditure reassignments. But for now, these must be thought of only as future possibilities.

In this chapter, we speculate about these issues: how might the lost business tax revenues in Shandong be replaced from existing resources, what new tax for provincial and local governments might eventually be introduced, and how would Shandong fare under a change in regime for central-provincial transfers. We also speculate about whether such changes would require a more centralized (provincial government driven) financing system in the province.

Replacing The Business Tax

The business tax is being merged into the value added tax. While this is good tax policy—it will allow sellers to claim credit under the VAT for tax paid on all input purchases—it will have important consequences for the revenue base of provincial and local governments. The "swap"—business tax for VAT—is not a good one for subnational governments because business tax revenues accrue fully to them whereas their share of VAT collections is only 25 percent. It might be argued that the revamped VAT base may grow faster in the long run , but this still would not likely address the shift in revenue capture from the local to the central government level.

The potential revenue loss is not easily calculated. To date the local governments have been held harmless against any revenue loss due to the restructuring. We can, however, illustrate the possible magnitude of the problem. In 2014, the budgeted amount of business tax revenues was 113,592 million RMB. The business tax accounts for about 30 percent of all tax revenues, and so would not be easy to replace in the provincial revenue structure. Note for example that business tax collections in 2014 were nearly twice as large as the local share of VAT collections.

To illustrate the reform options, we provide some very rough estimates based on rearranging revenue sources that are already in the Shandong system (See Table 14). In row 1 we show the revenue impact of removing the business tax, had that happened in 2014. If there were no changes in other revenue sharing rates, the local government 25 percent share of VAT collections would recapture some of the lost revenue. For purposes of illustration, let us assume that about a 100 billion RMB revenue increase would accrue to the central VAT if it had fully assumed the business tax in 2014.[1] In this case, about 25 billion RMB would automatically come back to the Shandong governments and the net revenue loss would be reduced to about 88 billion RMB. To recover all of the revenue loss would require a VAT sharing rate of 50 percent in this illustration. But such an increase would pose a significant incremental burden on the central government budget.

Another choice would be to impose a heavy surcharge on the urban construction and maintenance tax, the education surcharge, and the individual income tax. As shown in Table 14, an additional 100 percent surcharge on tax liability could reduce the revenue loss by 30 billion RMB. This option would be more feasible in the new arrangements where receipts are not earmarked.

There has been considerable discussion about backfilling for some of this revenue loss by increasing taxes on real property. The four taxes now levied on real property—house property tax, urban land use tax, land

1 Actually, the replacement of business tax for VAT is more complicated than a straight "25 percent for 100 percent" swap. VAT revenues would increase by less than 113 billion RMB because of the increase in credits allowed. Moreover, the rate and base structure of the business tax and VAT are different. And finally, the business tax is collected by the local tax bureau, and VAT by the central tax bureau, and their different procedures may lead to different collection rates. Note the following: The effective rate of business tax in Shandong is about 2 percent of GDP. That for the VAT in Shandong is 4 percent and the effective rate of the local share of VAT is about 1 percent. This is suggestive of why we can only roughly illustrate what might happen as a result of the swap, under a particular set of assumptions.

appreciation tax, and deed tax—produce revenues in amount equivalent to about 1.7 percent of GDP in Shandong. As shown in Table 14, increasing these existing taxes on real estate to 2 percent of GDP, by raising the tax rates and improving administration, would recapture about 16 billion RMB of the revenue loss. But 2 percent of GDP is a burden that approaches the level of real property tax in industrial countries and might be seen as too heavy a burden (Bahl and Martinez-Vazquez, 2008).

A major question to be answered is whether and how much new revenue will be captured from the new regulations that mandate reducing or eliminating tax preferences, and by collecting full taxes due under current law. No estimates (that we can report) have been made of the revenue potential of these actions. However, we know that Shandong's taxes as a percent of GDP are 3 percentage points below the national average. If one percentage point is raised from reduced tax preferences and full collections according to legal liability, as is called for in the Shandong proposal, about one-half of the business tax revenue loss would be recouped. Eliminating tax preferences is a good policy innovation with many benefits, but it does not appear that it can fully resolve the business tax problem. Moreover, there is a sequencing issue. The loss of business tax revenues is almost upon local governments. The time it will take to implement a program of reducing or eliminating tax preferences will be longer. Moreover, the new State Council regulations call for a slower approach to making these changes, than was originally envisioned.

The gist of this discussion is that replacing the business tax will be complicated matter and the amount of revenue implied is not inconsequential. This is one factor that might cause government to entertain the possibility of assigning new tax sources to subnational governments. It is to this subject that we now turn.

New Local Taxes

A second option to which the State Council might turn in its next deliberations is the authorization of new taxes for subnational governments. We discuss three possibilities here: a new property tax, increased motor vehicle taxes and increased sales tax. The property and sales tax options have been discussed by Congress, by the government and by others, but no concrete proposals have been made. Motor Vehicle taxes are presently used in China, but arguably there is more revenue potential from this source.

The property tax

The property tax has great potential as a revenue source in China, and it may be an opportune time to realize this potential. Most important, it could help to fill a revenue gap at the subnational government level, and could be especially productive in larger urban areas. To get some idea of the revenue potential, note that industrial countries raise more than 2 percent of GDP in property tax while low income countries raise about 0.6 percent of GDP on average (Bahl, 2009).

International Experience

The property tax is a favorite among the English speaking federal countries, but it is less important among non-English speaking countries and among unitary countries in general (Bahl, 2010; Lotz, 2006). It is mostly an urban tax. Property tax revenues account for one-half or more of local government financing in the Toronto, Montreal and Melbourne metropolitan areas, and it accounts for 34 percent of the budget in New York City.

Different patterns emerge for some metropolitan area local governments in other OECD and transition countries. Municipalities in the Netherlands, including those in the Randstad region, receive less than 5 percent of revenues from the property tax. There is no local government property tax in Norway (OECD, 2006, p176). In Copenhagen, the primary revenue source of municipalities is the income tax, and property taxes play only a minor role. The same is true in Stockholm, Tokyo and in the Swiss cities. The property tax is somewhat more important in Madrid at the city level, but financing is dominated by income taxes levied at the regional government level. In Busan and Daegu Korea, the property tax is an important source of local government financing, but most of the revenue is derived from a tax on property transfers.

Governments in most developing countries do not seem to have bought fully into the idea that the property tax is a good fit for financing local public services provided in metropolitan areas. While it is true that property values are growing in most metropolitan areas, valuation usually fails to capture this growth. This seems to be the case even in countries with large metropolitan areas (Mathur, et. al. , 2009; De Cesare, 2004). Moreover, delays in general revaluation are commonplace, significantly lowering the revenue-income elasticity of the property tax. The property tax as practiced in low income countries generally fails the tests for a good subnational government tax because of its low revenue yield, high administrative cost and unpopularity with voters.

There is a great deal of variation in the extent to which the property tax generates meaningful revenues for metropolitan cities. In Cape Town, South Africa, about 20 percent of metropolitan government revenues are derived from a tax levied against the capital value of land and improvements. This is about the same share of revenues that is received from intergovernmental transfers.

The primary source of revenue for municipalities in the Mexico City metropolitan area and in the Istanbul metropolitan area is the property tax. However, in neither case are the local governments empowered to set the tax rate or determine the tax base. There is some local government discretion in metropolitan cities in India but the results are much the same. The low yield is largely attributed to the poor administration of the tax. For example, in Mumbai only about 70 percent of properties pay tax, and in Kolkata properties are assessed at about 20 percent of their value (Mathur, et al., 2009).

Advantages and Disadvantages

Because the ownership of real property wealth is usually concentrated in the highest income classes, the burden of the property tax tends not to fall heavily on low income households. To the extent that higher taxes are paid on properties that have better public services, the property tax might be seen as a benefit levy. Again, it may not fall heavily on low income families. Finally, since residential property taxes are capitalized into reduced property values, market decisions will be more rational because owners will pay a charge for the benefits of local services delivered, and speculators will face a real cost of holding their land off the market. These advantages could be very important to China given its history of rapid increase in property values. But this will depend on the level of effective property tax rate that is imposed.

The major problems with the property tax have to do with its difficult administration and its unpopularity with property owners and leaseholders. Good administration requires identification of all parcels and their ownership, valuation and revaluation, collection from individual owners, and it requires extensive recordkeeping and updating. All facets of the administration must be done well to realize the full revenue benefits from the tax. [1]

The political unpopularity, and the resistance by taxpayers that can

1 A survey and analysis of the practice of property taxation in cities of developing countries is in McCluskey and Franzsen (2013). See also Bahl and Martinez-Vazquez (2008) and Bird and Slack (2004).

observed in developing countries around the world, seems disproportionate to the tax burden. It has to do with the tax falling on accrued income rather than realized income, the judgmental nature of the assessment, and the visibility of the tax. China will no doubt face many of the same unpopularity problems.

Potential in China

China is one of the few countries in the world that does not levy an annual tax on residential property. In theory, China could generate considerable revenues with such an urban tax. An annual property tax that would yield the equivalent of one percent of GDP might be a feasible reform target in China. This effective rate would be equivalent to about twice the average for developing countries and one-half the average for industrial countries.

Certainly there is considerable property wealth that can be taxed. By one estimate, the level of urban household wealth held in the form of property is about 200 percent of GDP (Gan, 2013). Even a relatively low effective tax rate of 0.5 percent on this gross measure of the tax base would yield the equivalent of 1 percent of GDP in revenues. Moreover, property values are likely to continue growing over the long run, though probably at a lower rate. The size of the base elasticity, and important question for local revenue mobilization, is an important consideration. Ideally this base elasticity would match up well with the growth in local government expenditures.

Revenue mobilization is of course an important objective, but the property tax also can be structured to encourage land use patterns that might lead to reductions in external costs. If the base of the tax is the assessed market value of the user right, for example, it could approximate an annual charge on location rents. This would provide an incentive for all users to develop land more intensively and could be made more consistent with an infill strategy for urban development. So would a tax on vacant property in the built-up area if it is imposed at a differentially higher rate. Again, this would not be a tax directly on the land, but on the market value of the user right. If the market value increased, so too would the tax. Liability would rest with the holder of the user right.

Other property-related financing instruments might be useful in achieving the objectives of recapturing some of the value created by public investment, and increasing the density of cities. These might include CEPACs as used in Brazil (Wetzel, 2013)[1], special assessments, betterment levies, valorization, and tax increment financing (Smolka 2013).

If China continues with its interest in property taxation, the door would be open to move toward the design of a comprehensive tax on property in urban areas. There is already an existing array of real estate taxes operating in China—land use tax, deeds tax, and land value added tax. Together these now account for revenues equivalent to about 1.6 percent of GDP (Man, 2013). These might be combined into a new property tax regime that would include the new annual property tax, a capital gains tax on transfers of real property, and a set of value capture and land use taxes on real estate. Valuation, cadaster and even collections could be unified or tightly coordinated, and the revenue yield could be quite significant. The new comprehensive property tax structure could be harmonized with the income and value added taxes to insure full coverage of property related income and to avoid double taxation.

Implementation Concerns

Adopting a broad based tax that is new to the country, and to the taxpaying culture, is always difficult. In China, three questions have continuously

1 The CEPAC, used in Brazil, is a bond issued by the municipal government and sold in public auction that grants its holder the right to augment the construction area in excess of legislation or to construct buildings that deviate from the guidelines and use foreseen by the legislation (Wetzel, 2013, p336).

come up when the property tax has been discussed. In fact, none of these three sets of concerns is a serious roadblock to property taxation.

(1) The first concern is whether a property tax can be imposed when the owner of the land is the state? The answer is that the tax can be levied on the user right to the land, and the liability to pay the tax is with the holder of the user right. When the lease expires, the user right reverts back to the state.

(2) The second issue is whether the property tax can be a local government levy but imposed under a national law. There are two arrangements that can work. Under one, the tax can be imposed under a national law and be administered by the national government, but tax rates can be set by the local government. The other is that the tax can be imposed under national law but be administered by the local government with rates set by the local government. Under either of these arrangements the property tax would be a local levy.

(3) The third issue is the confusion about whether a lease payment and a property tax amount to double taxation. These are two distinct payments for two different purposes. The lease purchases the right to use the land. The property tax is a payment for public services provided by the government. The lease purchase amount does not include the payment of any present or future taxes.

Design and Implementation in Shandong

The design of the property tax for each province will be a national matter, and there should not be great differences in the implementation concerns. An interesting issue relates to revenue mobilization, and the extent to which the property tax could pick up the loss due to the elimination of the business tax.

If the property tax is imposed as a new tax, and the effective rate is set to be equivalent to one percent of GDP, it could yield about 60 billion RMB (at 2014 levels). This would be equivalent to about two-thirds of the net loss from elimination of the business tax. However, implementation of the property tax will almost certainly be gradual because of administration concerns and because it will be a new tax that is levied more directly on people than are most Chinese taxes.

More likely, it will begin at a much lower effective rate than one percent of GDP (Bahl, Goh and Qiao, 2014; Hou, Ren and Zhang, 2015). There is another reason not to be optimistic about the property tax making a large and immediate contribution to recovering the revenue losses from business taxes. Shandong, like the rest of China, already levies a family of taxes on property. In Shandong, these account for about 1.7 percent of provincial GDP. Under one scenario, the new property tax would replace these or bring them under a comprehensive tax on property/land use values. In this case, the incremental revenues from a real property tax will be much less than one percent of GDP. For example, as shown above, a "replacement" property tax with a very high effective rate of 2 percent of GDP, would yield net revenues of only 16 billion RMB, which is 18 percent of the net loss in business tax revenue at 2014 levels.

There would be some difficult implementation issues with a new property tax in China. The tax could be assessed and collected by the local tax bureau. If it were structured with a standard deduction to protect low income households and small businesses, the base in rural counties might be close to zero. Conceivably, it might favor richer local governments even more than the present business tax or VAT. So, would the right choice be to subject the property tax to a significant amount of provincial revenue sharing because of the different revenue potential between the urban and rural areas? Or should it be an urban tax levied only in the large cities?

There also could be some difficult administration issues. If assessment is value based, there will be a strong argument for strict valuation guidelines, and possibly implementation to be led by the provincial level. The same may be true for the maintenance of the cadaster. At the same time, there is great value to using the great familiarity of the local government with its property market and real estate market. Defining the "right" administrative structure will be a formidable task. What if local governments were given some flexibility to set the property tax rate within limits, or if they were given some discretion to determine taxable values? Could the property tax "work" in a province such as Shandong? If the county or the district were the taxing authority, it might put in place a competitive model where counties or districts might use lower property tax rates to attract real estate investment. This potential problem might be resolved by levying the tax on a metropolitan area (prefecture) basis.

Motor vehicle taxes[1]

Increased local government taxes on the ownership and use of motor vehicles could fit a Shandong strategy for revenue mobilization and for coping with the costs of urbanization. The number of motor vehicles is growing faster than the population in urban areas in China (Bahl, Goh and Qiao, 2014), their use imposes infrastructure costs on urban local governments, and they generate external costs that are for the most part uncompensated by users. Nearly 80 percent of the vehicle fleet is privately owned. If structured properly, increased taxes on motor vehicles could be revenue productive, efficient, and green.

The rapid growth in motor vehicles compared to that of the road network has been an important contributor to the growing congestion levels and longer commutes. The result is a heavy external cost in terms of congestion and pollution. One study of Beijing has put the level of external costs at between 7.5 percent and 15 percent for all types of externalities (reported in World Bank and Development Research Center, 2014, pp. 187 - 262).

1 This analysis is drawn from Bahl, Goh and Qiao, 2014.

Given this situation, it is understandable that Chinese policy has focused on controlling automobile use in large urban areas, and a good start has been made in this direction in a few cities. However, there is arguably even more to be gained by giving subnational governments additional control over motor vehicle taxation. The result could be to discourage the use of private cars, at the margin, while generating new revenues to defray some of the costs involved.

Chinese cities could continue to use tax and charge policies either to increase the price of owning and using a car relative to using a public transport system, or to make a different housing location choice. This could be done by charging drivers for the full cost of using private vehicles, including environmental and social costs, through mechanisms such as higher registration fees, higher gasoline taxes, higher tolls and parking fees or various forms of congestion pricing. Depending on the price elasticity of demand, local governments could generate significant revenues from this to cover the general costs of urbanization. Structuring these taxes to have the desired impact on vehicle use is a more complicated matter than is suggested here, and is not independent of housing prices, land use restrictions and patterns of infrastructure investment. Still, at the margin, local government taxation of motors vehicle ownership and use can have environmentally friendly impacts, and potentially could generate significant revenue to cover the infrastructure costs related to urbanization.

At present, Chinese subnational governments are not funded to any significant extent by taxes on motor vehicles. The registration tax on motor vehicles produces only a small revenue flow, and the tax on motor fuels is a central government levy. The experience with parking fees, toll and congestion charges as resource allocation measures is growing but has not yet become a major subnational government revenue source.

The annual tax on motor vehicle registrations is based on engine capacity, as it is in most countries. At present, revenues from this tax are equivalent to only about 6 percent of that received in VAT revenue sharing. Motor vehicle registrations do meet the criteria for a good local tax. Given the number of motor vehicles, and the growth in these numbers, there is good revenue potential. For the most part, the burden of the tax (or charge) is borne locally. Administration of the tax is by the local governments and is straight forward. Higher registration costs can stimulate tax avoidance measures such as registration in a lower taxing jurisdiction, but this can be controlled by registration requirements, periodic inspections and stiff penalties. The revenue potential of motor vehicle ownership charges is much greater than is presently collected, and significant increases could be realized if local governments decided to tax automobile ownership at a higher level (and if they were empowered to do so).

The taxation of motor fuels is a much more lucrative tax base, and it would more directly tax the use of motor vehicles. The question is whether this could be locally administered in China's larger cities. Ideally, the tax would be collected at the pump. Alternatively, it could be assessed at the factory gate as it is now, but the destination of shipments could be tracked. This would put in place a system whereby the rate of motor fuel tax could vary from one local government to another. Even at the current central government excise tax rates, a motor fuels levy would enable local governments to mobilize significant revenue.

Would it be fair to levy a higher tax on motor fuels in large cities? China's gasoline prices are already above those in most developing countries, and above those in the US, but below the average in the European countries (World Bank and Development Research Center, 2014, pp. 439 - 535). On the other hand, Chinese gas prices do not appear to be high enough to cover the external costs imposed by the consumption of motor fuels.

Would it be efficient to levy a higher rate of gasoline tax in China's large metropolitan areas? At the margin, this would lead to a higher cost of living and would be a factor affecting migration decisions. Higher gasoline prices would be consistent with other urban planning goals, such as reducing the congestion and pollution that come with automobile use, and raising the price of urban sprawl. In all of this, however, it is not so clear that the elasticities of substitution are high enough to make much of a difference unless there were very large rate increases.

Congestion and emissions can be reduced by demand management. Shanghai, Beijing and Guangzhou have introduced vehicle ownership and/ or usage control. These municipalities set a cap on vehicle registrations and established a quota for newly registered license plates. The motor vehicle management agencies allocate these quotas via license-plate auction (e. g. , Shanghai), lottery (e. g. ,Beijing), or a combination (e. g. , Guangzhou) (World Bank and Development Research Center, 2014, pp. 439 – 535).

The World Bank (World Bank and Development Research Center, 2014, pp. 439 – 535) argue that road pricing and parking charges are the most direct way of assessing the costs of congestion and air pollution in dense urban areas. Fuel taxes and licensing fees are alternatives, but are less targeted. Road pricing is common on China's expressways and has been discussed for heavier use in several urban areas. Parking fees are another way to tax road users, and the experience with higher charges on parking has been good. Parking fees and taxes are price-elastic, and there is evidence that they are effective reducing car trips and reducing the share of cars in the modal split (OECD, 2010).

Could local governments in a province such as Shandong implement either a higher tax on motor vehicle registrations, or a tax on motor fuels? For either tax, a district or county level tax would not seem feasible unless the tax is levied at a uniform provincial rate. Otherwise, the potential for evasion would be too great. But if the idea is to charge a differential rate for motor vehicle ownership and use in urban areas, a uniform rate would not achieve the objectives.

Local retail sales taxes[1]

Local government sales taxes can be efficient instruments of urban government finance if collections can be shifted from an origin basis (place of manufacture or distribution) to a destination basis (place of consumption) (Bird, 2006). In the United States, for example, a local government retail sales tax is collected at the point of consumption. Under an origin-based arrangement, such as China's VAT, by contrast, collection is at the point of production or distribution and some of the tax burden may be borne by consumers who live in another jurisdiction. For example, Buenos Aires and Bogota levy a sales tax on gross receipts, which is not destination-based but still is revenue productive. There has long been a call to abolish the turnover tax in Buenos Aires but the absence of a "suitable" alternative has held off reform.

If administration on a destination basis could be made feasible, sales taxes on selected items of consumption could be revenue productive and would pass some of the tests of a good local tax. This might be done adequately for some items of consumption, for example, high end jewelry, durables and imported luxury goods. But for most consumer goods, a retail sales tax would encourage tax avoidance by providing an incentive to shift the point of consumption to informal traders that are not easily policed by the tax authorities.

The problems with collection from informal sector retailers is also the reason why the revenue productive excises cannot be converted to retail sales taxes with higher rates imposed on consumption in urban areas. Otherwise, particularly beer, liquor and cigarettes would be attractive revenue base. There is another option. All of the excise revenue could continue to be collected as at present, but the revenues could be assigned to

1 This section draws heavily from Bahl, Goh and Qiao, 2014.

cities on some formula basis. This would be a transfer of revenue, but would not give the local governments any power to increase or reduce rates, or to differentiate their rate from that in other urban areas. In effect, it would be an intergovernmental transfer.

China is in the process of folding its business tax into the VAT, mostly to broaden the base of the value added tax. Another reform direction, however, would have been to convert the business tax into a local business VAT imposed on the costs of factors of production. Bird (2013, p. 7) argues that the experience in France, Italy and Japan suggests that a local tax based on value added and levied on an origin basis may not only be a sensible way to charge business for benefits obtained from local public services but may also be administered adequately and with no serious economic costs.

A local tax on consumption, as discussed here, would have an intergovernmental dimension. If levied only in urban areas, it would leave open an important avenue for tax avoidance. If levied at a uniform rate and province wide, it would raise equalization issues. One option would be a province wide tax where a percentage of collections would be directed to a revenue sharing pool, and the remainder would be retained on a basis of derivation.

Piggyback taxes [1]

Some of the administrative problems with local taxation can be avoided by adopting a "piggybacking" approach, i. e., to allow the local government to select a tax rate to be imposed on a central government tax base. The piggyback approach is used to a considerable extent in industrial countries. The primary source of revenue for Swiss cities is a piggyback personal income tax; the city of Rome levies a piggyback income tax on a base

---

1 This section draws heavily from Bahl. Goh and Qiao, 2014.

defined by the central government, and Danish local governments tag on to an income tax base set by the central government. US local governments in many states impose a sur-rate on the state government retail sales tax base. At least three cities—Bangkok, Moscow, and Seoul—have their own surtax on the VAT (Martinez-Vazquez, 2013).

Piggybacking is already done in China with the urban construction and maintenance tax and the education surtax. In these two cases, the base is the aggregate tax collections from VAT, excise taxes and the business tax, and the revenues from this surtax are allocated fully to the local government. The sur-rate, however is set by the central government.

This piggyback tax might be viewed as a benefit charge, i. e. , a payment for using local government services. [1] Under such a reform, the existing UMCT and education surcharge would be replaced with an "urban service tax". The local government then could be given the option of increasing the piggyback tax rate above its present level. There would be some revenue potential here for Shandong. At present, the UCMT and the education tax surcharge account for 0. 51 percent of GDP. If the surcharge were increased to 100 percent as an "urban service tax", the revenue yield would rise to 1. 02 percent of GDP and the incremental amount would cover about one-third of the net 88 billion RMB loss of business tax revenues.

The individual income tax could be added to the list of options for piggybacking. In Shandong, a 50 percent levy on a base of individual income tax collections could generate enough new revenue to recover about 7 percent of the lost business tax revenue. The effective rate of the income tax would increase from its present level of only from about 0. 2 percent of GDP to 0. 3 percent. There are good arguments to use the individual income tax more intensively, including the lower likelihood that the burden

1 The benefit charge argument is sensible, because local businesses make use of local government services and so do the local residents that purchase their goods. But VAT and excise taxes are origin - based and so there will be some exporting of the tax burden to other jurisdictions, depending on the trading area of these firms.

will be exported. Unfortunately, the base of the individual income tax is so narrow that the revenue potential is very limited. And, the already high tax rate on labor is a major drawback. Unless the social security contribution rate can be lowered, this may not be a viable option.

There are other problems with this approach. It is still an origin-based tax, and some of the burden will be exported as is the case now. Another issue is that the revenue take will be vulnerable to changes in central government tax policies, such as increased thresholds or exemptions, or lower tax rates. On the other hand, this reform would be in line with the State Council regulation that the urban construction tax and the education surcharge should not be earmarked and should be moved into the general public finance budget.

A piggyback individual income tax would pose an equalization problem since collections would be concentrated in a few counties. Moreover, a higher income tax in district A might put that local government in a less advantaged position vs. district B where the tax rate is lower. Even if the tax rate is uniform, there is the problem of the tax accruing to the local government which houses the enterprise and shutting out the local government that is residence to workers who commute. One option would be to make it a provincial government tax and use the revenues to fund a sharing pool for equalization purposes. Another would be to make it an urban services levy and allow local governments to retain it on a derivation basis, and take this into account in forming the distributable pool for equalization.

Intergovernmental Transfers

Another possibility for allowing provinces to recapture the loss in business tax revenue is for the central government to fund the shortfall by increasing the level of general intergovernmental transfers. This might be done in one of two ways: (a) with a compensatory grant scheme or (b) with an increase in the vertical share of grants provided to all subnational governments in China. In fact, neither option would work very well if the intent is to replace lost business tax revenues.

Of the two, option (b) would be better public policy, but Shandong province probably would do better under the first scheme. To illustrate, take the case of the elimination of the business tax. In terms of 2014 budget amounts, the net revenue loss to Shandong would be 88 billion RMB. Under the compensating grant scheme the central government could give the province a grant of that amount to cover the loss. This would be equivalent to about 70 percent of the present level of earmarked and unconditional grants budgeted for 2014. Compensating grants schemes are used around the world to compensate subnational governments due to revenue losses from central government actions. The problem with this approach is that there is usually no provision made for the future revenue. In both South Africa and Pakistan, important local government taxes were abolished by the center but were not replaced by a grant that had the same built-in growth as the lost tax. The consequences are that the local governments have become more dependent on central grants, and they have much less elasticity to their taxing base.

The second approach would be much less favorable to Shandong but probably better public policy. Under this version, the central government would increase the size of the national pool for general grants by an amount that would match the loss of business tax revenues nationally. This amount would then be allocated in the same manner as are other unconditional grants. In this case, Shandong might not be reimbursed fully for the loss in business tax revenues, even for its first year loss, because Shandong receives a lower per capita amount of grants than do other provinces.

CHAPTER SEVEN CONCLUSIONS AND THE WAY FORWARD

Shandong province is undertaking an ambitious reform in its financial management system. The Shandong proposal fully adopts the State Council regulations but adapts these new regulations to the particular economic structure and governance of the province, and to the problems it faces. This program has the potential to significantly improve the public finance regime.

The provincial government has set high expectations for this program. Governor Guo Shuqing put it well:

"*Governments at all levels should further improve the understanding of the functions of public finance, strengthen the culture change of public finance, dynamically adjust the structure of fiscal expenditure, enhance the capacity of service delivery, improve the efficiency of the fiscal fund, comprehensively promote the reform of the fiscal and taxation system, and make best efforts to build a modern fiscal system*". [1]

General Commentary on the Shandong Proposal

Shandong Province proposes a modernization of its financial management system, a rationalization of taxation practices, and a revision of its approach to intergovernmental fiscal relations. The proposals are mostly consistent with international good practice, closely follow the regulations laid down by the State Council, and directly address many of the problems

1 http://www.sd.xinhuanet.com/ldhd/2013-06/22/c_116245333.htm

with the present intergovernmental fiscal arrangements in Shandong. In keeping with the general directions of the Congress, the proposed reforms will address issues of expenditure efficiency, revenue mobilization and intra-province equity.

Under the leadership of a progressive governor, the Shandong authorities have developed a strong proposal that once implemented can significantly strengthen the public finances in all three areas that have been targeted for improvement. Full implementation of the new budget law will improve the efficiency with which expenditures are planned and delivered, a rationalization of the practice of tax collections and a phasing out of the practice of giving tax preferences can increase the rate of revenue mobilization, and ongoing changes in the system of intergovernmental transfers within the province can lead to a better program of equalization.

One might think of the proposal as having three legs. The first is modernizing the financial management system by making it more transparent, and putting in safeguards against inefficient spending practices, over-borrowing, and corruption. The second is using the tax system to take an important step in the direction of separating the roles of the government and competitive sectors. The third is rationalizing the system of provincial finance to both simplify the system and make it fairer to both rich and poor regions.

Financial management.

The implementation of the new budget law is the most important of the financial management proposals. By requiring full coverage of all fiscal activities of governments in the province, it eliminates the possibility of extra budgetary activities. Moreover, it makes provision for more transparency by integrating the four sub-budgets of subnational governments. It generally shifts the focus of the budget from a control document to a planning document, and introduces multi-year budgets. By eliminating earmarks, it will increase the flexibility in expenditure planning. These are all important changes.

The budget law is complemented by the planned completion of the treasury system by 2017. This will enable better control of cash management. Moreover, the new regulations will phase out most special funds and will eliminate the practice of creating new budget lines. The reforms include the creation of a budget stabilization fund to smooth out short term deficits and surpluses and avoid the buildup of large cash balances in the general budget.

The creation of a debt framework will bring borrowing under control. All borrowing will be approved by the provincial government, and no borrowing will occur off-budget. The practice of using a financial platform will be eliminated and existing (illegal) debt will be "cleaned up".

The results of a successful implementation of the financial management component of the Shandong Proposal should be a more efficient system of government spending. Moreover, the new approach will lead to freeing up some expenditures from low priority uses and redirecting these to the provision of essential services. If this happens, there will be an indirect "revenue effect".

As in the case of most proposals, especially those that call for sweeping changes, there are questions. The clarification of the relationship among the four budgets of local governments is an important step forward. But still, there is no call for a current and capital budget. The question is whether capital investment planning and multi-year budgeting can be carried out effectively without a capital budget.

A second issue has to do with holding to a hard budget constraint. The proposal calls for allowing annual deficits with bailouts and a one year payback of the subsidy. This works fine when the underlying problem is irregular revenue flows, or delays in project spending, or unexpected economic disruptions. The use of a budget stabilization fund can work well in such cases if the government has the discipline to keep the fund balances at a safe level. But if the deficit is due to a structural problem (e. g., overspending or slow growing revenues) allowing annual budget deficits can be a risky policy. Safeguards need to be in place and are especially important in China because local governments have no autonomous sources of revenues to raise funds for current expenditure purposes. Policies to smooth out annual imbalances between spending and revenues with budget stabilization funds work much better when revenues are rising faster than spending, than they do when revenues are growing slowly.

On the debt management reforms, it is not clear how new debt will be repaid, and how the risk management analysis will be structured. The county/district governments have no independent revenue sources (other than land leases). But in the government fund, this source will be earmarked to support special projects. But what about the repayment of loans for general public finance budget projects? One possibility is that new debt will be serviced by intergovernmental transfers. But if so, the line between a loan and a grant might become blurred.

Finally, there is the question of implementation strategy and timing. In particular, there is the difficult problem of installing these improved practices in 140 counties that range from urban districts that are relatively sophisticated on financing matters, to rural counties with limited resource base and limited capacity. Successful implementation will require provincial government leadership and the provision of significant training, and continued oversight. This might lead to an overload that will further slow the progress.

Tax reform.

The second set of reforms are focused on rationalizing the relationship between the public sector and the competitive sector. The Shandong proposal argues for developing a fully integrated taxpayer information system to assist in improving collection rates, lowering collection costs, and lowering compliance costs. More important, the practice of giving subsidies to individual enterprises will be halted. On the tax side, preferences given to enterprises will end unless the preferences are approved by the State Council. Such preferences might now include exemptions and rebates. They can also include the collection of less tax than is assessed when revenue targets are reached.

Shandong does make good proposals to address the revenue problem—improve the tax administration efficiency with a better information system, and remove discretionary tax preferences from the present system. A significant amount of Shandong's low tax effort may be due to weak administration and overgenerous tax preferences, but no estimates are made in the Shandong fiscal reform proposal. We can say that the proposals are in the right direction, but we cannot say with any degree of accuracy how much of the tax revenue shortfall problem they can address. There is some indirect evidence that the revenue sacrifice may be quite significant. Shandong's collection rate against GDP is a full 3 percentage points below the national average. But such indirect methods of estimating revenue potential is not a good substitute for a formal practice of fully accounting for tax expenditures in each annual budget.

The implementation of this revenue program will almost certainly be problematic, and it will take time to fully embrace it. Tax preferences can be well entrenched and hard to pull back, and they may have a constituency within the government. Government officials have used this strategy for years in supporting their industrial policy, and they have identified tax preferences, rightly or not, as one factor contributing to the rapid economic growth of the past. The indirect path to encouraging economic development—provide good services—may seem less satisfying and harder to claim credit for. Moreover, reductions in what many see as effective economic development subsidies are especially difficult to eliminate when the growth rate in the economy has slowed. Note also the more recent State Council regulation that seems to call for a less aggressive approach to eliminating tax preferences. The limits on tax preferences is good policy, and it might be revenue productive, but implementing such a chance might be slow going.

Intergovernmental fiscal relations.

The three concerns in Shandong are: (a) the assignment of expenditure and administrative responsibilities may not be correct, (b) the distribution of revenues among the sub-provincial governments may not be adequately equalizing, and (c) the structure of the intergovernmental transfer system is flawed.

The Shandong proposal has addressed the key issues of concern, and has done so in a way that follows good international practice. First, the existing assignment of responsibility for all expenditure functions will be reviewed with an eye toward reducing the murkiness in assigned responsibilities. This review could lead to a change in expenditure responsibilities among province, prefecture and county in Shandong. The reform plan calls for drawing up these new assignments, and putting them into practice in 2015, on a trial basis, for education, health and transportation.

This is the right place for the reform to begin. To the extent the government finds that externalities and economies of scale have been given too little weight, they likely will move to a less decentralized fiscal system, i. e., a system where counties have less direct expenditure responsibility than under the present system, and more responsibilities are shifted to the provincial level.

The second major issue to be resolved is the large fiscal disparities among the local governments within the province. The goal of the reform is for the province to administer a unified revenue sharing mechanism to reduce this disparity. Despite a revision of the revenue sharing system in 2013, which improved things markedly, some important problems remain. Most importantly, the province will need to decide the important issue of how much equalization it wants to do. The specific revenue sharing plan is not yet worked out, but the reform proposal seems to be moving in the direction of a more rule-based approach to making the distribution.

Third, the proposal calls for changes in the structure of provincial-local grants toward a reduction in earmarked grants in favor of unconditional grants, and an end to matching provisions. This would create a less complicated and more transparent system, and it would give expenditure planners more flexibility. The proposed reforms in the intergovernmental transfer system are not yet developed in any detail, but the idea of reducing earmarked grants is in step with central government policy. A reform of the equalization grant system will almost certainly be considered, but there is not yet a discussion in the Proposal about how it will be financed or how large it will be relative to shared taxes, or how much equalization is desired.

This leg of the fiscal reform program in Shandong is not so far along as the others, i. e. , it is focused on describing the approach it plans to take in formulating the reform. The intergovernmental fiscal reforms that are proposed call on the Provincial Government to address some fundamental issues. These include whether more governance decisions will be made at the higher province level rather than at the grass roots county level, and whether a trade will be made between equalization of service levels and stimulating economic growth.

The Way Forward

Shandong has made a good effort on its fiscal reform program. It lays out a plan for modernization of its financial management system that can significantly improve expenditure efficiency and revenue mobilization, while reducing waste and addressing some facets of corruption. It adopts good international practices, follows the State Council regulations very closely, and could become a model for other provinces to follow. But for the Proposal to reach its full potential as a planning and guidance tool, it should be deepened in terms of providing hard evidence about what it intends to achieve, and updated to track its progress against these targets.

Policy leadership from the provincial government

Subnational governments in China do not have discretion to make many of the budgetary decisions that subnational governments make in industrial countries, e. g. they do not have any taxing powers. In effect, the envelope for the public finance budget is set by the central government. However, there are areas where the provincial and local governments do have discretion to influence the public finances.

In the next version of this reform document, the provincial government might address its policy stance about its intergovernmental fiscal policies. The main areas might include the following:

(1) Shandong is one of the most decentralized governance structures in China. Will the complexities of expenditure and revenue assignment cause a movement toward more centralization at the province level?

(2) Will the overall proposal lead to a continued separation of the government sector from the competitive sector? Will subsidies and preferential tax treatments be withdrawn in large amounts, and will the new funding proposed for industrial upgrading move government back toward a closer relationship with the competitive sector?

(3) Whether the system of provincial-local transfers will be shifted to a rule-based formula system or will hold to the present approach which gives province/prefectures more discretion to move money according to where it identifies needs.

(4) What is the right size for the equalization pool for revenue sharing?

(5) Will provincial-local transfers change in the direction of less earmarked grants and more unconditional grants? Will all matching requirements be dropped?

(6) How will local government general obligation borrowing be authorized by the provincial government when there is a limited capacity to repay debt? .

(7) How aggressive will provincial governments be in enforcing the hard budget constraint on local governments?

(8) Will the province be aggressive about removing perverse incentives to achieving the goals of the reform?

The need for an annual update of the Proposal

In order to continue using the proposal as a plan for upgrading the system of public finances, it needs to be deepened and it should be revised on a regular basis. A "one-off" study will not have a long life in guiding public finances. The present version of the proposal contains little by way of metrics. For example, there is no estimate of the amount of tax preferences that are now given, or of the amount of subsidy that is granted directly to enterprises for economic development support, or of the amount of equalization that is achieved by the system of provincial-local transfers.

The annual updates, with hard evidence and metrics as described above could be useful in several ways:

(1) Resetting targets for the reform;

(2) Budget planning;

(3) Grading and monitoring the progress of various local governments, and local government officials;

(4) Identifying constraints and roadblocks, and developing strategies to

address these.

Implementation problems

The major concern about the Shandong Proposal is whether it can be effectively implemented in a timely manner. Here there are four important concerns. The first is finding a way for some entrenched but counterproductive practices to be removed so that the reforms can be introduced. The separation of the private from the public sector will be no easy matter. The government has favored the competitive sector with subsidies and tax preferences of various kinds. It is not clear how easy it will be for subnational government officials to back away from these direct relations with the competitive sectors, or how long the transition to a separation of government and private sector activities will take. Tracking the progress in this area will be a high priority task.

A second and even more difficult area is upgrading the capability of local government staff. In one sense, the new budget law calls for far-reaching changes in how financial management is done. This suggests a considerable investment in training and supervision. Even without the complication of a new law, there is a knowledge gap of staff, especially in the more rural counties. To move forward with implementation, it will be important to establish a strategy for upgrading staff capabilities. This may turn out to be a major constraint to moving forward with the reforms.

Third, it will be important to track the impact of perverse incentives in the fiscal system and make necessary policy adjustments to address these.

Finally, because there is so much to do in implementing this reform, and so much possible shock to the system, there is need for an implementation plan to phase it in. [1] It would be useful for the provincial government to identify the order in which it will bring these reforms on line.

1 For a discussion of sequencing fiscal reforms, see Bahl and Martinez-Vazquez (2006).

APPENDIX 1：Tables and Figures

Table 1：Population Characteristics：Shandong Province

Year	Population(in million)	Rank in China	Urban Population(in percent)
2000	90. 0	2	26. 8
2001	90. 4	2	27. 8
2002	90. 8	2	29. 0
2003	91. 3	2	31. 1
2004	91. 8	2	32. 2
2005	92. 5	2	45. 0
2006	93. 1	3	46. 1
2007	93. 7	2	46. 8
2008	94. 2	3	47. 6
2009	94. 7	3	48. 3
2010	95. 9	2	49. 7
2011	96. 4	2	51. 0
2012	96. 8	2	52. 4
2013	97. 3	2	53. 8

Source：Wind and CEIC.

Table 2: Public Service in Shandong: 2013

Item	Shandong	National Average
Health (per 10,000 population)		
The number of beds in hospitals	50.32	45.5
The number of doctors in hospitals	62	53
The number of nurses in hospitals	25	20
Environment(in 10,000 Ton)		
Emissions of SO_2	164.5	65.93
Emission of NO	165.1	71.85
Emission of dust	69.7	41.23
Emission of solid waste	18,172	10,571
Emission of hazardous waste	509	105
Population (in percent)		
age 0 - 14	15.48	16.4
age 15 - 64	73.54	73.9
age >65	10.98	9.68
Infant mortality rate	2.42	2.69
Population to Civil Servants Ratio	30	27
Education		
The number of students in primary school per 100,000 person	6,463	6,913
Teacher to student ratio in primary school	16.16	16.76
The number of students in elementary school per 100,000 person	3,283	3,279
Teacher to student ratio in elementary school	12.08	12.76
The number of teachers in senior school per 100,000 person	3,213	3,227
Teacher to student ratio in senior school	14.43	14.95
Illiteracy rate	4.97	4.88
Transportation (kilometres per million persons)		
Railway mileage	44	75.81
Road mileage	2,606	3,202.09
Inland waterway mileage	11.52	92.57

Source: National Bureau of Statistics.

Table 3: GDP Level and Growth: Shandong Province

Year	GDP(in billion RMB)	Percent of China (in percent)	Rank	Per Capita GDP (in RMB)	Rank	Average for Prefecture Cities (in RMB)	Average for Counties (in RMB)
2000	834	8	3	9,326	9	10,951	
2001	920	8	3	10,195	9	12,150	
2002	1,028	8	3	11,340	9	13,570	
2003	1,208	9	3	13,268	7	16,267	
2004	1,502	9	2	16,413	7	20,034	14,094
2005	1,852	10	3	19,934	7	24,027	17,295
2006	2,208	10	2	23,603	7	28,404	20,540
2007	2,597	10	3	27,604	7	33,526	24,492
2008	3,093	10	3	32,936	8	39,942	29,235
2009	3,390	10	3	35,894	8	42,269	32,371
2010	3,917	10	3	41,106	9	48,615	36,317
2011	4,536	9	3	47,335	10	55,259	
2012	5,001	9	3	51,768	10	57,791	
2013	5,523	9	3	56,323	10	62,461	
2014	5,943	9	3				

Source: Wind and CEIC.

Table 4: Structure of GDP: By Sector

(In percent)

Year	Primary Industry		Secondary Industry		Tertiary Industry	
	Shandong	China	Shandong	China	Shandong	China
2000	15	15	50	45	35	40
2001	15	14	50	45	36	41
2002	14	13	50	44	36	42
2003	12	12	54	45	34	42
2004	12	13	56	46	32	41
2005	11	12	57	47	32	41
2006	10	11	57	47	33	42
2007	10	10	57	47	33	43
2008	10	10	57	47	33	43
2009	10	10	56	46	35	44
2010	9	10	54	46	37	44
2011	9	10	53	46	38	44
2012	9	10	51	45	40	46
2013	9	9	50	44	41	47
2014	8	9	48	43	43	48

Source: Wind and CEIC.

Note: 1. Secondary Industry includes Industry and Construction.

2. Tertiary Industry includes: (1) Transport, Storage & Post, (2) Wholesale & Retail Trade, (3) Hotel and Catering Service, (4) Banking and Insurance, (5) Real Estate, (6) Governments, Political Party Organs and Social Organizations, etc.

Table 5: Expenditure Distribution Between levels of Governments in China: 2013

Province	Amount(in billion)				Percent(in percent)		
	Total	Provincial	Prefecture	County	Provincial	Prefecture	County
Beijing	417. 4	170. 2	230. 3	16. 9	40. 8	55. 2	4. 0
Tianjin	254. 9	104. 1	135. 8	15	40. 8	53. 3	5. 9
Hebei	441	71. 5	84. 2	285. 2	16. 2	19. 1	64. 7
Shanxi	303	61. 9	58. 3	182. 9	20. 4	19. 2	60. 4
Inner Mongolia	368. 7	57. 6	85	226	15. 6	23. 1	61. 3
Liaoning	519. 7	64. 4	162	293. 3	12. 4	31. 2	56. 4
Jilin	274. 5	60. 4	76. 3	137. 8	22. 0	27. 8	50. 2
Heilongjiang	336. 9	78. 5	92	166. 4	23. 3	27. 3	49. 4
Shanghai	452. 9	159. 1	281. 9	11. 9	35. 1	62. 2	2. 6
Jiangsu	779. 8	87	175. 1	517. 8	11. 2	22. 5	66. 4
Zhejiang	473	48. 2	84. 7	340. 2	10. 2	17. 9	71. 9
Anhui	435	59. 6	125. 2	250. 1	13. 7	28. 8	57. 5
Fujian	306. 9	42. 1	75. 3	189. 4	13. 7	24. 5	61. 7
Jiangxi	347	54. 5	54. 4	238. 1	15. 7	15. 7	68. 6
Shandong	**668. 9**	**66. 7**	**161. 7**	**440. 5**	**10. 0**	**24. 2**	**65. 9**
Henan	558. 2	79	134. 5	344. 7	14. 2	24. 1	61. 8
Hubei	437. 2	48. 4	111. 1	277. 6	11. 1	25. 4	63. 5
Hunan	469. 1	80. 8	103	285. 3	17. 2	22. 0	60. 8
Guangdong	841. 1	118. 6	319. 3	403. 1	14. 1	38. 0	47. 9
Guangxi	320. 9	61. 7	64. 6	194. 7	19. 2	20. 1	60. 7
Hainan	101. 1	27	22. 9	51. 3	26. 7	22. 7	50. 7
Chongqing	306. 2	96. 3	135	74. 9	31. 5	44. 1	24. 5
Sichuan	622. 1	84. 2	114. 9	423	13. 5	18. 5	68. 0
Guizhou	308. 3	65	36. 5	206. 8	21. 1	11. 8	67. 1
Yunnan	409. 7	87. 3	63. 3	259. 1	21. 3	15. 5	63. 2
Tibet	101. 4	49. 5	20. 3	31. 6	48. 8	20. 0	31. 2
Shanxi	366. 5	80. 8	87. 3	198. 4	22. 0	23. 8	54. 1
Gansu	231	47. 3	36. 9	146. 7	20. 5	16. 0	63. 5
Qinghai	122. 8	48. 8	16. 3	57. 7	39. 7	13. 3	47. 0
Ningxia	92. 2	21. 9	23. 1	47. 3	23. 8	25. 1	51. 3
Xinjiang	306. 7	80. 9	46. 7	179. 1	26. 4	15. 2	58. 4

Source: Local Government Fiscal Operation Analysis 2013, Ministry of Finance.

Note: Taiwan、Hong Kong and Macao data are not included.

Table 6: Comparison of Fiscal Outcomes between Shandong and other Provinces in 2014

Items	Shandong	China
Per Capita Expenditure		
Public Finance Budget (in RMB)	7,331	9,438
Government Fund Budget (in RMB)	4,047	3,540
SOE Operation Budget (in RMB)	27	42
Social Security Budget (in RMB)	2,197	2,462
Expenditures as a percent of GDP		
Public Finance Budget (in percent)	12.08	20.28
Government Fund Budget (in percent)	6.67	7.61
SOE Operation Budget (in percent)	0.04	0.09
Social Security Budget (in percent)	3.62	5.29
Per Capita Revenue		
Public Finance Budget (in RMB)	5,135	5,546
Government Fund Budget (in RMB)	4,059	3,655
SOE Operation Budget (in RMB)	27	45
Social Security Budget (in RMB)	2,470	2,865
Revenues as a percent of GDP		
Public Finance Budget (in percent)	8.46	11.92
Government Fund Budget (in percent)	6.69	7.86
SOE Operation Budget (in percent)	0.98	0.10
Social Security Budget (in percent)	4.07	6.16
Grants from Central Government		
Per Capita (in RMB)	2,054	3,773
Percent of GDP (in percent)	3.4	8.1
Debt Outstanding in June, 2013		
Per Capita (in RMB)	7,261	17,040
Percent of GDP (in percent)	11.96	28.11

Source: Ministry of Finance, Shandong Budget Discloser Journal Feb 2015, National Audit Office.

Table 7: Consolidated Public Finance Budget Revenue 2014

Item	Budget Execution (in million)	Per Capita Amount (in RMB)	As a share of GDP (in percent)
Total Tax Revenue	396,564	4,051	6.7
Value Added Tax	59,696	610	1.0
Business Tax	113,592	1,160	1.9
Corporate Income Tax	48,289	493	0.8
Individual Income Tax	11,518	118	0.2
Resource Tax	11,957	122	0.2
City Maintenance and Construction Tax	23,133	236	0.4
House Property Tax	12,249	125	0.2
Stamp Tax	6,056	62	0.1
Urban Land Use Tax	26,469	270	0.4
Land Appreciation Tax	25,774	263	0.4
Tax on Vehicles and Boat Operation	4,665	48	0.1
Deed Tax	27,367	280	0.5
Other Tax Revenue	25,800	264	0.4
Total Non-tax Revenue	106,107	1,084	1.8
Special Program Receipts	15,352	157	0.3
Charge of Administrative and Institutional Units	30,220	309	0.5
Charge of using state-owned resources or assets	38,195	390	0.6
Other Non-tax Receipts	22,340	228	0.4
Total Tax and Non-tax Revenue	502,671	5,135	8.5
Debt Revenue	16,200	165	0.3
Local Government Bond Revenue	16,200	165	0.3
Transfer Revenue	275,036	2,810	4.6
Repayment Revenue	42,685	436	0.7
Unconditional Transfer	86,443	883	1.5
Earmark Transfer	71,942	735	1.2
Transfer from Other Budget	19,586	200	0.3
Surplus from Previous Year	54,380	556	0.9
Total Public Finance Budget Revenue	793,907	8,110	13.4

Source: Shandong Budget Discloser Journal Feb 2015.

Table 8: Comparison of Financing Model for a Rich District and Poor County in Shandong Province

(in million)

Item	Shizhong District[a>]		Shanghe County[b>]	
	Amount (in RMB)	Percent of total(%)	Amount (in RMB)	Percent of total(%)
Total Tax Revenue	7,637	93.13	513	76.68
VAT	980		47	
Business Tax	2,628		198	
Corporate Tax	1,554		44	
Total Nontax Revenue	563	6.87	156	23.32
Total Public Finance Budget Revenue	8,200	100	669	100
Total Public Finance Budget Expenditure	3,207		2,102	
Transfers In	-4,993		1,433	
Per Capita Expenditure	6,286		3,681	

Source: Shizhong Government Website and Shanghe Government Website.

Note: a > Shizhong District data are for 2014;

b > Shanghe County data are for 2013.

Table 9: Consolidated Fiscal Position in Shandong Province in 2014

Item	Amount (in million)	Per Capita Amount (in RMB)	As a share of GDP
Public Finance Budget			
Public Finance Budget Revenue	793,907	8,110	13.36%
Tax and Nontax Revenue	502,671	5,135	8.46%
Transfer from Central Government	201,070	2,054	3.38%
Transfer from other Budget	19,586	200	0.33%
Transfer from previous year or surplus	54,379	555	0.92%
Debt Revenue	16,200	165	0.27%
Public Finance Budget Expenditure	793,907	8,110	13.36%
Expenditures	717,590	7,330	12.08%
Transfer to upper - level Government	8,333	85	0.14%
Debt payment	5,332	54	0.09%
Budget Stability Reserve	17,801	182	0.30%
Transfer to next year	44,283	452	0.75%
Surplus	567	6	0.01%
Government Fund Budget			
Government Fund Budget Revenue	476,584	4,868	8.02%
Revenues	397,366	4,059	6.69%
Transfer from Central Government	8,782	90	0.15%
Transfer from other Budget	2,879	29	0.05%
Transfer from previous year or surplus	67,556	690	1.14%
Government Fund Budget Expenditure	476,584	4,868	8.02%
Expenditures	39,6171	4,047	6.67%
Transfer to upper - level Government	197	2	0.00%
Transfer to other Budget	7,602	78	0.13%
Transfer to next year or surplus	72,613	742	1.22%
SOE Operation Budget			
SOE Operation Budget Revenue	3,050	31	0.05%
Revenues	2,672	27	0.04%
Transfer from previous year	378	4	0.01%
SOE Operation Budget Expenditure	3,050	31	0.05%
Expenditures	2,631	27	0.04%
Surplus	419	4	0.01%
Social Security Fund Budget			
Social Security Fund Budget Revenue	241,778	2,470	4.07%
Social Security Revenue	187,930	1,920	3.16%
Subsidy	40,573	414	0.68%
Social Security Fund Budget Expenditure	215,068	2,197	3.62%
Expenditures	208,907	2,134	3.52%

Source: Shandong Budget Discloser Journal Feb 2015.

Table 10: Shandong's Expenditure Perform

(in RMB)

Year	Per Capita GDP	Rank	Per Capita Revenue[a)]	Rank	Per Capita Expenditure	Rank	Per Capita Grants[b)]	Rank	Grants[b)] as a percent of GDP	Rank
2000	9,326	9	515	9	681	21	212	31	2	30
2001	10,195	9	634	9	834	21	231	31	2	30
2002	11,340	9	672	9	948	22	311	31	3	31
2003	13,268	7	782	9	1,108	21	361	31	3	30
2004	16,413	7	902	9	1,296	21	450	31	3	31
2005	19,934	7	1,160	10	1,585	22	497	31	2	28
2006	23,603	7	1,457	10	1,970	22	620	29	3	28
2007	27,604	7	1,789	10	2,415	22	727	29	3	27
2008	32,936	8	2,078	11	2,872	24	892	28	3	27
2009	35,894	8	2,322	11	3,451	28	1,205	28	3	26
2010	41,106	9	2,868	12	4,323	27	1,382	28	3	27
2011	47,335	10	3,586	13	5,190	29	1,783	28	4	25
2012	51,768	10	4,191	14	6,097	29	2,007	28	4	25
2013	56,323	10	4,685	15	6,872	28				

Source: Wind and CEIC.

Notes: a) Revenue includes tax revenues and non – tax revenues, it does not include grants.

b) Grants refers to transfers from the central government.

Table 11: Shandong Fiscal Disparities

At the prefecture level:

Per Capita GDP Prefectures[a) (in RMB)	2004	2005	2006	2007	2008	2009	2010	2011	2012
Average	20,034	24,027	28,404	33,526	39,942	42,269	48,615	55,259	57,791
Highest	49,909	64,606	79,766	90,928	111,574	111,543	127,654	143,921	144,778
Lowest	4,147	5,090	5,961	7,504	8,933	10,190	12,798	16,105	21,436
Standard Deviation	12,046	15,048	18,241	20,646	24,637	24,575	28,030	31,233	29,203
CV	60%	63%	64%	62%	62%	58%	58%	57%	51%

Per Capita Expenditure Prefectures[a) (in RMB)	2004	2005	2006	2007	2008	2009	2010	2011	2012
Average	1,250	1,564	1,869	2,338	2,762	3,254	4,138	5,048	5,673
Highest	3,052	3,541	3,534	4,237	4,877	5,702	7,678	9,669	10,055
Lowest	457	569	765	1,045	1,256	1,503	1,950	2,396	3,361
Standard Deviation	719	841	879	1,050	1,215	1,368	1,728	2,148	1,972
CV	57%	54%	47%	45%	44%	42%	42%	43%	35%

Source: Wind and CEIC.

Note: a) Including all 17 prefecture cities in Shandong Province.

At the county[1] level:

Per Capita GDP Counties[a)] (in RMB)	2004	2005	2006	2007	2008	2009	2010
Average	14,094	17,295	20,540	24,492	29,235	32,371	36,317
Highest	46,669	53,036	63,624	75,714	90,483	100,786	116,316
Lowest	3,457	3,922	4,496	5,473	6,625	7,401	9,125
Standard Deviation	8,683	10,903	13,172	15,755	18,675	21,246	23,761
CV	62%	63%	64%	64%	64%	66%	65%

Per Capita Expenditure Counties[a)] (in RMB)	2004	2005	2006	2007	2008	2009	2010	2011	2012
Average	777	958	1,209	1,518	1,808	2,106	2,680	3,335	4,066
Highest	2,668	3,436	3,489	4,566	6,346	7,062	8,970	9,901	11,108
Lowest	307	370	505	670	849	1,075	1,102	1,556	2,030
Standard Deviation	426	548	649	781	982	1,101	1,366	1,684	1,964
CV	55%	57%	54%	51%	54%	52%	51%	50%	48%

Source: Wind and CEIC.

Note: a) including out of all the 92 counties in Shandong Province, Changqing is not included because there are no available GDP data for Changqing, Jinan, because Chanqing changed from a county of Jinan to a district of Jinan in 2001. Counties do not include the districts in Shandong Province.

1 Including 91 counties in Shandong.

Table 12: Land Lease Revenue for China and Shandong

Year	China		Shandong	
	Amount(In billion)	As percent of GDP	Amount(In billion)	As percent of GDP
2010	2,710	6.6		
2011	3,150	6.5		
2012	2,889	5.4		
2013	4,125	7.0	286.5	5.2
2014	4,260	6.7	309.8	5.2

Source: Ministry of Land and Resources of China, and Shandong Budget Report.

Table 13: Subnational Debt for China and Shandong in June, 2013

Type	China		Shandong	
	Amount(In billion)	As percent of GDP	Amount(In billion)	As percent of GDP
Direct Debt	10,885.92	17	449.913	8
Implicit Debt	2,665.577	4	121.868	2
Contingent Debt	4,339.372	7	138.999	3
Total	17,890.87	28	710.78	13

Source: National Audit Office of China.

Table 14: Recapturing the Revenue Loss from Eliminating the Business Tax: Hypothetical Examples Using data from 2014 budget

(in billion RMB)

Item	Proposal	Net Revenue Change
Business Tax	Eliminate	-113
VAT: Plan A	No Change in Sharing Rate	25
VAT: Plan B	50 percent Sharing Rate	110
Urban Construction Tax Plus Education Surcharge	Additional Surcharge of 100 percent on Tax Paid	30
Piggyback Individual Income Tax	50 percent Surcharge on Tax Paid	6
Four Property Taxes	Raise rates to increase yield to 2 percent of GDP	16
Tax Administration Improvements	Remove Preferences equivalent to one percent of GDP	59

Source: Shandong Budget Discloser Journal Feb 2015.

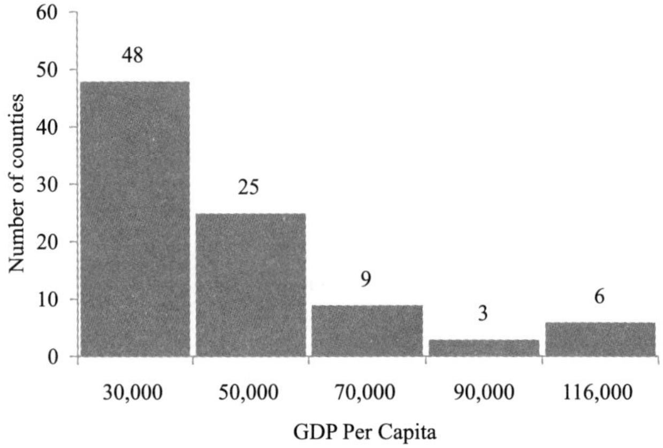

Figure 1：Distribution of Counties according to level of Per Capita GDP in 2010

Source：wind and CEIC.

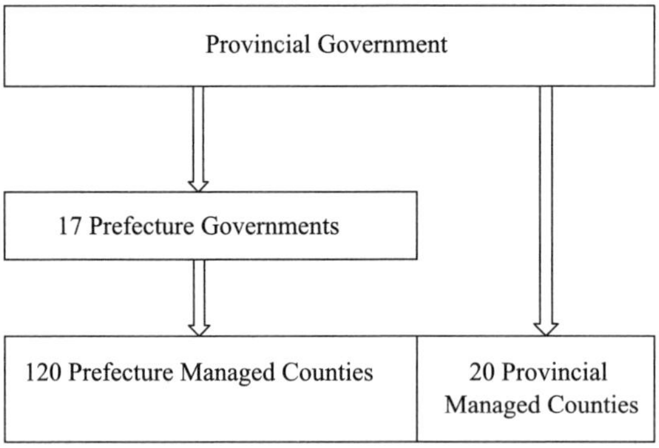

Figure 2：Shandong's Governmental Administration

APPENDIX 2: Regression Results

Regression A. Calculating Tax Effort for Shandong

We use a standard regression approach to calculate tax effort for Shandong province. Taxable capacity (T/Y) is estimated as a function of a set of exogenous variables (X_i) where

T_i = tax collections of ith province

Y_i = GDP of ith province

(x_1) per capita GDP to measure the size of the tax base

(x_2) percent of secondary industry in GDP

(x_3) percent to tertiary industry in GDP

(x_4) urbanization rate

All independent variables are expected to have a positive effect on taxable capacity. The results for three different specifications are presented in Table A - 1. We find that the primary determinants of taxable capacity are shown in Table A - 1.

Table A－1：Regression Results for Taxable Capacity

VARIABLES	Shared and Local taxes as a Percent of GDP		
	(1)	(2)	(3)
X_1	0.00948 **	－0.0103 **	0.00662
	(0.00471)	(0.00429)	(0.00490)
X_2	0.0969 ***		0.0870 ***
	(0.0211)		(0.0219)
X_3	0.0939 ***		0.0974 ***
	(0.0148)		(0.0153)
X_4		0.00652	0.00724
		(0.00529)	(0.00524)
Constant	－0.0758 *	0.137 ***	－0.0539
	(0.0428)	(0.0351)	(0.0441)
Observations	537	524	524
R－squared	0.755	0.725	0.753
Number of provinces	30	30	30

Standard errors in parentheses：*** $p<0.01$，** $p<0.05$，* $p<0.1$.
All variables in logarithms.

Tax effort (E_i) is measured as

$$E_i = (T/Y)_i / (\hat{T/Y})_i$$

The tax effort measure for Shandong is presented for each of the three specifications in Table A - 2.

Table A - 2: Shandong Tax Effort and Rank

year	Specification 1		Specification 2		Specification 3	
	Effort	Rank	Effort	Rank	Effort	Rank
1994	0. 67	27	0. 67	26	0. 69	26
1995	0. 67	27	0. 68	25	0. 68	25
1996	0. 72	27	0. 73	24	0. 73	25
1997	0. 80	25	0. 80	22	0. 82	22
1998	0. 85	24	0. 84	22	0. 87	20
1999	0. 89	20	0. 87	18	0. 91	18
2000	0. 92	17	0. 89	19	0. 94	15
2001	0. 94	15	0. 92	13	0. 96	14
2002	0. 93	18	0. 89	18	0. 95	16
2003	0. 94	16	0. 89	18	0. 96	15
2004	0. 89	19	0. 83	20	0. 91	18
2005	0. 86	22	0. 82	20	0. 87	22
2006	0. 84	23	0. 82	21	0. 85	22
2007	0. 80	23	0. 80	22	0. 81	23
2008	0. 75	25	0. 76	26	0. 76	25
2009	0. 75	25	0. 74	25	0. 76	25
2010	0. 75	25	0. 76	24	0. 75	25
2011	0. 73	28	0. 74	26	0. 73	28

Regression B. Calculating Grants Gap for Shandong

We use a simple approach to calculate the grants gap for Shandong province. We use a regression to estimate the determinants of grants of provinces in per capita terms. We run the regressions for total grants, unconditional grants and conditional grants respectively.

The independent variables include

(x_1) Per capita GDP

(x_2) the number of residents served by one public servant .

(x_3) Population density

The results, presented in Table B – 1, show that all the independent variables have the expected sign and are significant.

Table B – 1: Regression Results for Grants

ariables	(1)	(2)	(3)
	Total grants	Unconditional grants	Conditional grants
Per capita GDP	– 0. 6 ***	– 0. 6 ***	– 0. 6 ***
	(0. 16)	(0. 15)	(0. 18)
Population – per public employee	– 2. 1 ***	– 2. 1 ***	– 2. 1 ***
	(0. 22)	(0. 22)	(0. 25)
Population density	– 0. 3 **	– 0. 3 **	– 0. 3 *
	(0. 14)	(0. 13)	(0. 16)
Constant	23. 97 ***	23. 38 ***	23. 44 ***
	(2. 39)	(2. 34)	(2. 75)
Observations	30	30	30
R – squared	0. 82	0. 82	0. 79

Standard errors in parentheses: *** $p < 0.01$, ** $p < 0.05$, * $p < 0.1$.

All variables in logarithms.

We calculate expected per capita grants for Shandong, based on this equation. We find that there is a significant gap between the expected level of grants and the level of grants that Shandong received. The gap for total grants is 859 RMB per capita, and the amounts are 562 and 297 for unconditional and conditional grants respectively.

Table B-2: Grants Gap for Shandong

Indicators	(1)	(2)	(3)
	Total grants	Unconditional grants	Conditional grants
Shandong			
Expected	2,888	1,818	1,070
Actual	2,029	1,256	773
Gap	859	562	297
National (average)			
Actual	5,232	3,236	1,996

Total grants, unconditional grants and conditional grants are in per capita terms.

Regression C. The Determinants of Per capita Expenditure in 30 provinces[1] of China

We use a standard regression approach (OLS model with year dummy) to estimate the per capita expenditure equations for 30 provinces in China, using pooled data for the years 2000 – 2013.

In the first model, the independent variables include per capita GDP. In the second model, the independent variables include per capita GDP and Population.

Table C – 1: Regression Results for Per capita Expenditure in 30 provinces of China

Variables	(1)	(2)
	Per Capita Provincial and Local Government Expenditures	Per Capita Provincial and Local Government Expenditures
Per capita GDP	0. 64***	0. 59***
	(0. 03)	(0. 019)
Population	—	– 0. 33***
	—	(0. 012)
Constant	2. 3***	8. 55***
	(0. 29)	(0. 33)
Observations	420	420
R – squared	0. 88	0. 96

Standard errors in parentheses: *** p < 0. 01, ** p < 0. 05, * p < 0. 1.
All variables in logarithms.

1 Exclude Tibet.

Regression D. Estimating the income elasticity of county government expenditures in Shandong

We use a fixed effects model to estimate the income elasticity of county level per capita expenditure for 91 counties in Shandong province. The dependent variable is Per Capita Expenditure. The independent variable is per capita GDP.

The results are presented in Table D – 1.

Table D – 1: Regression Results for Per Capita Expenditure in 91 counties of Shandong

Variables	County Per Capita Expenditure
per Capita GDP	0.70***
	(51.75)
Constant	−0.04
	(−0.32)
Observations	637
R – squared	0.90

Standard errors in parentheses: *** $p < 0.01$, ** $p < 0.05$, * $p < 0.1$.

All variables in logarithms.

REFERENCES

[1] Bahl, Roy (1971) "A Regression Approach to Tax Effort and Tax Ratio Analysis" International Monetary Fund Staff Papers, Vol 18. No. 3.

[2] Bahl, Roy (1999). Fiscal policy in China: Taxation and intergovernmental fiscal relations. (San Francisco: 1990 Institute and University of Michigan Press).

[3] Bahl, Roy (2009) Property Tax Reform in Developing and Transition Countries (Washington D. C. : USAID).

[4] Bahl, Roy (2010). "Financing Metropolitan Areas" in Local Government finance: The challenges of the 21st Century, Second Global Report on decentralization and Local democracy (Cheltenham, UK: Edward Elgar).

[5] Bahl, R and Jorge Martinez – Vazquez (2006). "Sequencing Fiscal Decentralization". World Bank Policy Research Working Paper 3914, Public Sector Governance Group. Washington D. C. : World Bank.

[6] Bahl, Roy, and Jorge Martinez – Vazquez (2008). "The Property Tax in Developing Countries: Current Practice and Prospects" in Making the Property Tax Work: Experiences in Developing and Transitional Countries, ed. by Roy Bahl, Jorge Martinez – Vazquez and Joan Youngman. (Cambridge: Lincoln Institute of Land Policy), pp. 35 – 57.

[7] Bahl, Roy, Chor – Ching Goh and Baoyun Qiao (2014). Reforming the Public Finance System to Fit a More Urbanized China (Beijing: China Financial & Economic Publishing House).

[8] Bahl, Roy and Richard Bird (2008). "Subnational Taxes in Developing Countries: The Way Forward" Public Budgeting & Finance, Volume 28, Number 4, pp. 1 – 25.

[9] Bird, R. M. (2006). "Local and Regional Revenues: Realities and Prospects", in R. M. Bird and F. Vaillancourt, eds, Perspectives on Fiscal Federalism. WBI Learning Resources Series (Washington D. C.: World Bank), pp. 177 – 96.

[10] Bird, Richard (2013). "The VAT as a Local Business Tax" Tax Notes International, September 16, page 1 – 7.

[11] Bird, Richard and Enid Slack, editors (2004) International Handbook of Land and Property Taxation (Cheltenham, UK: Edward Elgar).

[12] Chen, Shiyi, and Jun Zhang (2008). The Efficiency of China Local Expenditure: 178 – 2005. China Social Science. 2008 (4) (in Chinese).

[13] De Cesare, Claudia (2010). "Overview of Property tax in Latin America". Working Paper WP10CD1 (Cambridge Ma: Lincoln Institute of Land policy).

[14] Gan, Li (2013, updated). "Findings from China Household Finance Survey" Powerpoint Presentation, (Texas A & M University).

[15] Hofman, Bert and Susana Cordeiro Guerra (2007). "Ensuring Inter – Regional Equity and Poverty Reduction" in Fiscal Equalization: Challenges in the Design of Intergovernmental Transfers edited by Jorge Martinez – Vazquez and Bob Searle (Springer) pp. 31 – 60.

[16] Hou, Yilin, Qiang Ren and Ping Zhang (2015). The Property tax in China: History, Pilots and Prospects (New York: Springer).

[17] Li, Junsheng, Baoyun Qiao, Lezheng Liu. (2014). "Building Sound Governance through Clearly Assigning Intergovernmental Resposibilities" [J]. Journal of Central University of Finance and

Economics, 0(03):3 (in Chinese).

[18] Liu, Lili and Baoyun Qiao (2013). "Restructuring of Legacy Debt for Financing Rural Schools in China" in Until. *Debt Do Us Part: Subnational Debt, Insolvency, and Markets* edited by Octaviano Canuto and Lili Liu (Washington D. C.: The World Bank), pp. 81 – 108.

[19] Lou, Jiwei. 2013. Rethinking of intergovernmental fiscal relations in China. Beijing: China Finance and Economics Press. [13] Lotz, Jorgen (2006). "Local Government Organization and Finance: Nordic Countries" in Local Government in Industrial Countries, ed. by Anwar Shah (Washington D. C.: World Bank) pp. 223 – 264.

[20] Lotz, Jorgen and Elliott Morss (1967). "Measuring Tax Effort in Developing Countries" International Monetary Fund Staff Papers. Volume 14, no. 3, pp. 478 – 499.

[21] Man, Joyce (2013). "Evaluation of Property Tax Reform and Experiments in China" Background paper prepared for world bank urbanization project, August 23, 2013.

[22] Martinez – Vazquez, Jorge (2013). "Local non – property tax revenues" in Financing Metropolitan Governments in Developing Countries edited by Roy Bahl, Johannes Linn and Deborah Wetzel, (Cambridge: Lincoln Institute of land Policy) pp. 183 – 212.

[23] Mathur, Om Prakash, Debdulal Thakur and Nilesh Rajadhyasksha (2009). "Urban Property Tax Potential in India" (New Delhi: National Institute of Public Finance and Policy).

[24] McCluskey, W. J. and Riel Franzsen (2013). "Property taxes and Land Taxes" in Government Finance in Metropolitan Areas in Developing Countries edited by Roy Bahl, Johannes Linn and Deborah Wetzel (Cambridge: Lincoln Institute of land Policy).

[25] OECD (2006). "Stockholm, Sweden", OECD Territorial Reviews.

[26] OECD (2010). Governance in Guangdong, Territorial Reviews, (Paris: OECD).

[27] Qiao, Baoyun and Lezheng Liu, 2013, Intergovernmental Fiscal Relationship and Risk – sharing Function: Background and Framework. Intergovernmental Fiscal Relationship and the Risk – sharing Function of Public Finance, edited by Baoyun Qiao and Lezheng Liu. China Financial and Economic Publishing House: Beijing.

[28] Qiao, Baoyun, Lezheng Liu, Yin Xundong, Guo Shen. (2014). "A Comparative Study on Local Government Incentives" [J]. Economic Research, 2014(10):102 – 110(in Chinese).

[29] Research on the Establishment of Modern Fiscal System in Shandong, Shandong Province March 2, 2015.

[30] Smolka, Martim (2013) Implementing Value Capture in Latin America: Policies and Tools for Urban Development, Policy Focus Report (Cambridge: Mass, Lincoln Institute of land Policy).

[31] Wetzel, Deborah (2013). "Metropolitan Governance and Finance in Sao Paulo" in Government Finance in Metropolitan Areas in Developing Countries edited by Roy Bahl, Johannes Linn and Deborah Wetzel (Cambridge: Lincoln Institute of land Policy). Pp. 309 – 338.

[32] Wong, Christine (2012). "Toward building Performance – Oriented Management in China: The Critical role of Monitoring and Evaluation and the Long Road Ahead" ECD Working Paper no. 27 (Washington: World Bank).

[33] Wong, Christine (2013) "Paying for Urbanization in China: Challenges of China's Municipal Finance in the Twenty – First Century" in Government Finance in Metropolitan Areas in Developing

Countries edited by Roy Bahl, Johannes Linn and Deborah Wetzel (Cambridge: Lincoln Institute of land Policy), pp. 273 – 308.

[34] Wong, Christine, Christopher Heady and Wing T. Woo (1995), Fiscal Management and Economics Reform in the People's Republic of China, Hong Kong: Oxford University Press.

[35] World Bank (2013). Beyond the Annual Budget: Global experience with Medium Term Expenditure Frameworks (Washington D. C.: The World Bank).

[36] World Bank (2015). "China Economic Update: Reform Priorities in China's Financial Sector" (World Bank, Beijing, June).

[37] World Bank and Development Research Center (2013). China 2030: Building a Modern, Harmonious, and Creative Society, (Washington D. C.: World Bank).

[38] World Bank and Development Research Center (2014). Urban China: Toward Efficient, Inclusive and Sustainable Urbanization (Washington D. C.: The World Bank).

（汉英对照）

地方财政体制改革的选择：山东财政案例

OPTIONS FOR REFORMINGS SHANDONG'S FISCAL SYSTEM

罗伊·鲍尔
吴卓瑾　著
乔宝云
刘乐峥　译

中国财政经济出版社

图书在版编目（CIP）数据

地方财政体制改革的选择：山东财政案例：汉英对照 /（美）鲍尔，吴卓瑾，乔宝云著；刘乐峥译．—北京：中国财政经济出版社，2016.3

书名原文：OPTIONS FOR REFORMINGS SHANDONG'S FISCAL SYSTEM

ISBN 978－7－5095－6647－3

Ⅰ.①地…　Ⅱ.①鲍…②吴…③乔…④刘…　Ⅲ.①地方财政－财政改革－研究－山东省－汉、英　Ⅳ.①F812.752

中国版本图书馆 CIP 数据核字（2016）第 037646 号

责任编辑：杜　剑　　　　责任校对：黄亚青
整体设计：郁　佳　　　　版式设计：董生平

中国财政经济出版社出版

URL：http：//www.cfeph.cn
E－mail：cfeph@cfeph.cn

（版权所有　翻印必究）

社址：北京市海淀区阜成路甲 28 号　邮政编码：100142
发行处电话：88190406　财经书店电话：64033436　84041336
北京财经印刷厂印刷　各地新华书店经销
787×1092 毫米　16 开　17.25 印张　269 000 字
2016 年 4 月第 1 版　2016 年 4 月北京第 1 次印刷
定价：48.00 元
ISBN 978－7－5095－6647－3/F·5346
（图书出现印装问题，本社负责调换）
本社质量投诉电话：010－88190744

打击盗版举报热线：010－88190492、QQ：634579818

目　录

致　谢

在为“世界银行中国财政分析与贷款管理研究”课题撰写论文的过程中，我们产生了写作这本书的想法。2015 年年初，正值山东省提出深化财税改革、加快建立现代财政制度之际，我们开始了此项研究。在此，特别感谢山东省财政厅厅长于国安先生、副巡视员王晶先生以及其他参与此项研究的山东省财政厅同事们。此外，本书还得益于山东省地税局、省发改委、省卫计委、省教育厅、人力资源和社会保障厅、省国税局等部门与我们进行的座谈研讨。山东省财政科学研究所崔宗涛所长及同事们也为写作本书提供了很大的帮助。2015 年 4 月，我们在济南市商河县和市中区的实地调研也充实了本书内容。本书得以成型离不开山东省财政厅同事们的重要贡献。

2015 年 6 月 6 日，我们以圆桌讨论会的形式完善了本书初稿。感谢山东省财政厅的同事们来北京参与讨论会。同时，感谢参与讨论会并给予宝贵建议的以下政府官员和学者：杨元伟、王道树、胡贺波、梁昌新、王朝才、杨远根、黄然和李承霖。此外，感谢参与讨论会并提出有益建议的以下专家和学者：杨运杰、孙殿明、郑新业、刘乐峥、王永超、马念谊、张洪战、胡云归、马昊、丛培德、赵慧和梁洪波。

最后，最终书稿的形成离不开一些人的出色工作。感谢中国财政经济出版社的赵力编辑提供专业的指导，使本书出版成为可能。中央财经大学李雯睿为本书提供了宝贵的研究帮助。

作者简介

罗伊·鲍尔 美国乔治亚州立大学安德鲁·杨政策研究学院杰出经济学教授和荣誉退休教授。他作为顾问曾为全世界许多国家的公共财政改革提出建议。他曾发表了许多学术专著和论文。

吴卓瑾 世界银行中国、蒙古和韩国区首席经济学家。在北京工作之前，她是世界银行埃塞俄比亚、苏丹和南苏丹地区的首席经济学家。在这之前她曾是世界银行俄罗斯区的高级经济学家，研究对象包括前苏联国家和新欧盟成员国家。吴卓瑾是经济地理学报告《2009 年世界发展报告》的副主管。2000 年到 2007 年，她作为东亚和太平洋国家区域办公室的经济学家，专门研究贫困、公平和劳动力市场问题，主导关于柬埔寨、蒙古和菲律宾的报告和对话。吴卓瑾在耶鲁大学作为优秀毕业生获得学士与硕士学位，随后在哈佛大学获得经济学博士学位。

乔宝云 中央财经大学中国公共财政与政策研究院院长、经济学教授。他著有许多学术专著和论文，也曾为许多国家就公共财政、地方治理和经济发展问题提供建议。他毕业于美国乔治亚州立大学，获得经济学博士学位。

本书译者刘乐峥 中央财经大学中国公共财政与政策研究院助理教授。他曾出版多部关于中国财政和税收的专著，主持或参与多项财政部与国家税务总局的研究课题。他在美国西密歇根大学获得经济学博士学位。

前　言

为减少对竞争性部门的直接补贴和税收优惠，并对地方政府间财政关系进行再思考，全国人民代表大会号召地方政府采用更加现代化和更加有效的财政和债务管理方法。2014 年，国务院推出了该项改革的指导性规定，并计划随后推出关于省与地方政府的税收和支出划分等全国人大关注的其他问题的规定。

在正在推行的一项财政改革中，山东省将国务院的规定与自身的情况结合了起来。在改革过程中，山东省力求解决财税管理上的问题。此外，为了响应国务院关于平衡政府间关系以及“创新财政资金支持产业发展使用方式”的号召，山东省也制定了许多相应的政策和措施。山东省的改革方案将有可能成为其他省份改革的范本。

本书对山东省改革方案进行了分析和评价，以更好地认知省与地方政府在新一轮改革实施时可能扮演的角色，更好地理解地方政府对全国人民代表大会提出的一些更深入的财政改革会作何反应。

山东省的人口和经济基础

山东省拥有近 1 亿的人口，是中国人口第二大省。从 2000—2013 年，山东省的城镇化率翻了一番，达到 54%。为了满足新增城镇人口的公共服务和基础设施需求，政府预算承担着极大的压力。人口结构的变化也对预算产生了新的要求，特别是人口年龄分布的改变

意味着劳动力供给的萎缩、养老和医疗支出的增多，以及解决环境问题需求的迫切。

山东省地区生产总值占全国生产总值的9%，人均GDP在全国各省市中排名第10位。城市地区的平均收入比县城地区约高34%。县城地区人均收入跨度很大，大部分集中在低于3万元人民币每人的水平，另有12个县的人均收入高于城市地区的平均值。各地居民平均福利水平的不均等加上地方政府平均征税能力的不均等，迫使山东省急需实施财政均等化改革。

在山东省，政府治理和服务供给并不集中在省政府，而是分散在140个区县政府和17个地级市政府中。实际上，省级政府支出仅占政府总支出的10%，属于全国最低水平。而被视为我国地方政府基石的区县政府，公共支出比例约为66%，属于全国最高水平。一般公共财政预算中的税收和非税收收入约占山东省全省GDP总额的8.46%，低于其他省份的11.92%。此外，山东省土地出让金收入以及债务余额占GDP的比例均低于其他省份。

山东省80%的政府服务所需资金是通过共享税和地方税筹集的，另外20%由中央的转移支付补贴。几乎所有收入均在市县政府层级征收。山东的省级与地市级政府分享地方政府收入，并且决定转移给有预算赤字区县政府的数额。这一转移支付通常由一系列程序决定，包括专家的论证、专有公式的计算以及相关方的协商等。

问题与关注点

尽管山东省的综合财务状况仍保持着平衡状态，但一些问题的出现开始逐步打破这一平衡。

（1）省与地方政府的支出比例较低。山东省人均GDP在全国排名

第10位，然而人均公共财政预算支出仅排名第28位。造成这一结果的原因主要有两点：征税努力不够；获得的中央政府转移支付相对较少。

（2）在人均公共服务支出上，最高的区县的支出额约为最低区县的9倍，最高地级市的支出额也约为最低地级市的9倍。问题是，如此大的差距在未来能否仍为人们所接受。

（3）山东省城镇化所带来的基础设施需求，加上日趋老龄化的人口结构，将会对基础设施和公共服务的融资造成巨大压力。

（4）随着土地出让收入的减少，如何为基础设施建设筹资尚未可知。山东省政府负债率低，可以进行举债融资，然而如何还本付息也是一个问题。

（5）政府与竞争性部门保持着直接联系。相当数量的企业仍然在不同程度上为政府所拥有，因此政府可以借助这些国有企业通过多种渠道直接或间接地影响私人部门的活动。对某些行业和企业的税收优惠和税收返还不但形成了政府预算的沉重负担，同时也扰乱了市场的决策。

（6）体制中存在反向激励，这些激励有的不利于增加财政收入，有的使投资倾向于经济发展而非公共服务，有的造成土地过度出让，并且过度分权本身也会导致区县政府被分配到一些有溢出效应或规模经济效应的职能而产生效率损失。

（7）公共资源分配并未如愿建立在规则之上，这使得体制更加复杂。三个问题能够说明这种复杂性：第一，每一级省与地方政府的收入和支出均在四本独立的预算中披露。其中有三本预算包含现金和资本支出，同时也包含各级政府的转移支付等。第二，部分省级—地市级—县级政府间的转移支付靠专家论证和商讨的方式决定，转移支付带有限制条件等都增加了复杂的程度。第三，过去用土地出让权为基础设施投资作贷款担保的做法已经造成了地方政府在还本付息义务上

的困惑。

山东省改革方案

山东省人民政府针对国务院的规定和目标制定了改革方案，出色地完成了工作。这一方案有三个重要支撑：第一，建立现代化的财税管理体制，设定低绩效支出、过度举债和腐败方面的警戒线；第二，利用税收制度进一步将政府与竞争性部门分离开；第三，构建更加合理的政府间转移支付体系，保持合适的均等化水平。如果执行顺利，山东省财政改革将会提高政府支出效率，促进财政收入的增加和税收的公平，同时提高政府间财政体制的均等化水平与规则管理水平。

财政管理

《预算法》的实施是财政改革的一个重要举措。通过要求地方政府将所有收支活动纳入预算，预算法消除了预算外收支的可能性。此外，地方政府需要整合四本预算以增加透明度。总的来说，预算法将预算的重心从控制转向了规划，并引入了跨年度预算的概念。随着专项转移支付的减少，地方政府支出规划的弹性也会增加。

预期于2017年完成的《国库管理制度》作为新预算法的补充，将使有效地控制支出成为可能。与此同时，新规定将逐步取消大多数特殊基金，禁止新增预算项目的做法，要求设立预算稳定基金平滑短期赤字与盈余。

构建债务管理框架能够控制债务规模。所有举债行为都必须得到省政府的批准，并列入预算。利用地方融资平台举债的做法将被禁止，同时现存的（不合法的）地方债务将被逐步甄别和清理。

这一新的进程势必将一些资金从低优先级的支出中释放出来，转而投入到必需的公共服务中去，这会产生间接的收入效应。

然而，像其他许多改革方案一样，山东省的方案也存在一些问题。方案并未提及经常性预算和资本预算。在设立预算稳定基金后，允许地方年度预算列赤字，实施年度紧急救助也许会取得成效，但必须注意应限制赤字仅用于解决短期的现金流问题，防止为软预算约束开后门。在债务管理改革方面，方案未明确地方政府如何偿付新债务。区县政府不拥有独立的收入来源（除了土地出让金收入）。用政府间转移支付来还本付息是一种可能，但这会模糊贷款和转移支付的界限。

最后，实施改革需要策略，即需要一项缜密的计划来逐步引入这些变革。特别由于山东省的140个区县政府情况复杂，有的在财政事务上富有经验，而有的农村县市的资源基础和能力则较为薄弱，要推进这些改革措施将遇到困难。

税收改革

另一方面的改革集中于推动实现公共部门和竞争性部门关系合理化。山东省改革方案提出，要建立综合全面的纳税人信息系统，帮助提高征税率，降低征税成本和纳税遵从成本。更重要的是，除得到国务院批准的条款外，对企业提供补贴和税收优惠的做法将成为过去。由此产生的收入可能十分可观，尽管方案文件中并未给出具体的收入估算。然而，山东省相对GDP的税收征收率低于全国平均值3个百分点，这也说明通过减少税收优惠来增收的潜力可观。

税收改革的实施必定会遇到一些困难。税收优惠的做法根深蒂固，完全取消阻碍重重，特别是在政府中仍不乏支持这一做法的官员。此外，在山东省经济增长率已经减缓的情况下，要削减被许多人视为刺激经济发展有效手段的企业补贴也十分困难。就这一点而

言，近期国务院新的规定似乎也要求地方在取消税收优惠时应采取较为温和的方式。

政府间财政关系

山东省政府间财政关系的三个问题是：(1) 支出和管理责任的划分不清晰、不合理；(2) 收入在地方政府间的分配可能不够均等；(3) 政府间转移支付的管理框架有待完善。改革方案充分汲取了国际先进经验，以求解决以上三个问题。但是，其中政府间转移支付体系的改革尚未有具体方案出台。

第一，由于省政府、地级政府和县市政府间的支出责任可能有所改变，现有支出职能的划分可能需要重新论证。改革方案要求实现责任的重新划分，并于2015年在教育、医疗和交通领域进行试点。

第二，省以下地方政府之间巨大的财政差异应当得到解决。具体的收入分享计划尚未出台，但改革方案似乎寻求为地方政府间的收入分配建立一个更加基于规则的方法。

第三，改革方案要求省给地方政府的转移支付中应当减少专项转移支付，增加一般性转移支付，并且取消地方的资金匹配。

弥补营业税收入损失

山东省需要应对的另一个问题来自于营业税取消后财政收入减少所产生的缺口。部分缺口可以随着改革的实施自然填补，如减少的税收优惠、提高财税管理效率带来的成本降低和支出减少等。改革方案未就各类措施变动对山东省财政收入的影响做出估计。然而，如果把对企业的税收优惠占GDP的比重限制到最多占1%的话，营业税收入

中的一半损失就可以得到弥补。

还有部分收入损失可以通过增加新的收入来源进行补偿，当然，开征新税必须得到中央政府的批准。目前看来，这种想法短期内难以实现。

展 望

山东省在财政改革上进行了极具探索意义的尝试，其制定的改革方案将会极大地提高支出效率和收入激励，同时减少浪费，抑制腐败。改革借鉴了先进的国际经验，遵循了国务院的新规，将成为其他省市的学习典范。需要指出的是，为了让改革方案充分发挥其作为指导规划文件的潜力，我们应当更明确地说明方案的预期目标，跟踪改革进度，制定实施策略和时间表。同样地，假如将方案作为完善财政制度的规划，山东省则需要定期对方案做出修订。“一次性”的研究在指导山东公共财政改革方面不具备长久生命力。目前版本的方案包含的可度量指标较少。例如，对当前税收优惠总额、支持经济发展的企业补贴的总额和为实现均等化在省与省以下政府间进行的转移支付的总额等均未进行相应的估算。

对山东省改革方案的一个主要担忧在于其能否按时有效实施，主要包括以下几点：

其一是需要寻求一条路径来取消部分根深蒂固却适得其反的做法，以此作为改革的切入点。完全分离私人部门与公共部门并非易事。政府通过各种各样的补贴和税收优惠施惠于企业。地方政府官员要从与竞争性部门的这些直接联系中抽身出来有多困难，或者分离政府与私人部门职能需要多长时间，都尚未可知。

其二是在提高地方政府工作人员的专业能力方面存在困难。在某

种意义上，新预算法对财税管理方式深层次的改变提出了要求。我们需要在培训和管理上花更多的精力。即使不考虑新预算法提出的要求，政府工作人员，特别是乡镇的政府工作人员也仍有很大的提升空间。因此，为了改革方案的顺利实施，制定一个政府工作人员能力提升策略十分重要，这可能成为改革成败的关键。

第一章 导 论

中国的财政体制已落后于其经济社会的发展。无论是税收制度、公共支出、中央与地方的财政关系，还是财税管理的手段，都难以与当前的政府职能相匹配。与此同时，大环境也发生了变化。中国的经济增速放缓，人口结构日趋老龄化，环境问题愈加严重，且面临着加速城镇化时加大的基建投入所带来的一系列问题。

全国人民代表大会意识到了这一问题，突出强调了进行财政改革的必要性。国务院制定了新的法规，同时对完善财税结构的长期目标展开研究。新预算法和新规定的出台，成为了中国税收体系和财税管理迈向现代化的重要一步。

在调整地方政府收入预算结构、重新划分支出责任，以及改革政府间转移支付制度等方面，中国还有很长的路要走。虽然这些重大改革目前仅有一个大概的方向，尚未出台明确规定，但改革似乎不仅将涵盖制度上的变化，还将触及中国地方政府的角色定位这一基本理念的改变，核心依然是建立一个能够更加明确地将政府的传统职能（公平有效地提供公共服务）和竞争性部门的投资生产职能分离的财政制度。

由于情况复杂，加上体制上的一些做法已经根深蒂固，中国的财政改革需要时间和耐心。改革应该循序渐进，不可一蹴而就。即便是财政改革的第一步——本书的核心——财税管理改革，也非一日之功。理论上，国务院的改革指导意见随时可以付诸实施，但中国经济的低速增长将会拖延改革进程。

研究目的

近年来，许多宝贵的研究对中国的财政问题进行了思考和探讨[1]。然而，几乎所有关于省级财政和政府间财政关系改革的文章都采用了自上而下的分析思路，提出的论点多为“为实现改革目标，中央应当制定的政策和改革措施”（Bahl，Goh and Qiao，2014；世界银行中国发展研究中心，2014；Qiao and Liu，2013）。毫无疑问，这与中国自上而下的传统政府财政制度结构相一致（Bahl，1999；Wong，Heady and Woo，1995）。具体来讲，地方政府总是被动地实施中央的改革方案，却极少主动开创改革的局面。

相对而言，省和省以下政府在财政改革中发挥的作用不那么重要，自下而上的改革很少出现。尽管如此，一些省政府已经开始探索如何将中央领导的财政改革与地区具体情况相结合，以提高支出效率，实现额外收入。山东省的财政改革方案就是这样的一个典型案例。

本书的目的在于对山东省财政改革方案作进一步的分析，主要包括两个方面：第一，省和省以下地方政府在改革中的角色定位；第二，省和省以下地方政府在面对全国人大提出的长期改革时可能会有的反应。

以此为基础，我们提出了两个常见的问题。第一个问题是，假设中央立法不改变，省和地方政府如何能够提升财政绩效？这一问题的重点在于现有体制下地方政府已经拥有的财政自治的三个方面：财税管理、省与地方政府之间的收入分配和支出责任划分，以及政府性基金预算和社会保障预算相关的收入活动。山东省的改革方案主要关注

1　Lou，2013；Li，Qiao and Liu，2014；Wang，2013；Chen and Zhang，2008。

了前两个方面，特别是如何将国务院的规定与该省的经济和政府治理环境相结合。

第二个是山东省的收入实现问题。一方面，现有改革将会导致营业税收入减少，这会多大程度上影响总收入？现在看来，这一问题已不遥远。另一方面，山东省是否应该在国家财政体制内进行结构化改革？如，推行日益增强的收入自主权、对收入分配体系进行完善等。如果答案是肯定的，山东省又应该怎么做？全国人民代表大会和财政部均对增加地方政府税收收入的可能性进行过探讨。尽管这些改革带来的成果可能在短时间内难以显现，但仍然是我们分析的重点。分析可能从两个方面产生积极影响：一是我们会重新审视中央政府推行的政策方向与地方政府面临的财政问题之间的一致性；二是我们能够帮助中央决策者对省和地方政府的政策和管理进行进一步的研究，指出应如何完善制度以支撑下一轮改革。

研究方法

山东省提出了一整套财政改革方案，涵盖了预算管理以及省级以下政府的融资等问题。该方案的成果可参见《山东建立现代财政制度研究》。方案在遵循了国务院规定的同时，充分考虑了山东省政府治理和政府间财政结构的现状。

我们不对山东省能够在多大程度上代表其他省份这一问题进行过多探讨。需要指出的是，山东省与其他省份采用了许多相同的做法，共同面临着中国普遍存在的人口结构和城市化改造问题，同时在同样的财政体制内行事。因此，山东省在财政改革中的发现和做法可能对其他省份具有借鉴意义。另一方面，山东相对富裕，人口在全国省份中位居第二，工业基础较为雄厚，在财政方面尝试了一些不同的做法。

从这一角度来讲，山东省改革方案所具有的特点可能与其他省份的实际情况不符。因此，在推广山东省做法之前，应当根据其他省份的不同特点重新对方案进行修正。

本书将分为两个部分。第一部分，研究山东省的改革背景：人口、经济、政府治理、财政结构、财政绩效，以及公共财政的相关问题。随后，我们将分析评价山东省政府推行的改革方案。该方案遵从了党的十八届三中全会提出的公共财政体制改革方向，可以说是国务院出台的新法规中所阐述的综合性财税管理改革的具体实施方案。

第二部分，探讨中央政府将如何进一步完善政府间财政关系。到目前（2015 年 6 月）为止，中央政府的长期财政改革已进行了三步：一是对政策方向的讨论与确定；二是已通过决议并待实施的新法规；三是仍在进行的关于新财政制度的争论。中国的政府间财政改革仍在进行中，但对个别省份的改革举措进行评价也十分重要，有可能推动措施的实施和推广。

我们将以营业税取消后面临的收入问题作为第二部分的开始。随后，关于如何解决收入激励问题，我们的回答仅仅是启发性的，然而更具有激励作用的应当是类似于政府间财政改革的一些措施。财政部、国际机构和学者们已经对大部分的改革措施进行了讨论。改革方案包括赋予地方政府新的征税权利和对政府间转移支付制度进行结构化改革等内容。有趣的是，我们发现部分改革可能难以在山东现有的省和地方结构中推进，必须在省政府层面进行适当的调整。

第二章　山东省基本情况

山东省的这一财政改革才刚起步。改革的措施符合中央当前的政策和法规。理解改革方案在地方人口与经济结构、政府治理与财政结构，以及现有财政体制的影响下是如何形成的十分重要。我们从这一点开始分析。

人口特点和经济结构

山东省是中国人口数量第二大的省份，拥有近 1 亿的人口（表 1）（各章的图表均见附录 1）。在 2013 年，山东省约 54% 的人口居住在城市，这与吉林省（54%）和海南省（53%）的城镇化率相近。和其他许多省份一样，山东经历了快速的农业人口向城镇转移的过程。从 2000 年到 2013 年，山东的城镇化率翻了一番。从绝对数字来看，城镇人口在这一时间里增加了大约 2 400 万人。人口结构的这一变化对城市公共服务和基础设施的预算提出了严峻的考验（Bahl、Goh 和 Qiao，2014；世界银行中国发展研究中心，2013），同时也造成了部分农村地区的空心化。

人口结构的其他变化也会对预算产生巨大压力。年龄分布的变化意味着劳动力的减少，并需要对养老金和医疗健康进行更多的投入。如表 2 所示，该省约 11% 的人口年龄超过 65 岁，高于全国平均水平 1 个百分点。

山东省的地区产出占全国总产出的9%，是国家经济的重要部分。在过去的15年里，山东省的GDP增速与其他地区基本保持一致。人均GDP普遍被认为是衡量经济发展的重要指标。依据这一指标，山东可以在全国省份人均GDP排名中位列第10（表3），属于发达地区。2013年，山东省人均GDP为56 323元人民币（折合9 091美元），比全国平均水平43 320元人民币高约23%。换个角度来看，山东的人均GDP（9 091美元）与东亚太平洋沿岸国家平均水平（9 116美元）、罗马尼亚（9 490美元）以及毛里求斯（9 477美元）旗鼓相当。

同所有省份一样，山东省的收入分配并不均等。城市地区的平均收入大概高出县市地区约34%。图1中的频数分布表明，县市人均收入水平的分布很广，但大多数集中在少于30 000元人民币的分组，同时也有12个县市的人均收入水平高于城市地区的平均水平。这种居民人均收入的不均等，及其带来的平均纳税能力的不平等，都意味着想要在城市与农村地区以及县市之间提供均等化公共服务将会遭遇重大挑战。

山东省经济基础较其他地区而言更集中于工业部门，第三产业的支出比重较低（见表4）。因此，山东保持了在制造业上的比较优势，生产效率比服务业要高（世界银行中国发展研究中心，2013）。

政府治理

图2显示了山东省政府治理的三个层级：省级政府、17个地级政府和140个区县政府。在这140个区县中，有20个是作为试点由省级政府直接管辖，其余均由相应的地级政府管辖。正如我们要讨论的，地级市管辖的48个市区对财政结构具有重要意义。因为这些市区是该省税收收入的重要来源地，辖区居民也享受着比农村地区更高水平的

公共服务。

政府治理和公共服务供给出现了向地级政府和区县政府层级分权化的趋势。省政府担负着极少的服务提供直接责任，更多的时候作为地方财政的管理者来行动，对来自中央的转移支付和专项资金分别进行分配和发放。事实上，如表5所示，山东省级政府支出仅占该省政府总支出的10%，在全国各省份中属于最低水平。相反，被看作地方政府基石的区县政府，其支出占政府总支出的66%，在全国属于最高水平。

地级政府在提供直接公共服务上扮演着比省级政府更重要的角色。在一些政府有责任提供如自来水和公共交通等区域性服务的城市地区更是如此。地级政府还需要在省政府领导下对赤字或者盈余地区的收入进行再分配。如我们将要讨论的，省政府在2013年改变了其实现均等化的方式，这也成为山东省政府治理结构改革的重要组成部分。

从这些制度安排上的数据和观察来看，我们或许可以说山东省的政府治理和财政状况在中国属于较为分权的。

公共服务水平和财税成效的比较

我们根据公共部门的工作量和绩效指标对山东省和全国平均水平进行了比较（表2），以期对山东政府的工作水平有一个大致的印象。我们看到的结果有些复杂。在部分服务上（例如，医疗专业人员），山东的公共服务水平似乎较高，这与收入较高省份的情况类似。在其他方面，例如环境质量和教育系统的覆盖程度上，山东却低于全国平均水平。

然而，正如对表2中的延展性指标分析的那样，数据对山东省公共服务水平的描述并不全面。例如，我们会看到关于医疗服务基础设施（例如，床位数和专业人员数）的强有力数据，但改革规划（2014）中更深入的讨论指出，城乡之间的公共服务能力存在着巨大

的差异。

从预算的角度来看，情况更加清晰。财税数据表明，山东省政府规模比相同公共服务水平所对应的政府规模要小。此外，山东省的政府支出、人均支出占 GDP 的比重、公共财政预算、综合预算以及人均未偿债务余额与全国平均水平相比均较低。

公共服务融资

山东省公共财政预算中的收入（不包括中央的转移支付）约占 GDP 的 8.46%。而全国平均来看，这一指标约占 GDP 的 11.92%（表 6）。相对于 GDP 规模而言，山东省政府性基金收入以及土地出让金收入也比全国平均水平低。

公共财政预算的收入部分见表 7。其中，税收收入占比很大（约占税收收入和非税收入总额的 79%）[1]。营业税占税收收入的比重最大（28.6%）。同时，对中央转移支付（返还收入、一般转移支付和专项转移支付）的依赖很严重，这部分收入约占公共预算总收入的 25%。依赖中央的拨款是山东省省级财政的重要特点，这对于了解山东省的预算平衡至关重要。

几乎所有的收入都在地级和县级政府进行征收。省级政府征收的税收只占 3%。但由于各个区县的纳税能力差别很大，山东省采用横向均衡以更好地实现收支平衡。在 2014 年之前，省级政府和地级政府会决定收支盈余的区县可以将多少收入进行保留，以及预算列赤字的

1 人们对“地方税”的概念有时会有误解。在中国，“地方税”是指全额由地方政府获得的税收。例如，25% 的增值税和全部的营业税都由地方政府拥有，但地方政府没有调整税率和税基或者开征新税的权利。在大多数西方工业国家，“地方税”是指地方政府能够决定税率和税基的税收。按照西方的定义，中国所说的地方税和共享税其实也是政府间转移支付的一种形式。在下文中，我们将使用中国的定义。关于该问题的更多讨论，请参见 Bahl 和 Bird（2 008），Ebel 和 Tallercio（2008）。

区县应当得到多少转移收入。2014 年，山东采用了一个更加传统的分配方法，给予省级政府一定的增量税收入，由其进行均衡性分配。地方政府得到的转移支付通过结合特定设计法和计算公式共同得出。在前者中，地方政府被赋予一个叫作“标准化支出需求”的指标，上级政府以覆盖该指标为目的对收入短缺的地方政府进行支持。

我们对一个富裕的市区和一个贫困的县在 2014 年的财政预算进行比较分析，以说明这一计算体系（见表 8）。接下来的例子则说明了 2013 年横向分配的方案。较富裕的市区（济南市市中区）被赋予的支出指标为 32.07 亿元人民币，由于收入高达 82 亿元人民币，则必须将差额部分的 49.93 亿元人民币上交给地级政府或者省级政府用于再分配，这大概占了该区收入的 65%。较贫困的县（济南市商河县）的支出指标为 21.02 亿元人民币，约 32% 的资金依靠自有收入，剩下的 68% 都将通过转移支付获得。这两个区县的例子表明，这一分配体系实现了均衡，但并非完全意义上的均衡。因为从另一个角度来看，富裕的市区人均支出为 6 286 元人民币，而贫困县的人均支出仅为 3 681 元人民币。

预算绩效

山东省的综合财政状况目前仍处于平衡状态，四类财政预算的情况见表 9。依赖于中央政府一般和专项转移支付，公共财政预算得以扭亏为盈。否则，地方税收加上共享税税收难以覆盖预算支出。政府性基金预算和国有资本经营预算目前也保持着盈亏平衡。其中，政府性基金预算的大部分收入来自土地出让金收入。

目前社保基金预算的支出有 82% 由缴费收入支撑，另外 18% 由一般预算账户的财政补贴以及微量的累计余额支付。2014 年，社会保障基金余额为 2 417.78 亿元人民币，约为该年社保基金预算总支出的 112%。

第三章　公共财政问题与关注

山东省目前并没有财政危机。财政改革的目的是为了实现政府工作的现代化、公共部门与私人部门在经济中的分离，以及遵循国务院新规提高透明度。假如改革能够合理推进，省与地方政府财政将得到加强，尽管这并非主要由融资缺口引起。

山东省经济基础雄厚，足以产生更多的财政收入，其财政收入与中国其他地区保持着同样的增速。在财税管理和税收征管方面的改革措施将会产生效率收益，在节省支出的同时增加收入。然而财政支出需求也十分巨大。城镇化率的大幅度提高，对现有的城市基础设施造成了压力，140 个区县之间在公共服务水平上也存在较大的不均等。社会保障预算目前虽有财政补贴的支持，但随着人口老龄化，劳动力的萎缩，预算的负担会进一步加重。

尽管税基具有较强征税潜力，营业税的逐步取消依然会造成地方财政收入的紧张。财政改革将通过减少税收优惠政策实现税收增收，也会产生支出推迟收入增加的效应。

山东省政府已经面临的很大难题是未来也许存在收入缺口。同时，其他结构性问题也亟待解决。随着新预算法的实施和财税管理改革的推进，以上许多问题都可以逐步得到解决。至于剩下的问题，则需要等待中央政府层面的下一轮财政改革。下面我们将主要集中讨论以下问题：

（1）山东的省与省以下地方政府支出是否过低？是否有充足的征税空间供省与省以下地方政府为更高水平的公共服务、公共基础设施

和社会保障融资？

（2）省以下地方政府之间的财政差异应当在多大程度上得到减少？减少财政差异应当使用哪些政策工具？

（3）省与省以下地方政府是否过于直接地参与了竞争性部门的活动？山东省公共部门是否过于复杂而导致难以有效管理？

（4）山东省财政体制中是否存在逆向（不利的）激励？

政府支出是否足够高

山东省的政府支出是否能满足需求？这个问题回答起来并不容易，因为无论支出再高，总是有着尚未满足的公共服务。更多的支出有时好，有时不然，这要看现在所提供服务的质量和效率如何，也即 A 省是否可以用更低的成本提供与 B 省相同质量的公共服务。所以，我们无法绝对地评价山东政府的支出是否达到“正确”的水平。

然而，我们可以从另外两种途径来考虑这一问题：一是可以比较山东与其他省份在公共服务水平方面的指标；二是可以与其他省份比较政府支出水平的高低。

对公共服务投入产出的粗略估计，可以作为公共服务需求在多大程度上得到满足的指标。从服务水平、产出、投入，以及省级政府的特点等方面来看，似乎不能说山东在公共服务提供上有多大不同（表 2）。因为山东省的工业集中，它的环境并不好，文盲率相对较高。另一方面，医疗服务投入显得较高，教育投入处于正常水平。我们不能仅凭这些非直接证据就说山东省公共服务水平很低。但由于数据有限，公共服务水平难以衡量，所以以上可以作为一个粗略的评价。

第二种途径是比较山东省和其他省份的省与省以下地方政府支出水平。我们发现了一个有意思的结果，至少在一般公共财政预算上，

山东省的省以及省以下地方政府的支出率相对较低。山东省人均 GDP 全国排第 10 名，但人均公共服务预算支出仅排第 28 名，与最后一名的水平十分接近（表 10）。2013 年，山东省人均支出约为 6 872 元人民币，为该年人均 GDP 的 12%。同时，中国所有其他省份的人均支出为 8 836 元人民币，相当于人均 GDP 的 19%。当然，这并不是说山东省政府便应当提高其公共支出占 GDP 的比率，但这是一个很重要的现象。山东省的决策者可以从分析山东省支出模式以及为何与其他省份存在差别中获得有益思考。

地方政府较高的支出水平往往与较高的发展水平以及这种发展水平带来的较大公共服务支出需求相联系。在我国，地方政府用以满足这些需求的收入是固定的，由中央政府的共享税分成和转移支付，以及被授权在地方征收的税种组成。地方政府不拥有征税权。此外，如之前所指出的，一些省份的人均支出较高，也可能是由较高的政府服务需求、较多的工业政策支出，或者政府支出的效率造成的。但作为实务性的问题，高支出水平是由预算收入方面的因素引起的，即可能与不同的征税能力、征税努力水平、税收优惠政策，以及中央政府转移支付水平有关。

为了更好地估计山东省政府支出低于平均水平的程度，我们研究了中国各省人均 GDP 和人均地方政府支出的关系。结果显示，一个省的人均 GDP 如果增加 10%，政府支出将会增加 5.9%（见附录 2 的回归 C）。也就是说，我国政府间财政体制中存在一个均等模式。但该体制并未实现完全均等化，一些富裕省份比贫穷省份支出要多得多。这很大程度上是因为不同省份的禀赋差别很大，共享税的划分以不同地区的经济为基础，同时营业税则属于经济水平决定的税种。Bahl、Goh 和 Qiao（2014，第二章）指出，2009 年我国中央对地方的所有转移支付中有 49% 其实是共享税，因此转移支付在各省之间的分配与该省的人均 GDP 和人类发展指数高度相关。Hofman 和 Guerra（2007，p34）

认为财政差异从时间的角度来看一直很大，他们用从 20 世纪 90 年代到 21 世纪前期的数据支持了这一观点，也即我国的财政体制并没有成功解决地区均等问题。

根据附录 2 中回归 C 的等式我们可以大概估算，一个与山东省拥有同样人均 GDP 的省份，在 2013 年人均政府支出应当达到 8 196 元人民币，但山东省事实上只有 6 872 元人民币，低于预期水平 16%。假如以全国平均水平（预测值）为标准，山东省必须增加人均支出约 1 964元人民币。

如何解释这一结果？为什么山东省政府支出比全国大多数其他省份要低？有三个假说也许可以解释：

（1）山东省征税努力程度较低；

（2）山东省得到的中央政府转移支付较少；

（3）山东省的 GDP 被高估了。

较低的征税效率

在与其他省份相比时，我们发现山东省的征税效率较低。有若干原因可以解释这一现象。在以全部税基为对象评估山东省地税局或国税局，其在征收税收上可能不如其他省份那样努力，或者有一大部分经济活动并未被囊括进税基之中（可能因为税收减免或是税收优惠）。造成该情况的原因可能是税收监管有问题，抑或是政府官员有意将减少税负作为工业政策的一部分。

从表 6 我们可以看到，山东省从自有资源上征收的人均税收约为 5 135元人民币，全国平均水平为 5 546 元人民币。山东省征收的全部税收（共享税分成和地税局征税收入）相当于 GDP 的 8.46%，相比较而言，全国平均水平则为 11.92%。

实际税率的平均水平不是衡量征税效率的充分指标，因为它没有

考虑到其他可以提高财政能力的因素（例如，城镇化率、工业和第三产业的经济份额、人均国内生产总值）。这些因素暗示我们其实可以很容易的达到一个更大的税基。在衡量征税效率的时候，我们对各省的实际征税和期望各省正常努力水平下可能达到的征税状态之间的关系是非常感兴趣的。

我们考虑了这些有助于提高财政能力的因素，并且在此书的附件2中对这些因素所做的回归分析结果进行了说明，即回归分析A[1]。这项研究的结果表明山东有能力征收相当于2011年全省GDP的11.2%的共享税和地方税，但实际上，只征收了8%。也就是说，山东的征税效率（实际税收与纳税能力的比率）为27%，这个比率是低于全国平均水平的。通过分析，山东省一直以来都是一个低征税效率的省份（表A－2）。假设山东将征税率提高到全国平均水平，也就是增长到全省GDP的11.2%，那么，2011年的人均支出就可以提高1 833元，并且山东的人均支出排名也将由第28名上升到第19名。

较低的转移支付

对山东省支出率低的第二种解释是中央政府对山东省的一般和专项转移支付低于其他省份。通过表10可以看到，2012年山东省是获得人均拨款最低的。山东省收到的转移支付仅为全省GDP的4%，远低于全国平均水平。如上所述，山东省的人均支出缺口是1 324元，其中的65%可能来源于其获得的低于平均水平的一般和专项转移支付。

接下来进一步解释山东省获得的一般和专项转移支付低于平均水平的原因。附录2的回归分析C表明，中国一个省的人均GDP如果增加10%，政府补助就会减少5.9%。在这个估算中，我们考虑了人口

1 Lotz and Morss（1967）、Ball（1971）有关于衡量税收努力回归方法的更完备说明。

密度以及每个省份地方政府雇员对应的人口数。正如预期的那样，中央政府拨款的分配是以均等化为基础的，但是山东省获得的补助水平却低于一个类似省份应获得的预期水平。按照山东的人均 GDP 水平，预期的人均补助应该是 2 888 元，但事实上，只有 2 029 元。

将这两个分析综合起来考虑，我们可以发现山东的人均支出水平低于全国平均水平的数额中，1 833 元是由于其较低的征税效率，859 元是由于均等化的转移支付系统。在对平均征税效率和补助金的平均水平进行回归分析后，可以得到一个结论：山东省政府有能力将人均支出定在 9 564 元，并且在人均支出上可以排到第 15 名而不是第 28 名。

高估的 GDP 值

对山东省支出率低的第三种解释是省 GDP 被过高估计。这一解释很有趣。如果山东省在 2013 年将 GDP 高估了 22%，那么真实 GDP 与支出的比率将会与全国平均水平持平，GDP 与税收的真正比率将会是 10.3%，并且山东省的征税效率将会排在第 22 名。对 GDP 的过高估计还会减少政府间的转移支付。[1]

财政差距是否过大

山东省的均等化体系可能不足以缩小当地政府间的财政差距。如表 11 所示，县与县之间经济发展水平和人均支出水平的差距很大，人均 GDP 变动幅度从 11 万 6 千元到 9 千元，人均支出从 9 千元到 1 千

1　罗伊·鲍尔、吴卓瑾、乔宝云（2014）发现对于各省来说每个有条件的、分类的、均等化的转移支付项目的人均转移支付额与人均 GDP 都存在显著的负相关关系。

元。总的来说，支出额最高的县的公共服务的人均支出是支出额最低县的9倍，在市级政府中最高的人均支出额与最低的比值也是9比1。目前在制定公共政策的时候需要关注人均支出的差距是否过大，已超过可接受范围。

如果政府认为在公共服务领域的支出差距过大，那么省政府可以通过一系列的均衡转移支付来减少差距。均等化的理念是指低收入县相比高收入县人均会得到更多的转移支付，以便用来平衡高收入县越来越高的收入。山东省已经采用了这种方法，在2013年，52个有财政困难的县获得了省/地级行政区提供的大约370亿元的转移支付。这种均等化转移支付分配方案更多是临时性的，而不是基于公式化的。省/地级行政区的官员主要基于每个县的基本信息和专家判断地区间财政差距评估。

我们可以预测这个临时性质的分配制度能多大程度上降低富县相对于穷县在开支方面的优势。例如，如果人均支出的离差（它反映了税后–转移支付后的结果）小于人均GDP的离差，这个体系一定程度上是均等化的。如果人均支出的离差大于人均GDP的离差，那么这个体系实际上会导致财政差距增大，也就是说这个体系是非均等化的。

用山东省90个县的数据进行的横向分析表明，当人均GDP有一个百分点的提高，人均支出水平提高0.7%（附件2，回归D）。这说明目前的体系有一定程度的均等化作用，也就是说，由于地级政府和省政府将富县的财政盈余分配到赤字县，支出差距有所减小。但问题是目前的均等化程度是否能满足省政府的目标。山东省政府间的转移体系应该更均衡吗？省级补助应该更均衡的理由是：支出差异仍然很大，并且在中国大多数的财政收入分配有利于高收入地区。例如，共享税（在山东省所有的税收收入中占比超过60%）是基于来源地进行分配的，这有利于具有较高征税能力的地方。对于其他的“地方税”的征收也是如此。

最后，值得注意的是，取消营业税也会产生一种反均等化效应，因为这个税种会有不少盈余可用于分配给贫困县。这笔款项相当于约三分之一的营业税征收额。没有营业税的替代税种，或者不汲取额外收入来弥补损失，可能会危害到政府的均等化目标。

城市公共服务需求会对预算产生压力

在山东省城市地区，支出仍然不足。其中一部分原因是有约 2 800 万人口在 15 年时间内陆续迁移到城市。并且，随着城镇化的不断推进，即使以缓慢的速度扩张，也会给城市基础设施建设和公共服务带来压力。山东省目前约有 4 500 万人居住在城市以外的地区。在过去的 20 年间，我国约 30% 的农村人口迁移到城市，有的是临时工，有的是新居民，有些移居者来自省内农村地区，另外的来自其他省份。为了更加清晰地阐述，我们可以观察到，如果 30% 的山东农村人口迁移到城市，那么在未来 20 年内，新城镇居民的数量将在 1 300 万人左右。然而，我们也要注意，较低的国内生产总值增长率可能会延缓移民迁入。尽管如此，如果没有大量新基础设施投资以及增加的经常性预算支出，是不能满足移民迁入以及自然增长的人口所带来的支出需求的。

那么最后一个问题就是，税收是否可以实现全面覆盖增加的支出需求量。至少从中期来看，税收收入在中国可能会增长得很缓慢。预计在未来几年，GDP 增长率会从 2014 年的 7.4% 以及 1990—2012 年期间年均的 10% 下降到 7% 。我们可以举个例子来说明增长放缓的影响。假设税收收入弹性不变，那么在 2015 年到 2020 年期间，如果以 12% 的 GDP 增长率计算，会增加 200 亿元（人民币）的税收收入，而以 7.5% 的增长率计算，只能增加 170 亿元人民币。未来可能有 4 万亿人民币的资金缺口需要通过紧缩开支或增加收入来解决（世界银行中国

发展研究中心，2013）。

土地出让收入和基础设施融资的减少

在一定程度上，第一次城市化浪潮时，中国通过出让土地，已经成功地解决了新增基础设施融资这一问题。表 12 说明了中国土地出让收入占国内生产总值的比例。2014 年，土地出让收入相当于 GDP 的 6.7%。这个规模是惊人的，相当于地方政府一般公共预算总额的 56%，并且占到地方政府性基金预算收入的 85%。对房地产需求的大幅增长推动了税收收入的增加。[1]

但这种对土地出让的严重依赖产生了一系列问题，包括地方政府担保的基于土地的债务数额、地方较差的投资选择、相对于其他城市而言在基础设施建设上的过度投资、城市扩张以及土地从农业用途转向工业时带来的社会公平问题[2]。或许土地财政融资最重要的问题是：它挑战了地方政府债务管理。土地融资具有更多的财政风险，因为不切实际地认为这是一个持续的收入流会鼓励地方政府超支。因此，地方政府很可能会在基础设施的融资上借钱过度。此外，当房地产市场面临负面冲击时，使用土地出让会有风险，并且也会刺激土地和房地产市场泡沫。较差的财政透明度和财政纪律使局势进一步恶化。

通过城市发展投资公司进行融资已经成为基础设施融资的主要渠道，同时也造成了地方政府债务的快速增长。但城投债的增长带来了一些问题，例如不合规的经营和非法的政府担保。为了控制不断增长的债务风险，国务院在 2010 年 6 月 13 日发布了［2010］19 号文件，

1 房地产价格上涨的原因有很多种。一方面，城市化规模创造了大量的房地产需求和财产增值，刺激地方政府参与土地市场；另一方面，地方政府从土地出让中获得的利益也推动了住房成本的上升，使得住房价格更高，进一步巩固了财富效应。

2 对问题的全面分析，见世界银行和经济发展中心（2013）。

《国务院关于加强地方政府融资平台公司管理有关问题的通知》，要求各级政府清理融资平台，以便确保信贷安全。新的债务管理制度和新的预算法旨在避免重蹈城市发展投资公司的问题。

山东省政府土地出让收入占 GDP 的比例低于全国平均水平，且未偿还的债务水平较低（表 12 和 13）[1]，土地使用权的转让收入占政府财政收入的 77%，相当于 2014 年全省总税收的 78%。虽然使用强度比中国其他地区的低，但土地出让收入仍然是山东省一个非常重要的融资来源。例如，在 2013 年，土地出让收入覆盖了 83% 的政府资金支出，并且几乎等同于一般税收的征收额。

虽然这看起来是为借贷提供财政空间，但是却导致山东省基础设施融资来源出现了问题。市政债券不是一种收入来源，而是一种在资产寿命期内分期支付的付款安排。问题在于用来偿还贷款的收入流是有限的。土地出让收入增长率在 2013 年第 4 季度开始下降，在 2014 年第 4 季度出现了负值（世界银行，2015），并且现在使用融资平台是非法的。如何在省内收入结构中找到一种还款方式是目前需要关注的问题。取消营业税可能会进一步减少可用于偿还债务的总收入。

公共部门和私营部门尚未完全分离

理论上来说，公共部门的作用应该是提供那些自由市场不能进行有效供给的服务和活动和公平收入分配。（不能提供有效供给的原因或许是因为很难制定收费价格，也可能是因为共同消费所带来的益处）。虽然中国在某些行业已经存在私有化，但是很多其他行业还没有正式私有化。政府的支出范围仍然十分广泛。

1　对未偿还的或有债务没有可供参考的信息。

人大和政府都提倡在地方政府和竞争性的经济领域之间建立一种合作关系。政府应该将角色转向提供公共服务，并且要间接介入经济发展，也就是说，政府应该提供一个有利于经济发展的环境而非直接参与经营活动。举个例子，政府应该为生产和贸易提供必需的基础设施，例如交通、港口、水利和电力，并且还可以通过提供良好的便利设施（学校、卫生保健、公园、环境清洁等）来协助具有竞争性的产业，这样可以帮助企业吸引质量高的劳动力。政府应该负责打造一个监管框架——此监管框架可以造福于人民并且对于企业来讲也是公平的。

在山东省，政府部门和竞争性行业间存在直接的关联，这个关联体现在几种形式上。各级政府仍拥有（或控制）大量企业，并且政府部门可以通过国有企业去直接或者间接地影响私有企业。近些年，城市发展投资公司在公共和私人部门之间创建了一个更加复杂的联系。

此外，在竞争性行业中政府对企业还有一定的补助。这些补助的机会成本是对一般政府性服务均等的投资。另一种类型是给某些特定企业税收优惠或者退税。最后，借贷中存在或有债务。这些情况中，我们无法收集到可以准确衡量政府介入竞争性企业程度的数据，然而根据国务院规定以及山东省相应的一些政策性建议，所有这些领域显然都有公共部门的重度参与。

有一个对山东省来讲可行的办法是先清除政府对企业的补贴，然后取消税收优惠、退税，以及其他导致企业不全额纳税的政策。这样便可以为公共服务释放投资资金，并且有助于解决取消营业税导致的收入缺口。它还为企业提供了“公平竞争”的平台，可以让市场更有效地发挥作用。国务院监管条例及山东的研究方案通过省级政府对政府担保借款的审定和废除来控制债务，这样一来，有助于分离政府—企业间关系。

然而，继续分离山东省政府和竞争性行业将不会是一件容易的事，

尤其是在经济增长的速度正逐步放缓的时候。事实上，国务院已经对以这么快的速度撤销税收优惠政策这一行为提出了警告。不过，据报道，2015 年提出的大量关于税收优惠政策的申请都已经被驳回了。

不合理的激励机制

中国的政府间财政体系被一些（无意的）动机破坏了，这些动机激励地方政府做一些有悖于国家和省政府政策目标的事情。如何克服这一结构性困难将会是山东省财政可持续性面临的另一个挑战。

将预算支出集中在公共服务的改善上而不是经济发展上存在很大障碍。省级政府和地方政府的首要任务应该是为公民以及在其管辖范围内的企业提供足够的公共服务。在很多西方国家，公民在选举省级和地方政府官员的时候主要参考官员所提供服务的质量。在中国，省级和地方政府官员是由更高级别的政府来任命的，有领导才能的官员会带来经济增长和投资，许多人认为这极大地影响了官员的任命。这导致相对于给潜在的或者现存的企业提供公共服务和税收优惠政策而言，对官员并不愿意给家庭提供较多公共服务。[1]

山东省的方案通过列举政府投资某些区域的竞争性产业，例如制造业、企业技术升级、资本贷款等来说明目前存在着对经济的过度投资。方案指出对经济事务的支出占山东省公共支出的 34%，但是 OECD 的平均水平只有 12%。

另一个不合理的激励机制是对经济发展所取得的成就进行奖励，这样会造成我们看到的 GDP 数据要比实际的高很多。我们没有证据证明这个现象存在于山东省或者中国其他地方，但是可以肯定的是这种

1 这是一个很复杂的问题，从长远来看，成功就业可能会增长为家庭所提供的福利。参考对评估问题的一般性讨论，黄佩华（2012）。

不合理的激励机制是存在的。

目前的体系抑制了税收的增长。在山东省，区政府在收入汲取能力方面存在很大差异。遵循着“以富济贫”的收入共享方案，一些筹集了大量资金的地区（市区和一小部分县城）可以保留一部分份额来满足自己对公共服务的需求，剩下的被转移给地区政府或省政府，地区政府或省政府可能自用或者转移给贫穷的地方政府。从边际的角度看，区政府增加的税收都会被转移到市一级。这激励区政府（以及一部分县）为了经济发展给企业提供税收优惠，这最终降低了税收。改革将改进方式方法，在很大程度上削弱了不合理的激励制度。然而，如果省可以分享一部分增加的收入，对增加财政收入的抑制效应也会减弱。

收入共享也会对一些贫困县税收的增加产生抑制作用。根据目前的安排，收入较少地区的县政府期望它们的财政缺口可以通过填补赤字的转移支付来弥补。那么为什么要在财政缺口可以被转移支付填补的情况下做出更大的努力来获得更多的收入呢？同样的道理，在支出方面，成本节约产生的益处并不会归于提高支出效率的当地政府。

对于增加财政收入存在障碍这个问题可以通过改变收入共享方式来解决。每一个（接受的）县会被给定一个财政收入增收水平的目标，这个目标由省/地级行政区设定，是给定征税努力水平下区县政府可以征收的财政收入估计值。需要提供资金支持的财政缺口是标准支出需求与想要达到的收入水平目标之间的差额。在这样的体制下，那些收入水平在设定目标之下的县区将会得到较少的补助金。

这一体制带来的另一个负面激励源自分权化的支出责任划分。对于基层县级政府来说，繁重的分配任务可能会导致其在做一些财政决策的时候效率低下。例如，县政府在一些可以阻止环境恶化的服务上面花费少、投入的成本低，这样一来环境的恶化就会蔓延到邻近的地区。解决这个问题的方法就是审视山东省的支出责任划分体制并确保

已将外部效应和规模效应考虑在内。

资本融资体系更偏向于土地出让方面。2014 年，山东省大约有78% 的政府基金收入都是来自于土地出让。对土地出让依赖的原因是很明确的：土地出让相比税收来讲，可以获得更多的收入，并且土地出让相对提高地方税来讲少了很多争议。最重要的是，它们是当地政府无须等待中央批准的一个收入来源。但是，正是因为土地出让的好处太大了，当地的政府领导会留存过多的土地用来发展当地经济，而远离支持一般公共服务的资本支出，这导致了大量不可持续的债务。因此应设法减少土地出让带来的负面激励。

财政体系或许过于复杂

基本上山东省的公共资源配置不是基于规则的，因此，那些可能导致特殊结果的因素并不透明。这也是国务院提倡财政实践应该更现代、更透明的一部分原因。

当决策的制定是基于特别的个例或协商而不是基于规则的时候，一系列问题便出现了。其中一些问题可以通过山东省提出的财政改革建议直接解决，但是还有一部分问题没有在改革方案中解决，这是发展省财政体系过程中妥协的结果。接下来讨论的四个问题阐明了财政体系复杂性的本质。

第一，每个省级地方政府的收入和支出体现在四个独立的预算中：一般公共预算、政府基金预算、国企经营预算和社会保障预算。一般公共预算、政府基金预算、国企经营预算包含经常性支出和资本性支出。在这些账户里有每个层级政府内的转移支付，也包括政府层级间的转移支付。复杂性源于对地方政府预算的国家层面的界定就要求四个独立预算。如果想要合并这四个独立预算以给出地方财政的全景是

非常难实现的，因此财政实践透明化这一目标更加难以实现。

第二，复杂性来源于在省—市—县/区各级政府间分配转移支付所用的方法。举个例子，决定分配给某个县的转移支付的总额的决策过程不是完全透明的。对于这个问题的解决方案是通过一个公式化的体系来重新分配资金，使资金从富县流向贫困县，这一点在之前也讨论过。

第三，地方政府基金的专项转移支付在整个体系中是一个非常复杂的问题。最近的改进是将省级专项资金由 243 项压减到 99 项。然而，仍有很大空间来进一步减少这些转移支付。

第四个问题源自于以往的实践中使用土地出让抵押来使基础设施投资获得贷款。在过去，一些预算外的贷款是由省级和地方政府预算来担保的，但是由于当地政府所承担的贷款偿还责任存在一定的模糊性，因此实际的担保强度是不清晰的。

第四章　山东省财政改革

到 2020 年建立现代财政制度是山东省在全面深化改革背景下的财税体制改革目标。更准确地说，是到 2020 年时建立起现代化的政府治理体系及财税管理体系。为了实现这一目标，山东省政府对如何贯彻党中央全面深化财税体制改革总体方案进行了深入研究。

山东财政改革方案得益于郭树清省长的领导。这一方案旨在率先建立现代财政制度，山东省的目标是率先在中国建立全面、统一、法治、有效的现代财政制度。改革方案指出山东作为中国经济的重要组成部分，有必要率先承担财税改革的责任，做出示范。[1]

这一改革方案虽然宏伟，但与中国建立现代财政制度的目标是相吻合的。改革方案以良好的国际经验为出发点，结合中国的实际情况，并包含了政府治理及改革政策的内容。值得一提的是，这一改革计划的内容均是在中国现行的法治框架下设计的，并未超出现有法制框架，并且严格遵循了中央的政策导向。中央和地方之间的支出责任划分、收入划分等属于中央决策的事项并未出现在该计划中。

改革基础

2010 年至今，山东省财政状况较为良好。目前良好的财政状况将

1　山东省是中国的人口第二大省，山东省 GDP 约占全国 GDP 的 9%。

有助于山东省实现“到2020年建立现代财政制度”的财政改革目标。这一财政改革计划并不是彻底地更替原有财政体制，而是在现有体制上深化改革。这一原则与中央政府深化财税体制改革的思路一致。中央政府提出建立现代财政制度，厘清政府和市场的边界。在此基础上，山东省还提出了一些新的财税体制改革方向。

山东省在以下几方面取得了明显的改革成效：

（1）公共服务的供给明显增加。数据显示，山东省人均财政支出由2000年的681元提高到2013年的6 872元，相当于年均增长18%，超过同期山东省人均GDP的增长速度。山东省人均GDP由2000年的9 326元提高到2013年的56 184元，年均增速为13%。

（2）山东县级政府财政补助计划与2010年开始实施。截至2013年，52个财政困难县累计获得补助374亿元用于消化2010年至2013年的基本财力缺口。2013年起，该体制进行了改革，以提高富裕区县的增收积极性。

（3）预算管理改革取得较大成效。山东省各级政府初步建立了全口径预算，建立起包括收入分类、支出功能分类、支出经济分类的政府收支分类科目体系。

（4）国库集中支付改革在山东各级政府全面推行，提高了资金的拨付效率。公务卡制度全面建立，将过去使用现金结算的公务消费改为刷卡结算。资本项目的管理逐步加强 。这些措施使得财政体系逐步简化明了。

（5）中央政府对山东省的转移支付占山东省GDP的比例由2000年的2%上升到了2012年的4%。但是，山东省获得的转移支付仍然位于全国的较低水平。

（6）山东省人均财政收入由2007年的1 789元上升到2013年的4 685元。

（7）山东省的财政状况良好，预示着山东省良好的财税管理水

平。4 个预算都保持着平衡状态。2014 年，所有基金的总预算平衡相当于总支出的 63%。

目　标

山东财政改革方案旨在全面改善财税体制。这一计划并未涉及中央制定新措施，而是在中央政策既定的条件下设计山东省的改革方案。因此这一计划主要旨在如何将中央政策贯彻实施到山东省，以及在法治框架内为山东本省设计一些改革计划。山东财政改革方案侧重于财税管理，逐步有序地进行改革，并提出了较为重要但尚未完全明确的政府间转移支付改革。

山东财政改革的目标大致可以归纳为以下 9 方面：

（1）一个主要目标是继续转变财政职能，使其专注于提供高效且公平的公共服务，并避免直接参与竞争行业的投资和生产环节。特别是，财政管理应该避免当前过多介入经济事务的情况。

（2）改革方案应解决那些导致目前山东省财政体制运行效率不高的问题。

（3）本项目的结果应该是一个综合的财政管理体系，涵盖全省所有的财政活动。所有预算科目应该是统一的，这样每一项支出都会包含在 4 个预算中。不应该再有预算外账户或预算外活动，所有的或有负债都应充分报告和解释。

（4）该系统应根据法律运行。税收应根据税法征收，定向或非定向的拨款都应根据法律法规，应该有一个最低限度的协商安排。

（5）预算编制过程（所有的支出和收入活动）应该是透明的，便于接受社会监督。这将使财政计划更加有效且有利于获得公众的支持。预算执行也应该是透明的，这可以通过国库管理和会计核算的改革

实现。

（6）财政体制应该是稳定且可持续的。如果支出和增加收入的活动规则不经常更换，各级政府能够更好地规划自己的活动，应尽量减少引起财政风险的做法。

（7）省及省以下地方政府需要平衡四个总目标：足够的公共资源、经济发展、经济效率和公平。确定这些平衡有利于引导资源配置。

（8）财政计划的评估必须既考虑直接影响，也考虑长期影响。将建立一个为期三年的滚动财政计划。新的债务管理框架将抑制低效的借贷行为。

（9）应该更好地协调财政政策和其他对经济和社会发展有影响的方案。

山东财政改革方案

按照党的十八届三中全会和省委十届八次全体会议的部署，山东省提出了一项具有深远意义的财政体制现代化建设方案。该方案借鉴了国际经验，致力于解决当前山东省政府间财政安排存在的问题。

预算管理改革

近年来，山东省管辖的地方政府在预算管理方面取得了显著的进展，但为了建立一个更加透明高效的系统，仍需要深化预算披露改革。这项改革方案的报告指出，政府预算并没有披露足够的政府支出信息，县一级的预算在这方面尤其薄弱。截至 2015 年 7 月，山东省政府预

算、部门预算和“三公”经费[1]预算披露率在市级为88%、82%、82%，县级为67%、43%、42%。根据改革方案，预算管理改革会涵盖以下内容：稳步扩大公开范围（例如，包括所有的特殊基金和债务）；逐步细化公开内容；积极推进专项资金信息公开标准化分开程序。

该方案指出要健全一般公共预算、政府性基金预算、国有资本经营预算和社会保障基金预算，建立定位清晰、分工明确、有机衔接、相互补充的“全口径”政府预算体系，深化综合预算改革，将部门所有收支全部纳入部门预算，切实做到“收入一个笼子、预算一个盘子、支出一个口子”，把包括特殊基金和债务在内的所有政府收支全部纳入预算管理，这些改革措施将会切实提高预算透明度。

深化预算改革还包括一些措施：

（1）建立跨年度财政预算规划。

（2）将预算收入从约束性转向预期性，当前的做法客观上容易导致预算执行“顺周期”问题，即当经济形势好时，完成收入任务后有税不收，经济热上加热；当经济紧缩时，为完成收入任务无税强收，经济冷上加冷。

（3）建立预算稳定调节基金以发挥“以丰补歉”的作用。执行中一般公共预算如出现超收，可用于冲减赤字或补充预算稳定调节基金；如出现短收，通过调入预算稳定调节基金或其他预算资金、削减支出实现平衡。

（4）改变注重支出的局面，推进预算绩效管理。

（5）完善年度预算审计与控制体系。

采纳中期预算和规划的建议十分重要。好处包括增强计划与预算之间的联系，提高财政政策解决人口和经济结构性变化的能力以及公

1 “三公”经费是指说明单位因公出国（境）团组数及人数，公务用车购置及保有量，国内公务接待的批次、人数等信息。

共支出的效率（世界银行和发展研究中心，2014 年，第 424—425 页）。已有证据表明中期预算框架能带来这些好处（世界银行，2013 年）。

预算管理方案的有些建议是针对政策的变化而不是针对行政和管理的变化的。大部分都是有助于合理化支出的政策，将支出计划从预算刚性转变为更具灵活性，能够增加收入以支持公共服务的提供。山东的改革要做到以下几点：（1）尽可能减少专款专用的范围；（2）清理和规范重点支出同财政收支增幅或生产总值挂钩的事项；（3）加快建立政府性基金预算中统筹使用部分列入一般公共预算的机制；（4）扩大国有资本经营预算实施范围，加大国有资本经营预算调入一般公共预算支持社会民生的力度；（5）发挥预算稳定调节基金“以丰补歉”的作用。

预算管理改革：述评

预算管理改革的建议经过了精心设计，并借鉴了国际经验。这些建议可以提高政府支出和政府财政规划的效率。总的思路是建立全面规范、公开透明的现代预算制度，使四类预算实现真正意义上的统筹融合，从而明确各个预算的盈余和赤字，并且能随时掌握各类资金之间转移的情况。

另一个思路是改变注重支出的局面，推进预算绩效管理。换句话说，预算方案将成为一个重要的规划和评估工具。

实现这些目标需要大幅度改变目前的一些做法，这需要时间。

构建更加透明的预算结构和报告体系，包括所有预算交易、借款和专项资金，是评估该省财政支出政策的重要步骤。在这种形式下，可以统筹融合各类预算，替代性支出政策的影响可以更容易和准确地被掌控。减少专款专用、减少支出指标，是预算规划能够更灵活地配置资源的另一步。举例来说，使政府性基金收入（如地方教育附加）

纳入一般公共预算，取消一些支出规定（如城市建设税）。另一受欢迎的举措是提高国有资本收益分成比例，加大国有资本经营预算调入一般公共预算支持社会民生力度。省级国有资本收益上缴公共财政的比例将在2020年达到30%，支出管理的重点从先确定支出总额再安排具体项目的方式转变为重点关注财政支出的绩效。这一套新的财政管理举措如果得以实现，将具有重大意义。

关于新的预算改革有以下四个问题。

第一，一般公共预算和政府性基金预算，都包括资本支出和经常性支出。此外，这些预算之间可以进行资金转移。在这样的安排下，资本支出规划如何控制？最终，政府性基金预算能否转变为资本账户，一般公共预算能否转为经常性账户？

第二，涉及预算稳定基金管理短期赤字的问题。据推测，这个想法是为了解决由于不可预见的情况或现金流异常，又或公共支出和收入正常的不规律现象导致的短期赤字（或盈余）问题。在这种情况下，预算稳定基金可以成为一个有用的工具，用于预算管理。但这一举措可能会用来平衡每年的预算，并为救助政策提供支持。但是，关于稳定基金将如何管理，或具体什么样的情况会被允许年度预算赤字，却尚未提供相应的细节。例如，年度预算赤字、救助和仍存在的税收优惠如果放在一起，将无法较好地与改革目标相统一。所有这些问题引出了一个更常见的问题——预算稳定基金是否可以被地方政府作为一种避免硬预算约束的手段来使用？

第三，如果对国企经营预算的转移没有专项拨款，那么还需要这个预算吗？是否可以取消？

第四，这项预算改革会在多大程度上引起收入增长尚不清楚，但是经过改进的财政体制应该能使支出更有效。当前对支出规划的一些限制会被取消，所以几乎可以肯定一些资金将被重新决定其支出方向。此外，透明预算和绩效管理将盘活其他资金。但支出的再分配需要时

间，现有预算的做法根深蒂固，需要加强政府工作人员的培训工作。可能营业税的替代税种在山东省落地后，地方政府的支出效率才能得以提升。

国库管理改革

山东省政府力争在 2017 年，所有下级政府的全部支出实行国库集中支付管理。监管机制现代化、培训和自动化都是这项改革的一部分。

国库改革的一些内容直接关系到支出控制。例如引进标准化的财政账户，今后一律不得新设专项支出财政专户，并逐步撤销各级党政机关等预算单位的实有资金基本账户。现有财政专户除经国务院批准，其他在 2016 年年底前一律予以取消，所有财政资金全部通过国库单一账户核算支付。严禁向非预算单位及未纳入年度预算的项目借款和垫付财政资金。积极开展国库现金管理，保持国库现金余额稳定在一个较低水平。

该方案还要求对预算进行更严格的控制。改革的目标在于三个方面。第一，对预算额度的调整将实行严格控制，所有的变更都必须向全国人大报告。第二，未经财政部批准，不得修改预算科目。第三，严格控制结余结转规模（拟议的限制是从 2015 年起各级结余结转资金规模占本级当年财政支出的比重必须控制在 9% 以内）。

为了提高支出效率，解决腐败问题，方案建议将采取一种新的更严格的采购政策。最后，政府在 2017 年以前将建立权责发生制的政府综合财务报告制度，以更好地管控政府债务风险，加强政府资产管理。从今年开始，所有设区的地市本级都要编制政府综合财务报告，并选择部分县（市、区）开展试点，明年将这项改革扩大到全省所有县（市、区），2016 年要力争以市为单位编制政府综合财务报告，2017 年编制全省合并的政府综合财务报告。

国库管理改革：述评

国库管理改革进行较为顺利，预计2017年将在全省实现，这是一个令人瞩目的目标。新制度在全面实施后，预期能显著提高对支出管理的控制。通过限制新的专项支出财政专户和新的基金账户，能加强新的预算管理规划并禁止预算外的任何借贷活动。对预算支出的严格控制是值得欢迎的，因为它使政府更关注预算的真实性。如果政府能成功限制预算科目间的支出转移和新设预算账户，预算规划则将得到显著改善。

严格控制结余结转规模是可以理解的，但也产生了一些难题。首先，特殊情况导致的结余结转是否意味着这一限制将会放松。例如，由于资本项目延迟或出于预防目的导致的未使用余额，在未来需要结转至家庭保障计划，然而据推测，上述来源的收入将被转到预算稳定基金。其次，余额超过9%后怎么处理，以及如何防止在年底滥用之前的结余？

如预算管理改革类似，国库管理改革预期会有一些储蓄问题出现。更好的采购政策下，必然会产生积极的影响，也能更好地管理未使用的余额。然而，改革方案并未对可能的成本节约额、资金减少额或重新分配用途资金额进行任何的估算。

最后，也许最困难的是财政管理制度的落实，特别是在县级政府。在许多县建立一个新的系统，意味着对培训进行较多的投资。目前山东省还没有制定培训计划以及评估该成本。

债务管理改革

方案指出，山东省遵循国务院规定的地方政府债务管理规范。贷款的基本规则由中央制定，但地方政府在实施细则上有一定的自主权。

借债的框架包括省政府经国务院批准可以适度举借债务（市县级政府确需举借债务的由省政府代为举借）。所有的借贷必须纳入预算，债务计划应获得上级政府批准。

方案提出要围绕控制和化解地方政府性债务风险，从五个方面健全债务管理机制。一是把地方政府债务分门别类纳入全口径预算管理。例如，将一般债务收支纳入一般公共预算管理，将专项债务收支纳入政府性基金预算管理。二是健全审批机制。三是建立相应的风险预警机制。四是完善债务报告和公开制度。五是建立关于非法或过度举债相应的考核问责机制。

该债务框架将明确还款责任，并硬化政府的预算约束。政府债务不可由企业代发或代偿。在政府与社会资本合作的情况下，应明确合同责任。发展有一定收益的公益性事业，如确需政府举借专项债务的，由地方政府通过发行专项债券融资，以对应的政府性基金或专项收入偿还。该方案还提供了应急措施，以应对可能出现的偿债困难。

该方案还涉及“清理”和减少现有债务。地方政府所借债务应分为一般债务和专项债务，并有相应的预算。为防止出现“半拉子”工程，过渡期内在建项目可优先通过债券融资，但融资平台将不再有为地方政府举债的权限。

债务管理改革：述评

即使山东省政府负债问题并不严重，债务管理改革也十分重要。建立一个明确拥有举借政府担保债务权限范围的制度意义重大。所有债务均由山东省政府来举借的做法受到大家的欢迎，因为山东省财政支出较为分权化，而且山东省地方政府间的财政差异十分巨大。甄别融资平台债的归属也是应有之举，清理其他的“非法”债务将有助于未来的发展，未经授权的借款会受到处罚。

然而，中国的地方政府性债务在过去的十年里已经积累成了一个

很严重的问题，即使是在山东省这样借贷水平不高的省份，仍然不易清理。至少我们可以提出三个问题。第一，也是最重要的，地方政府如何偿还债务？营业税的损失会让地方税务局的税收减少，这使省/市政府将共享税和转移支付成为偿还的主要来源。省/市政府会在收入共享安排上做出什么样的调整以适应新的借贷？

第二，由省级机构评估地方政府风险。特别是在一些欠发达的县，较差的经济基础令其不能放弃太多的共享税。这里就可能需要由省政府批准贷款，然后通过增加转移支付作为担保。但这种做法会模糊了借贷和转移支付之间的界限。

第三，关于对新专项支出财政专户和新基金账户的严格限制与政府性基金预算专项借款之间一致性的问题。

税制改革

山东税制改革方案强调要完成增值税改革，这就意味着营业税将不再是地方政府的财政收入来源。然而，这意味着地方政府需要找到额外的收入，以取代营业税的损失，并为升级服务和新的基础设施提供资金。这种替代策略将是山东财政体制改革的重要组成部分。但是山东省必须等待中央政府的行动才能确定一条完整的行动路线。不过，有几个领域省级政府有权收费，以进一步改进税收制度、增加税收收入，这些权力是由国务院规定的。

改革方案建议在现行体制下清理和调整税收优惠政策。一般来说，这些优惠待遇以减税、免税或退税的形式存在。山东省的方案中没有给出这些税收支出的一般会计统计数据，所以没有办法对税收损失的数额做出较准确的估计。此外，还有一个更微妙的税收优惠政策，即按“目标”税收来收税，而不是按应收税来收税。政府打算甄别所有这些非法或没有得到国务院批准的税收优惠，并予以取消。这项政策

应该能够带来积极的收益，也对该省的纳税人更加公平。

发展现代财政制度的另一项政策是使税收管理（中央和地方政府税）更有效。山东省的方案认为，搭建全省统一规范、共享高效的涉税信息管理平台，加快构建面向自然人的税收征管服务体系和第三方涉税信息报告制度，强化涉税信息的采集比对和分析利用。依法打击涉税违法行为，增加收入。进一步降低征纳成本、提高征管效率。

山东省的报告指出，合适的税制改革是实现税收收入的重要措施，建议对已有的针对房地产使用和转让的征税制度进行改革，完善其管理机制。但是，最终新的财产税结构则须由中央政府决定，且尚在在讨论中。在中国，征收财产税可能仍需几年的时间。从现有的房地产税收收入增加情况来看，有效税收与 GDP 的比值大约是 1.6%，且不具有进一步提高的空间。此外，房地产市场已经降温，税基的自动增长速度放缓。

报告也提出要清理现行的行政收费制度。截至 2013 年年末，山东省正在执行的行政事业性收费有 125 项（其中中央批准的收费项目 101 项，省级立项的 24 项）；正在执行的政府性基金项目有 20 项，全部为中央批准的项目。山东省的财政改革方案需要采取合适的做法，以消除这些费用，而在目前税收制度中尚未实施这类做法。例如，将一些收费合并为适当的税种，而使其他成为更合法的收费或成本回收费用。这属于结构性的变化，将提高效率，调动收入，服务于优先保障的财政支出项目，但不太可能产生更多的新增收入。

税制改革：述评

增加税收对山东省至关重要。营业税很快将被取消，而目前还没有相应的替代税种。一般税收收入的增长很可能会同 GDP 一样增速放缓，而城市化、环境问题和老龄化造成的支出压力将越来越大。山东省能做的很少，因为省政府不能开征任何新的税收。

山东省也提出了积极的方法来解决税收问题——使用信息系统提高税收管理效率，清理规范财税优惠政策等。较差的管理和税收优惠可能是导致山东省税收效率低的原因之一，但山东在财政改革方案中没有对税式支出做出估计。我们可以说这些建议都是正确的，但是我们不能确切地说出这些政策能在多大程度上解决目前的问题。

然而，有直接和间接的证据表明，山东省的改革如果实施成功，可以显著地增加税收。最直接的证据是将以“目标”税收征税转变为按应收税款征税，之前的做法导致了大量的漏税现象。间接的证据是，山东省在努力地提高现有的征税效率。2013 年，山东省所征税收为 GDP 的 6%，而全国平均水平为 9%。如果这一差距的一半是由于税收优惠政策造成的，则这一改革可以顺利解决取消营业税所带来的税收损失问题。

最后要关注的是该政策的执行。税收优惠政策实施多年，很难改变，这些企业和政府可能或多或少都有些关系。此外，许多人认为随着经济增长速度放缓，经济发展的补贴很难取消。还要注意最近出台的国务院规定，对清理和规范税收优惠政策似乎不太积极。清理规范税收优惠政策的速度可能无法像省政府设想的那样可以快速推进。

地方财政体制改革

现行财政体制与建立完善的社会主义市场经济体制的要求相比，离推进政府治理体系和治理能力现代化的目标还有较大差距。山东省有三个问题：（a）地方政府间的事权和支出责任划分还不够清晰；（b）地方政府间收入分配不均衡；（c）地方政府间转移支付管理不规范，不符合基于法制的现代财政体制要求。

首先，现代政府间财政体制应合理划分地方政府间的事权和支出责任，各级政府按事权划分各自承担相应的支出责任。前者应保证一

级政府、一级事权，没有重复，而后者则应确定地方政府应承担的责任。山东省的改革集中在三个基本问题。第一个问题是政府间事权和支出责任不明确，这导致了在某些情况下提供的服务重复，不清；第二个问题是，部分支出责任的分配并不合理，例如：有些具有区域外溢性或者规模经济效益的职能本不应该由县级政府来承担，而其他一些更适合由较低级别政府承担的职能却由省级或者地市级的政府承担了；第三个问题是，存在部分公共服务由多级政府共同承担的情况，而这会导致低效率。

山东省为了处理好上述这些问题，计划对当前所有支出责任的分配情况进行重新论证。通过列出各级政府相应的职能清单，解决支出责任分配不清的问题。支出责任的正确分配应取决于公共服务规模经济的大小或者外溢性程度，因为规模经济或者外溢性程度决定了一项公共服务是否应该由更高一级的政府来提供。如果一项公共服务的主要受益者是地方居民，那么相应的支出责任应该由县级或者地区政府来承担。应用这些规则，山东省各级政府之间的支出责任就会产生一定的变化。改革计划要求首先在教育、健康和交通运输行业进行试点，对各级政府的支出责任重新进行合理划分，并在 2015 年付诸实施。

其次，山东省另一个需要解决的问题是其各地政府之间的收入分配问题。目前的省级改革中，还有很多关于收入分配体制设计的改革尚未进行。改革文件中列出的指引并不明确具体，但其中有两条原则：第一条，包括与中央政府共享部分的税收收入在内，所有地方政府的税收收入都应归入为地级或县级政府的收入；第二条，省政府应该利用统一的收入分享机制，缩小各地方政府的财力差距。尽管相关的参数可能不同，这大概是目前仅有的关于收入分配体制的内容，但改革方向是要求有一套基于科学方法的机制。

最后，方案指出，山东省当前地方政府的转移支付体系也存在着一些问题。第一个问题是一般性转移支付和专项转移支付之间的平衡。

目前存在这样一种趋势，即各项专项转移支付应该合并，使之更加标准化，这样纵向的转移支付将在一定程度上减少。值得注意的是，专项转移支付的数量已经从243项下降到了71项，但仍然存在进一步下降的空间。现有方法的第二个问题是，转移支付中的匹配条款给地方政府带来了较大的财政压力，在国务院的文件规定中也体现了对此的关注。第三，有必要对部分转移支付的分配进行调整，例如，应该把外来人口更直接地纳入补贴项目的考虑范围；加大在生态方面的转移支付力度。第四，现有转移支付的结构还不是很理想，一般性转移支付的数量依旧低于专项转移支付的数量。

山东省这次改革要求通过以下办法来处理这些问题：

（1）完成对政府间财政关系的复核工作，使向地方政府转移的资金数额更为合理；

（2）明确专项转移支付制度，减少专项转移支付数量，并设立专项转移支付项目的退出条款；

（3）通过考虑区域管理、地市和县级政府履行承诺情况，以及一般公共服务需求等因素，创新分配专项资金的方式方法；

（4）建立对专项转移支付评估的一套监管系统，并规定专项资金是否持续供应将取决于政府的行政绩效。

省级以下财政体制改革：述评

山东省在这方面的改革和其他省份比并不突出，改革方案更注重说明其在改革中使用的方法。事实上，其中的许多方法已经为大部分政府用来对各自的政府间财政体制进行重新调整，同时，这也符合国务院有关规定的要求。

山东省计划首先对支出责任分配体制进行考察，判断职权责任的分配是否合理，这毫无疑问是正确的改革出发点。当发现政府在考虑外部性和规模经济方面基于的权重过低这一情况时，山东省可能会转

向更为集权的财政体制，也就是说，在这种体制下，县级政府将承担比过去更少的支出责任，因为更多的支出责任由省级政府承担了，而这一变革的影响将比想象中要大。

收入分配参照现代政府间财政体制的支出责任分配，如果支出责任有变化，收入分配也会进行相应的调整。然而这里面的一个主要问题是如何在重新分配各级政府的事权和财权的过程中处理好公平和均等化。现行做法和一般规律显示，至少应该考虑转向基于公式化的财政分配体制，而山东省的改革方案还没有涉及这方面，因此还不能判断这是否是其改革方向。但是，这是一个很重要的议题。

政府间转移支付体制方面的改革建议尚未完全展开，但改革方案粗略地提出了一些观点。改革的一系列目标中包括：降低专项转移支付、增加一般性转移支付、取消地方政府的配套要求。这些关于改革的粗略思考体现了均等化转移支付体系的大方向。然而，当具体到资金的来源、资金相对于共享税的规模，以及均等化程度等一系列问题时，目前还没有进行相关的讨论研究。

这些有关政府间财政的改革非常重要，因为这些改革要求省级政府而非市镇级政府处理一些基础性的问题，其中包括：是应该由高层级的还是底层级的政府做出更多的管理决策，如何在促进公共服务均等化和刺激经济增长之间进行取舍。

财政支出管理

山东省的改革方案要求在三个方面对支出管理进行改革：减少不必要的开销、削减市场竞争性领域的支出，以及寻找利用公共资金的新途径以支持经济发展。

第一个方面强调建立节约型政府，使那些旨在降低不必要的花费以提高一般公共服务支出效率的政策更加规范化。政府可能会引进一

套标准的费用管理系统，这套系统将覆盖政府接待、公务车、公务出行等方面的支出管理。当然，利用标准的程序还能在其他方面起到降低成本费用的作用，例如，政府采购、人员冗余、投资评估等情况，这些都在方案中有所说明。

山东省的改革方案要求省级和省级以下的政府，在市场竞争性领域要降低支出，该支出包括各种形式的补贴，正是这些补贴的存在导致政府在一般公共服务方面支出不足。改革方案要求政府支出逐步转向基本公共服务领域。

最后，改革方案还强调了一个目标：寻找利用公共资金支持工业发展和公共服务提供的新途径。方案鼓励地方政府退出旧模式下利用直接补贴和其他奖励的形式向私人公司提供资金的做法。而是通过建立特殊基金支持产业工作岗位的创造，目的在于引导社会资本投资，促进工业结构的转型升级。政府购买服务、政府与社会资本合作，以及其他促使社会资本在政府鼓励领域进行投资的新项目将会得到优先考虑；资金将来源于省级政府以及市场，而目标行业能否得到新的投资，将由一个委员会而非政府部门决定。

第二个方法是让市场投资甚至管理社会福利服务，如向老年人提供的服务。投资和服务的提供可能会涉及服务提供者竞争、定价、合同、特许经营权以及政府与社会资本合作等方面的内容。

财政支出管理：述评

改革方案提出了三条有关支出管理改革的方法，其中有两条都要求通过削减非必要支出、减少对竞争行业的直接支持，以及把资金转向一般公共服务来增加预算资金。

改革方案要求的厉行节约是一个好的倡议。要求减少非必要支持以实现更好的资金管理，这会对腐败现象有一定的限制并向社会和政府公务员发出了一个强烈的信号。但这并不意味着将产生较多的剩余

资金，因为这项工作通常需要行政方面进行投入，花费也颇多。

改革方案还要求削减支持竞争行业的资金支出，这与党中央的建议和国务院的有关规定相一致。改革方案给出的部分证据显示，相对来说，山东省在经济建设方面的支出比例较高，在社会公共服务方面的支出反而较低。减少企业补助将会增加一般公共服务方面的资金。据报道，目前政府已经拒绝了很多企业的补助申请。

国务院的规定还要求各省着力寻找支持经济增长的新途径。对此，山东省改革方案给出的建议是主要通过其他方式支持目标厂商和行业从而支持竞争性行业。由政府部门发放的补助将由基于经济发展战略的委员会发放的奖金取代。尽管改革方案并没有提供太多细节，但从中我们可以发现，资金的来源将会是省级政府和市场。上述建议是对原来部门通过补贴的形式给予奖励的改进，但却与区分公共与私人领域以及将政府工作集中在公共服务提供上这两个目标存在一定矛盾。

财政管理体制的现代化

目前的财政管理体制尚不成熟，原因有三个：一是结构缺陷；二是监管不力；三是政府工作人员能力有限。改革方案指出了其中存在的一系列问题：盗用公款、挪用公款、错误的会计记录、松懈的资产管理，以及特殊基金的浪费。山东省的改革方案要求财政管理方面所有领域的绩效都要有显著的提升，而且很有必要与法律，尤其是《预算法》，相契合。

第一个方面是改进监督机制，包括加大对非法行为和违规行为的调查力度。改革还要求加大预算和财政账户对公众开放力度，以便提高财政管理系统运行的透明度。这样将有利于更好地执行《预算法》，也更可能获得全国人民代表大会的认可，同时也会提高财政管理透明度。

第二个能改进的方面是地方政府财政管理运营效率的提升。在很多情况下，地方政府没有使用科学的方法进行财政管理，导致资金浪费的情况。出现这种情况，有时是对系统执行不彻底所造成，有时是员工能力不达标所造成。其导致的结果则是为了得到税收优惠需要付出巨大的代价，承担不必要的金融风险，产生非法开支等诸如此类的情况。为了解决这个问题，有必要提升财政管理人员的素质，在法律的规定下运作，并接受更好制度的监督。山东省改革方案要求，通过更科学的招聘方法和更多的培训对员工的能力进行较大的提升。

财政管理体制的现代化：述评

山东省改革方案在落实国务院新出台各项规定方面的工作值得肯定，因为山东省改革方案对这些规定给予了应有的重视。当然，目前的情况是，在现有的措施和最佳的措施之间还存在很大的差距。要达到用更加科学的方法对财政进行管理这一目标，并使用更加有效的方式提供服务，需要考虑三个方面的因素：

首先，实施的效果可能在省内各地市有很大的不同，在县市层级可能效果最差。处于偏远地区的资源有限，工作人员的工资水平较低，能力可能也不足以实施高质量的改革。

其次，一些区级政府很可能迫切需要提升它们的财政管理方法，但它们的需求和起点又可能不太契合。改革方案并没有针对不同类型地方政府的不同需求给出相应的处理方案。

最后，改革方案要求工作人员以更好的态度、更多的努力并采用更加科学的方法实施改革，但是对于如何把这些工作落实好，尚未给出一个具体的方案。例如，在培训工作方面，对于如何展开培训以及培训需要哪些资源这些问题都没有给出详细的解答。

第五章　国家背景：构建有活力的政府间财政体制

在 2014 年的秋天，中国高层国家领导人就国家税收体制、预算实施和中央与地方的财政关系等方面的财政改革出台了一个文件。这项文件的大致提议令人印象深刻，下面是文件的基本目标：

“财政是国家治理的基础和重要支柱。科学的财税体制是优化资源配置、维护市场统一、促进社会公平、实现国家长治久安的制度保障”。

中国已经为其财政系统的现代化制定了时间表。财政部声明，关于财政体制和税收体制的主要改革任务将于 2016 年完成，而一整套完整的现代财税体制也将于 2020 年建设好。在 2014 年 8 月 31 日，中国的立法机关通过了《预算法》的修正案，此次修订是自《预算法》在 1995 年生效以来的第一次修订。旧《预算法》是在中国深受计划经济思想影响的情况下制定的，这就留给政府大量的解释空间。《预算法》修正案与当今中国财政改革紧密相连，其获得通过历时之久是难以想象的：在 2011 年，修正案的初搞在花费了七年的时间后第一次拿出来讨论，又经过了四次讨论修改后才得以通过。在 2014 年的 9 月，国务院开始开展深化预算和债务管理改革的工作。

全会提供的指导方向[1]

2013 年 12 月 12 日，党的十八届三中全会通过党中央关于全面深化改革的一些主要问题的决定。党中央的决定明确提出一套深化财税体制改革的要求，改革的一些关键领域包括完善立法、明确权利和责任的划分、重建税收结构、稳定税收负担、预算透明化、提高办事效率，并为中央和地方政府建立一套现代化的财政系统。为了完成这些目标，党中央提出了三条主要的改革措施：完善预算管理系统；完善税收体制；建立起一套行政权力和支出责任相匹配的体制。

完善预算管理系统

一套完整、标准化、开放且透明的预算体制将被启用。同时，预算核查的重点将从财政预算平衡与赤字规模延伸到支出预算分析和财政政策方面。大部分与财政收入增长额或者国内生产总值增长额挂钩的主要支出将进行脱钩化处理，这将使得预算的灵活性大大增加。中国将建立一套跨年度预算平衡机制，一整套基于权责发生制的政府财务报告系统，以及一套对中央和地方政府都适用的标准化且合理的债务管理和早期风险预警机制。

一般性转移支付的影响因子将得到进一步改进，主要增加对老工业基地、少数民族聚集区、边远区域以及贫困地区的转移支付。由于中央政策要求增加支出导致的地方政府财政短缺将通过一般转移支付进行弥补。计划还包括对专项转移支付进行合并和规范，并逐步取消

1　以下材料来自乔宝云的翻译工作。

从地方政府流向竞争领域的资金补助。此外，进一步研究出于救济和急救目的以及其他的专项转移支付处理方案，如果涉及地方事务，则也将纳入进来。

完善税收体制

随着税制改革的开展，直接税的比重将逐步增加。同时，继续推进“营改增”的工作，简化税率结构。消费税结构的优化主要是对那些能耗高、污染重以及高端消费的产品征收消费税。税收改革计划还包括建立一套综合与分类相结合的个人所得税体系；同时，税收改革计划也涵盖了通过新的《房地产税法》，并要求适时征收新房地产税；加快资源税改革，逐步把目前收取环境保护费的做法改为征收环境税。

为了与统一税制、促进税收负担均等化与市场竞争公平化的要求相一致，推进税收优惠政策管理，尤其是要规范区域性税收优惠政策。与此相配套，关于税收优惠政策的法律会更加具体明确，相关法规也将出台，这些都决定了今后哪些税收优惠政策能继续使用，哪些将停止。另外，省级和地市级政府的税收征管系统也将进一步升级。

构建事权和支出责任相适应的体制

中央政府的事权和支出责任包括：国防、外交事务、国家安全，以及全国统一的市场规则和市场管理，所有这些在未来都将得到进一步强化。在社保项目和跨区域项目的建设和维护事权将由中央和地方政府共同分享。区域性公共服务将继续留给地方政府，中央政府将把一部分支出责任委托给地方政府，并通过转移支付向地方政府提供资金支持。

楼继伟部长关于党中央决定的看法

财政部部长楼继伟在谈到党中央的决定时指出，预算管理体制改革是根本，应该在改革中处于首要地位。收入分配改革应该在税收体制改革基本完成之后再进行。同时，建立起一套更完善的事权和支出责任相适应的体制可能需要耗费大量的时间以达成一致的计划。财政和税收体制改革的关键年份是 2014 年和 2015 年。就目前短期的情况来看，预算管理改革体制或许会取得实质进展，税制改革在法律和推进方面也将取得巨大进展，但事权和支出责任方面的改革可能最多只能进行到达成基本共识的程度。财政和税收体制改革的主要工作和任务将在 2016 年基本完成，同时各项改革也将陆续进行，但是要想建立起一套现代的财政体制可能要等到 2020 年。[1]

财政和税收体制改革的下一步将会是开拓一些重要的新型领域，这与党中央的决定一致：

（1）法律的改进将把重点放在财政运转法治化；

（2）中央政府和地方政府之间事权和支出责任的划分将更加清晰；

（3）税收体制的改革将包括逐步增加直接税种的比重，将各类行政收费税收化，强化所得税作为财政收入来源的地位，以及改进税收征管体系；

（4）财政收入占国内生产总值的比重应该稳定地保持在合理水平，税收负担的分配也应得到有效控制；

（5）将启用一套完整且标准化的预算披露系统，这套系统可以促进财政管理体制的民主化，可以帮助构建开放性政府，并且激励政府

1 这里报道的楼继伟部长的评论是来自于楼部长在 http：//news. xinhuanet. com/fortune/2014 －03/07/c_126233438. htm 的演讲。

依照法律运转；

（6）财政管理和预算评估的科学方法会有助于提高公共收入融资的效率。

楼继伟部长强调，深化财政和税收体制的改革是一项复杂的工作，改革的具体落实应该遵守以下原则：平衡政府与市场之间的关系，调动中央和地方政府的积极性，兼顾效率和公平，妥善处理长期和短期的问题。

国务院的规定

为了落实党的十八大和十八届三中全会的各项精神，国务院在2014年9月26日发布了《国务院关于深化预算管理体制改革的决定》。这个文件包括深化预算管理体制改革的具体决定，所有这些具体决定都是基于中国的新《预算法》，新《预算法》将引导预算体制逐步走向全面化、标准化、开放化和透明化。

国务院的决定列出了一系列需要解决的问题：由于缺乏长期预算的计划，预算管理和控制的方法存在不科学的问题；地方政府借款不受预算管理体制的约束；预算约束软化情况比较普遍；财政收支结构与政府目标不一致；财政盈余资金规模过大以及支出效率低下。所有这些问题都对中国财政的可持续发展带来了挑战。

新预算管理体制改革的原则包括：

（1）构建一套标准化和现代化的预算体系，并把这套体系与改进后的法律法规联系起来。

（2）在政府与市场之间划出明确的边界。各类财政补助和税收优惠政策应该进行复查，在合适的情况下应该予以撤销。

（3）推进预算的逐步开放和透明化。

（4）注重顶层设计，但同时也要注意外部环境和各种条件的约束，确保预算管理体制改革与行政管理体制改革之间能相互协调。

预算管理体制主要有八个方面需要进行改进：

第一，完善政府预算体系，积极推进预算公开。这可以通过明确一般公共财政预算、政府基金预算、国有资本经营预算以及社保基金预算的收支范围来达到。应该把所有的政府财政活动都纳入预算管理，并且预算的编制、执行和审计工作的过程也要更加清晰和现代化。

第二，健全预算标准体系。支出的水平应该根据政府机关运行的基本需要来决定、加强人员编制和资本管理。部门预算、政府预算和决算都应该遵循标准的经济分类编制。包括：

推进预算信息的全面披露。专项转移支付的预决算可按照功能、项目和地区披露。财政政策也将被披露，并且预算披露的范围可能会延伸到每个部门的最终账户中。此外，加大“三公”经费的公开力度。

改进政府预算的管理和控制，建立跨年度预算平衡机制。财政部门可单独或者联合其他部门编制三年期滚动财政规划分析和预测未来三年的重大收支情况。这项财政规划应该和国民经济和社会发展规划纲要以及国家的宏观调控经济政策相衔接。

收紧和重新聚焦预算控制。一般公共预算的审计应该从关注财政平衡和赤字规模转移到关注支出绩效和政策分析。为了强化预算约束，各级政府在向全国人民代表大会报告支出预算时都应该强调支出政策的内容。一般预算性支出的任何增加或减少都应该向同级的人大常委会汇报，提请审查和批准。收入预算应该从约束性转向预期性，根据经济形势和政策调整等因素科学预测。

对于中央预算来说，一般公共预算可能会由于宏观调控政策的需要而出现赤字，这可以通过发行国债来弥补。对于地方政府来说，在得到国务院的批准后，一般公共预算可能会出现赤字，这可以通过发

行一般债券来弥补。地方债的规模将纳入限额管理。国务院将决定并向全国人大及其常委会报告地方债的上限，并提请审议和批准。

政府性基金预算按照以收定支的原则，根据政府性基金项目的收入情况和实际支出需要编制。在得到国务院的批准后，为有一定收益的公益性事业发展地方政府可以在政府性基金预算下发行专项债。专项地方债的规模需要纳入限额管理。国务院要决定并向全国人大及其常委会汇报专项地方债的上限，并提请审议和批准。

国有资本运营预算要按照收支平衡原则编制，不列赤字。

建立跨年预算平衡机制。对于中央预算来说，中央一般公共预算的结余会被用于弥补赤字和补充到中央预算稳定基金中。中央一般公共预算的短收将通过来自中央预算稳定基金的转移支付、削减支出和经全国人大及其常委会批准后，在上限允许的范围内发行国债的方式弥补。对于地方预算来说，地方一般公共预算实现的结余将被用于偿还政府的债务或者补充到地方预算稳定资金中，而赤字则会通过地方预算稳定基金或其他预算性资金以及减少支出来弥补。如果仍然没有实现预算平衡，省级政府可以提高赤字规模并在得到省级人大及其常委会批准后向财政部汇报。增加的赤字需要用下一年度的年度预算来抵消。地级和县级政府可通过向上级政府申请暂时的紧急救助并在之后年度偿还的方式平衡预算。政府性基金预算的结余和省级国有资本经营预算的结余结转下一年安排，而其短收将会通过减少支出来抵消。

第三，加强财政收入管理，清理规范税收优惠政策。目标是加强税收征收和管理。税收部门严禁违反法律和法规，严禁越权征收超过应缴税额的部分，严禁提前征税、减少征税、豁免或延缓征税。

规范税收优惠政策。除国务院规定外，否则所有政府部门不得背离统一的财政和税收体制，自行制定税收优惠政策。这也包括禁止在起草其他法律、法规、发展计划和区域性政策时制定税收优惠。地区及政府部门不能在未经国务院批准的前提下为企业制定税收优惠政策。

具有经济和社会发展价值且没有法律法规限制的政策会在全国范围内尽快实施。原则上，具有专门时效性政策的实施应在到期时废止，并且未设政策实施的时间限制的应设定时限。

一些其他的行动应被提议来完善非税收入管理。其中最为重要的是规范清理行政性事业收费和政府性基金，以及废除非法的和不合理的收费基金项目；建立健全国有资源和国有资本的收益共享机制，落实国有资本的收益权；加强非税收入的分类预算管理；完善征收、支付和监管体制。

第四，完善财政支出结构，移除公共资金的刚性，加强结转和结余资金的管理。实现这些目标可采用以下几个步骤：

（1）为了最大化政府支出的效率，应严格控制诸如政府性楼堂馆所、财政供养人员和“三公”经费等一般性支出；

（2）清理规范重点支出与生产总值挂钩的事项；

（3）政府应逐步取消城市维护建设税、排污费、勘探和采矿权，以及矿产资源补偿费等专款专用的规定，深化税费改革；

（4）通过逐步整合所有预算性资金到财政部门统一分配，完善预算分配。

第五，改革和调整财政转移支付结构。包括：

（1）增加一般性转移支付的规模和比例，逐步提高其占总转移支付的比例至60%以上，完善一般性转移支付增长机制，并明显增加向革命老区、少数民族地区、边疆地区和贫困地区的转移支付。一般性转移支付（无条件拨款）应该弥补由于中央政策导致的地方财力缺口。

（2）落实专项转移支付体制改革。关于地方事务的专项转移支付将被纳入一般性转移支付。党中央将逐一调查竞争领域的专项转移支付，并且废除“小、散、乱”和效用不明显的专项转移支付。剩余的将被压缩规模并实施零增长。改进分配方式，减少行政性分配。合并

相似目的的专项转移支付。此外，党中央将会规范新的专项转移的设立，严格控制新项目，建立并完善专项转移支付的定期评估和退出机制。

（3）加快中央对地方转移支付管理办法的修订，对转移支付项目设立、资金分配、使用管理、绩效评价和信息公开等做出规定。建立财政转移支付和农业转移人口市民化挂钩的机制。在合理明确中央和地方支出责任的基础上，认真清理现行的配套政策。不再要求地方政府为公共事务提供配套资金。所有地区都应整合和调整本级政府安排的专项资金，完善资金管理办法，并提高资金的使用效率。

第六，加强结转和结余资金的管理。各级政府都应该：

（1）建立结转和结余资金的机制。之前年度的结转资金可被用于下一年的支出。连续两年没有被使用的结转资金应当作为结余资金管理，并且可以被用于补充预算稳定资金。所有的部门和单位之前年度预算的结转和结余资金按照财政部的规定办理。

（2）加大结余资金的使用力度。对不需按照原用途使用的资金，可被转移到经济和社会发展亟需资金支持的领域。

（3）建立管理和报告结转和结余资金的监管机制。

（4）建立科学合理的预算执行进度考核机制。

所有用于购买服务的资金都应该被列入财政预算中。鼓励所有政府部门根据相关规定购买服务，以有效地降低公共服务的成本并提升公共服务的质量。

第七，加强预算执行管理，提升财政支出绩效。在预算执行中应遵循下列要求：

（1）在年度预算执行中硬化预算约束。不在预算执行中发布增加支出的政策，除非发生如大灾害这样的需要支出的突发事件（这些支出将利用预备费来弥补）。一些有必要发布的政策中使用的资金将用未来年度的预算来弥补。涉及政府采购的预算根据政府采购相关的规定

执行。

（2）中央对地方一般性和专项转移支付应分别在全国人大批准后的 30 天内和 90 天内正式下达。在收到中央的一般性和专项转移支付后，省级政府需要在 30 天内将这些转移支付发放给包括县级政府在内的各级地方政府。

（3）所有部门和单位必须根据批准的预算执行预算性支出。如有需要，预算性资金可以根据财政部的规定在不同的预算科目间、不同预算级次或不同预算项目间调剂。

规范国库资金管理，提高收入和支出效率。因此，政府将：

（1）全面清理整顿财政专户。各地区不得设立新的专项资金账户。除了经财政部批准并报国务院批准予以保留的专项资金账户外，其余的应在 2 年内逐步取消。各级地方政府不可以开设新专项资金账户。

（2）规范权责发生制核算。地方各级财政除国库集中支付年终结余外，一律不得按权责发生制列支。按照国务院规定实行权责发生制核算的特定事项应该向同级的人大常委会报告。

（3）审查和清理现存的政府贷款和预付款。应从预算列支的贷款和预付款应根据相关规定支付。规定允许内的临时贷款和预付款应该及时收回，不合规定的应限期收回。

（4）严禁各级政府向年度预算外的单位或项目借款或垫付财政资金。另外，应该加强各级政府对国库的监督和管理。

健全预算绩效管理机制。绩效管理的范围可以逐步覆盖各级预算单位和所有财政资金，绩效评价的重点将从项目支出进一步拓展，并且评价的结果应作为制定未来支出规划的重要基础。

建立权责发生制的政府综合财务报告机制。当条件成熟时，政府综合财务报告将呈报给同级的人大及其常委会。这将成为评估地方政府绩效和预算工作的一项重要基础。另外，也应逐步建立政府综合财

务报告的披露机制。

第八，规范地方债的管理，设立风险管理程序。实现这一目的的第一步是建立标准的地方债融资机制和适当的地方政府债务融资主体。省级政府在国务院的批准下可以发行债券，而县级政府可以间接地通过省级政府发行债券。政府债务只能通过政府及其部门发起，不能通过企业和机构举借。地方政府可以通过债券的形式发起债务。应剥离地方政府融资平台为政府融资的功能。为了推行政府与社会资本合作模式，应鼓励社会资本通过特许经营等方式参与城市基础设施建设等有一定收益的公益性事业的投资和运营。

地方政府通过发行债券举借的一般性债务应纳入一般公共预算中，而通过发行专项债券举借的专项债务应纳入政府性基金预算中。

地方政府可在国务院批准的限额内举债，但必须得到相应级别的人民代表大会及其常委会的批准。地方政府应在举债时遵循市场准则。此外，应建立地方政府信用评级系统，完善地方债券市场。地方政府举债获得的资金只能用于公共福利功能的资本支出和适度偿还存量债务，不能用于经常性支出。

财政部可以根据如债务率、新增债务率、偿债率和逾期债务率等指标评估各地区的债务风险。对高风险的地区，应采取积极措施降低风险。在甄别和把地方存量债务并入预算管理后，为了减轻利息负担和优化债券期限结构，地区可申请发行地方政府债券置换现有的存量债务。为了硬化预算约束和防范道德风险，地方政府应对偿还它们的债务负责，中央政府实行不救助原则。

将地方债作为一个指标纳入地方政府政绩考核。省级政府应对辖区内的地方政府债务负责。各级地方政府应为它们的债务管理及预防和化解财务风险负责。政府的负责人应对这些政策的实施负主要责任。

通过设立适当的评价和监管机制、信息披露及警告体系、责任机制来严肃财经纪律。这可通过三种方式实现。一种方式是让所有地区

和部门都严格遵守融资和税收的各种法律法规，如《预算法》、《税收征管法》、《会计法》和《政府采购法》，同时，这些地区和部门要依法行使行政决策和财政管理权，自觉接受来自全国人民代表大会和公众的监督。为进一步完善审计监管，应建立决算审计体系。另一种建立财经纪律的方式是更好地规范理财行为。完善多种体系的建立和运营，包括预算编制、收入征收和管理、资金分配、国库管理、政府采购、财政监管、绩效评价，以及责任追究机制。第三种方式是各级地方政府对辖区内的所有部门和单位的财经纪律的执行情况进行全面的检查。财政部门和审计主体要指出存在的问题。责任意识也应通过根据诸如预算法的法律法规制定的惩罚措施得以加强，违规和违法行为包括虚报、冒领、截留、挪用、扣留财政资金，以及发布违反法律法规的税收优惠政策。

财政部关于收入管理的说明[1]

楼部长对收入管理做出了一个特别说明。他指出，现有的税收优惠政策过多，特别是区域的税收优惠政策过多。中国现在已经提出并实施了大约50种地区的税收优惠政策，几乎覆盖了所有省份（自治区和直辖市）。一些地方政府和财政税收部门发布“地方政策”，通过税收返还来达到减免税收的目的。这导致了税基侵蚀、利润向企业转移，以及出现税收“荒地”的问题。这些“地方政策”并不会优化税收使用，或实现社会公平的目标。而且，这些政策对公平竞争和市场环境的统一起到了负面作用，也和建立现代财政体系的要求不相符。

今后，地方政府起草的法律、法规、发展规划和区域政策不得打破统一的国家财政和税收体系，除税收法律和法规允许的特殊情况外，

1 这里并非楼部长的原话，而是我们基于其讲话的解读。

不得制定税收优惠政策。地方政府在没有国务院批准的情况下，不得为企业制定税收上的优惠政策。原则上，具有专门时效性政策的实施应在到期时废止，并且没有限期的政策应设定限期。财政部会定期检查和评估，违法行为将会得到严重的惩罚。

国务院于2014年11月27日发布了《关于清理规范税收等优惠政策的通知》（国发［2014］62号）（下文简称《62号通知》）。通过清理规范税收优惠等政策，《62号通知》的目的在于防止地方保护主义和不正当竞争，让市场在资源配置中扮演决定性的作用。

面对复杂的经济状况，国务院发布了《关于税收等优惠政策相关事项的通知》（国发［2015］25号）（下文简称《25号通知》）。《25号通知》列举了：（1）统一的全国性的税收优惠政策可以实施；（2）区域和部门的税收优惠政策应根据规定的时间限期实施，没有时间限制的，地方政府和相关部门应设立一个过渡期间，并在此期间实施；（3）部分与企业签订合同的地方优惠政策继续有效，已经履行的政策不能被追溯；（4）所有的地区和部门，新设立税收优惠政策和中央批准的非税优惠政策，需提交国务院批准。这些政策安排的支出不能与企业的税收和非税收入挂钩；（5）国发《62号通知》规定的专项清理工作在进一步部署前暂停。

财政部关于税收改革的说明[1]

税收改革的目标是建立一个具有科学发展、社会公平和统一市场特征的财政和税收体系。这项即将实施的改革现在还在讨论中，聚焦6个主要税种：增值税、消费税、资源税、环保税、财产税和个人所得税。

1　这并非楼部长讲话的原话。

增值税改革的目标是主要基于税收中性原则建立一个标准的消费型增值税体系。下一步“营改增”改革将会把范围扩大到生活服务业、建筑业、房地产业、金融业及其他产业。截至2015年，“营改增”改革将会按计划完成，涉及行业包括生活服务业、金融业和房地产业。楼部长提到，最困难的部分将会是把房地产业纳入到改革中。如果要把增值税改革的范围推广到建筑业和房地产业，那么还需要解决房产业增值税进项税额抵扣的问题。

中国的经济发展已经进入了“新常态”时期，即经济发展保持一个缓慢但是更加可持续的增长率。现行经济在一个总体平稳的条件下运行，但是正面临显著的下行压力。坚持放缓增长需要企业和政府的合作。企业应该发挥它们的主动性和创造力去适应经济新常态。政府应该为引导大批自主创业和创新营造环境。

一方面，政府应该颁布结构性减税和减少费用的政策和措施以减轻中小企业的负担并释放它们的增长潜力。另一方面，政府可以继续推行能适当激励市场主体活力的政策。

结构性改革的一些其他税收改革正在讨论中，但是还没有正式的行动。对于完善消费税体制，可能的结构性调整包括税基覆盖范围的扩大和税率结构的合理化。

为加速煤炭资源税的改革，政府可以推行资源税以价格为基础的改革，并逐步将资源税征收的范围扩大到自然生态空间，如水流、森林、草原和滩涂。

对于建立环保税，现存的排污费将被环保税取代。目的是根据重点调控和“费改税”的原则将税收作为一种保护生态环境的工具。

为加速财产税立法和及时推进财产税改革，我们可以增强对包括财产调查在内的税收结构问题的调研，并坚持立法的全面发展。

为探究逐步建立一个综合与分类相结合的个人所得税体系，政府应考虑修订《税收征管法》及其他相关的法律法规。

监管权在各级政府间的分配是一项重要的制度安排，并且一定要得到处理。维持现有的中央和地方财政模式的总体平稳是在中央和地方政府之间合理分配收入的前提。现在，与英国、法国、意大利、澳大利亚及其他中央财政收入占到总体财政收入比例70%以上的国家相比，中国的中央政府收入集中程度并不高。美国中央财政收入占总体财政收入的比例在一般年度也达到了65%左右。

为了推进中央和地方政府收入分配的合理化，我们可以做出合理的调整来帮助维持现在中央和地方财政模式的总体平稳。维持中央和地方政府财政模式的总体稳定和通过税收改革推进收入在中央和地方政府间分配的合理化都非常重要。税收收入变化很大的税种、有很强的再分配功能的税种和税基流动性大的税种都会被划分为中央税。在税收评估和征收必需的信息上地方政府有很大优势的税种，以及对地方资源配置有重大影响的税种，有很大比例将会被分配给地方政府。在实行收入分配之后，地方政府的财政缺口将通过中央的税收共享弥补。

对于在不同层级的政府间合理分配事权和支出责任，考虑那些能指导有效事权划分的客观要素非常重要。基于这些原则，考虑到统一市场规则和管理问题，可将国防、外交事务和国家安全的事权分配给中央政府。另外，人民代表大会应将地区性公共服务事权分配给地方政府并澄清中央和地方政府的共享事权。中央政府可能通过财政转移支付机制委托地方政府行使部分事权和支出责任。

第六章　财税管理改革与山东省财政

山东省的改革遵从了国务院 2014 年法规所设定的原则。尽管三中全会的决议似乎期待更大力度的财政改革[1]，但国务院目前仅出台了预算管理制度新规定。经济增速的下滑可能是改革脚步放缓的原因之一。

下一轮改革可能会在接下来几年里展开。我们或许可以用山东省的例子来说明这一点。第一，“营改增”后原来营业税税收的损失问题需要得到解决。在山东，营业税是省和地方政府最重要的税收来源。第二，如何应对山东省的收入缺口是一个更棘手的问题。支出方面，提高公共服务水平、偿还债务和社保资金支出等带来了支出的逐年增长；收入方面，由于土地出让收入减少和经济增速下滑，财政缺口会越来越大。

当然，改革方案会致力于解决这些问题。通过减少税收优惠、进行税费改革，以及提高财税管理效率节约成本，缺口可以得到一定的填补。国务院和山东省的改革方案对上述手段均有所提及，却未对成效进行估计。另外，中央政府批准的新增收入、补贴体制的完善、支出责任的再划分也会对地方政府收入的减少起到一定的补偿作用。然而就目前来看，这些要实现尚需时日。

在本章，我们将探讨以下问题：现有的收入如何替代营业税收入损失？省和地方政府最终应引入什么样的新税种？在中央与省之间转移支付发生改变时，山东省应该如何应对？进一步，这种改变是否需

1　请参见财政部部长楼继伟同样的评价。

要一个更集中化（省政府驱动）的财政体制？

营业税的替代

取消营业税改征增值税，这意味着经营者可以将购货款项所缴纳的增值税抵扣税款。尽管这是一个好的税收改革，但势必对省和地方政府的收入产生重大影响。“营改增”对地方政府来说并不是一件好事，因为营业税收入全额归地方所有，而增值税收入只有 25% 会分配给地方。有种说法认为，经过调整的增值税税基从长期看会增长得更快。但是，这似乎难以掩盖税收从地方向中央转移的本质。

潜在的收入损失难以计算。到目前为止，地方政府还可保留相关收入，因此在这个结构化改革中尚未受到伤害。然而，我们可以对该问题的严重性进行探讨。2014 年，营业税的预算收入为 1 135.9 亿元人民币，占总税收收入的 30%，在省级收入结构中难以被替代。需要指出的是，2014 年营业税收入约为增值税地方共享部分的两倍。

为了说明改革的可能选项，我们提供了一些关于山东省现有收入资源再分配调整的粗略估算数据（见表 14）。第一行表明了取消营业税对收入的影响。如果共享税分成比例没有变化，地方政府拥有的 25% 增值税收入可以一定程度上补偿收入的损失。为了便于理解，如果 2014 年“营改增”已经全面落实到位[1]，我们假设 1 000 亿元人民币的收入增加都来源于增值税，这样，约 250 亿元人民币为山东省政府的共享收入，收入的净损失便减少至 880 亿元人民币。为了覆盖所

---

1 事实上，“营改增”比简单的“100% 向 25%”转化要复杂得多。由于允许增加抵扣，增值税收入的增加会低于 1 130 亿元人民币。此外，营业税和增值税的税率和税基结构是不同的。营业税由地税局征收，增值税由国税局征收，不同的征收方法会导致不同的征收率。应当注意：山东省营业税的有效税率约为 GDP 的 2%，增值税为 4%，归地方所有的增值税部分则为 1%。这说明我们仅能在一系列假设下粗略估计“营改增”的结果。

有的收入损失，需要将增值税的分享率提高到50%。但这显然会给中央政府的预算造成极大的压力。

另一选择是多征城市维护建设税、教育费附加和个人所得税。如表14所示，在这些税种的现有纳税义务的基础上多征一倍的税收可以减少收入损失约300亿元人民币。如果这些税款不再指定用途，那么这个选择将在新的安排中变得更加可行。

也有很多讨论认为开征房地产税可以解决部分收入损失问题。目前以房地产为基础的四种税——房产税、城镇土地使用税、土地增值税和契税——收入大概占山东省GDP的1.7%。如表14所示，通过提高税率并完善征收管理，增加这些已经征收的不动产税至GDP的2%，可能减少约160亿元人民币的收入损失。但GDP的2%是工业化国家房产税的水平，对中国来说可能成为一个沉重的负担（Bahl and Martinez - Vazquez，2008）。

要弄清在现有法律下减少或取消税收优惠并进行全额征税后，是否以及会有多少新收入进账十分重要。目前尚无对这些行动所能带来的潜在收入的估计。然而，山东省税收收入占GDP的比重约为3%，低于全国平均水平。假如像改革方案中所描述的那样，其中1个百分点的收入可以通过合法地减少税收优惠和全额征税来获得，营业税收入损失的一半可以得到弥补。取消税收优惠是很有益的政策创新，但恐怕并不能完全解决营业税的问题。此外，政策施行顺序也很重要。由于营业税收入的损失完全由地方政府承担，实施减免税收优惠的政策又需要更多的时间。最近，国务院出台新规定又声称可以延缓税收优惠的减免。

综上所述，寻找营业税收入的替代是十分棘手的任务，特别是这部分收入还事关重大。地方政府可能以此为契机获得新的税收来源，我们接下来将讨论该问题。

新地方税收

第二个选择是赋予地方政府开征新税的权利，这也是国务院下一步将要研究的。我们在这里探讨三个可能性：开征新的财产税、多征机动车辆税和多征消费税。财产税和消费税的选择已经得到全国人民代表大会、政府和其他学者们的广泛讨论，但并未达成具体的措施。机动车辆税中国一直在征收，但它能成为具有更大潜力的税收来源。

财产税（房地产税）

在中国，财产税拥有巨大的收入潜力，如今可能是时候发挥这一潜力了。财产税可以帮助地方政府填补收入缺口，对于城市地区较大的地方政府更是如此。就平均水平而言，工业化国家每年的财产税收入超过 GDP 的 2%，低收入国家的财产税收入也达到了 GDP 的 0.6%（Bahl，2009）。

国际经验

一般来说，在以英语为母语的联邦制国家，财产税是最受欢迎的税种，但在非英语国家和单一制国家，它的重要性有所降低（Bahl，2010；Lotz，2006）。财产税几乎可以被看作城市税。在纽约市，财产税收入占地方政府收入的 34%；在多伦多、蒙特利尔、墨尔本等大都市区，这一比例可以上升至一半甚至一半以上。

在其他 OECD 和转型国家，一些大都市区的地方政府采用了不同的方式。荷兰的市政府，包括斯德区域在内，财产税收入的占比不到 5%。挪威的地方政府并不征收财产税（OECD，2006，p176）。在哥本

哈根、斯德哥尔摩、东京和瑞士，市政府的主要收入来源为所得税，财产税仅占很小一部分。相对而言，财产税对于马德里市政府更为重要，尽管其收入的主要来源也是在地区政府征收的所得税。在韩国的釜山和大邱，财产税是地方政府重要的收入来源，但以房产交易税收入为主。

大多数发展中国家的政府似乎难以认同财产税是城市地区地方政府筹集资金的有效手段这一观点。尽管在城市地区，财产价值一直在增加，财产的估值却没有完全反映这种增长趋势。即使在具有大都市区域的一些国家，这一情况也很明显（Mathur 等，2009；De Cesare，2004）。此外，迟迟不进行重新估价也十分普遍，极大地降低了财产税的税收的收入弹性。在低收入国家，财产税由于收入低、管理成本高以及不受民众欢迎，未能成为优质的地方税税种。

对于大城市来说，财产税能否产生足够的税收收入也难以确定。在南非开普敦，地方政府约 20% 的收入都是通过一种以土地和土地增值的资本价值为税基的税收来获得，数额相当于他们得到的转移支付收入。

墨西哥大都市区和伊斯坦布尔地方政府的收入主要来源均为财产税。但是，两者并没有被赋予设定税率和税基的权利。印度大都市的一些地方政府拥有财产税的立法权，但结果却没有什么差别。低收入主要是税收管理的低效率造成的。例如，孟买仅有约 70% 的财产缴税，而在加尔各答，财产仅以其价值的 20% 缴税（Mathur 等，2009）。

优势和劣势

由于财产财富的所有权一般集中由高收入人群拥有，财产税一般不会加重低收入阶层的负担。由于付了高税收的不动产通常位于公共服务较好的区域，财产税也被认为是一种受益税。最后，由于财产税已经通过资本化的方式弥补减值的财产价值，市场决策将更加理性，

因为财产所有者需要对当地政府为其财产提供的服务付费，而对于拥有财产的投机者来说，他们将面临一笔巨大的持有成本。中国的财产价值飞速增加，财产税的这些优点对中国很有用，但是否财产税能成为一个重要税种也依赖于财产税的有效征收税率。

财产税的主要问题在于管理困难，以及不受到财产所有者和租户的欢迎。良好的管理需要对所有财产和其所有权进行鉴定、评估和再评估。对个人所有者征税则需要大量的记录和更新。管理的方方面面必须做好，才能实现税收的足额征收。[1]

在全世界的发展中国家，我们都可以看到纳税人对财产税的不待见和抵制，就税收负担大小来看似乎是不相称的。这主要是因为财产税以累积的收入而非现阶段实现的收入为征税对象、评估具有主观性，以及税收具有可见性等。毋庸置疑，中国也将面临这一问题。

中国的潜力

中国是世界上极少数不对居民财产进行年度征税的国家之一。理论上，中国能从这一城市税中获得可观的财政收入。每年对居民的财产征收约为 GDP 总数 1% 的税收可能成为中国一个合适的改革目标。这一有效税率相当于发展中国家平均水平的 1 倍，以及工业化国家平均水平的一半。

毫无疑问，中国拥有足够的财产可以进行征税。有估计表明，城市居民房产形式的财富价值约为 GDP 的两倍（Gan，2013）。仅对这部分财产征收 0.5% 的低税率税收，便已相当于 GDP 的 1%。此外，财产长期来看会不断增值，尽管增速可能不高。从税基的弹性和地方财政收入的增收来看，财产税都是很好的举措。在最理想的情况下，税基的弹性会满足地方政府支出增长的需求。

---

1 关于发展中国家财产税实践的调查和分析见 McCluskey and Franzsen（2013）。同样参见 Bahl and Martinez – Vazquez（2008）以及 Bird and Slack（2004）。

虽然增收是十分重要的目的，但完善财产税结构可以推动土地使用模式的改进，减少外部性成本。例如，假如税基为使用者权益的市场价值，财产税大致就等价于土地的区位租金。这会激励土地使用者对土地进行集中开发，以支持紧凑使用土地城镇化建设策略。假如对建设地区的闲置地产以更高的税率征税，也能达到同样的效果。需要指出的是，这样做是对使用者权利的市场价值而非直接对土地征税。如果市场价值增加，税收也会增加。税收最终由使用权拥有者来承担。

为了那些因公共投资导致财产增值的价值不流失，增加城市密度，其他与财产相关的税收工具也都非常有用。这包括巴西使用的 CEPACs（Wetzel，2013）[1]、特殊的估值方法、不动产增值课税、限价以及税收增长额融资等（Smolka，2013）。

如果中国对财产税保持足够的兴趣，针对城市地区的财产建立一套综合性的财产税体系并非难事。中国已经有一系列的不动产税种，包括土地使用税、契税，以及土地增值税。这些税种的税收大概占 GDP 的 1.6%（Man，2013）。以此为基础可以构建新的财产税制度，包括新的年度财产税、不动产转让的资本利得税，以及一些关于房产增值和土地使用的税收。价值评估、房产价值清册甚至财产税的征收都会统一或者紧密地结合在一起，同时，财产税的收入也将会十分可观。新的财产税制度将与所得税和增值税进行协调，要确保所有财产相关收入覆盖，同时又要规避双重征税的情况出现。

方案实施的问题

征收一种对于中国及其税收理念来说全新的宽税基税种通常会有困难。在中国，讨论财产税时有三个问题不断显现。实际上，这三个问题对引入财产税来讲都不会形成太大障碍。

---

1 巴西用的 CEPAC 是有地市政府发行并公开拍卖的债券，债券赋予持有者超越法律规定的范围对建筑区域进行扩建的权力，或者建设与规定不一致但符合法律的建筑（Wetzel，2013，p336）。

第一个问题是，当土地所有者为国家时，能否实施财产税？答案是肯定的。财产税可以以使用者对土地的使用权为税基，谁使用谁纳税。租期期满时，土地使用权由国家收回。

第二个问题，财产税能否由国家立法，却由地方政府征收？有两种可行的制度安排。一是由国家立法，同时也由中央政府管理，地方政府可以决定税率。二是由国家立法，地方政府负责管理并决定税率。不管用以上哪一种安排，财产税都是一种地方税。

第三个问题是，土地出让金和财产税是否存在重复征税？答案是否定的，这是两种截然不同的政府收入。土地出让金是获得土地使用权所应支付的租金，而财产税是获得政府提供的公共服务所应缴纳的税收。因此，土地出让金并不包括任何现在或未来的税收。

山东省的规划与实施

各省的财产税设计是国家层面的事情，因此实施上不应存在太大的差异。可能人们对于财产税能够在多大程度上弥补营业税取消所带来的财政缺口问题更感兴趣。

假如财产税作为一个新税种实施，有效税率为 GDP 的 1%，每年将产生大约 600 亿元人民币的税收（以 2014 年水平为例），这相当于营业税收入损失的三分之二。然而，由于管理上的困难，以及作为一种更加直接对人民征税的新税种，财产税的实施必将是一个渐进的过程。

更有可能的是，有效税率在一开始会大大低于 GDP 的 1%（Bahl, Goh and Qiao，2014；Hou，Ren and Zhang，2015）。对财产税能够立刻产生大量收入以弥补营业税收入损失不能持乐观态度还有另一个原因。同中国其他地区一样，山东已有一系列的税收是以财产为税基的。在山东，这部分税收约占 GDP 的 1.7%。有一种可能是，新的财产税可能替代以上税收，或与这些税收一起构成一套以财产和土地使用价值

为税基的综合税收体系。在这种情况下，房产税能够产生的税收将会远小于 GDP 的 1%。例如，即使以 GDP 的 2% 这样高的有效税率来计算，“替代性”的财产税也仅能产生 160 亿元人民币的净收入，占 2014 年营业税收入损失的 18%。

中国实施新的财产税会遇到一些困难。财产税可以由地方税务局评估和征收。在设计财产税结构时，假如为了保护低收入居民和个体营业者而对其减免税收，则乡村地区的财产税收入可能接近于零。可想而知，相对于现有的营业税或增值税，富裕的地方政府可能会更加青睐财产税。因此，鉴于城市和农村地区的税收潜力差异巨大，是否应当将财产税作为省级政府收入共享的重要来源？或者是否应当将其作为一种城市税，仅仅在大城市征收？

财产税的管理也会遇到许多棘手的问题。如果资产评估以价值为基础，那么对价值评估的指导原则将会产生许多争论。财产税的征收，以及土地清册的日常更新和维护可能将由省级政府领导执行。同时，低层级的地方政府才真正对当地房地产市场十分熟悉，这对财产税的实施十分有帮助。我们很难对所谓“正确的”管理结构下一个定义。是应该给予地方政府一些空间，使其在一定的限制下设定财产税税率？或者赋予其自由量裁权来决定应税价值？在山东这样的省份，财产税能否起到应有的作用？如果区县政府可以对财产税拥有决策权，它们可能相互竞争降低税率以吸引房地产投资。要解决该问题，可以在地级市层面来征收财产税。

车辆税[1]

提高针对车辆所有权和使用权的税收，可以作为山东省增加税收，

1　这部分分析主要来自 Bahl，Goh and Qiao，2014。

弥补城镇化成本的有效策略。中国的机动车辆数目增速高于城市人口增速（Bahl，Goh and Qiao，2014）。机动车的使用给地方政府造成了基础建设负担，产生了使用者几乎没有承担的外部成本。有近 80% 的车辆归私人所有。假如设计合理，提高车辆税能实现增收的环境友好性和有效性。

路网建设速度跟不上机动车辆增长的速度，是造成拥堵愈加严重和通勤成本提高的重要原因。结果是产生了拥挤和污染等方面的外部成本。对北京的一个研究指出，这一外部成本约占所有种类外部成本的 7.5% 至 15%（世界银行发展研究中心，2014，pp. 187—262）。

因此，中国在大城市地区对机动车使用进行控制是合理的。在部分城市，已经形成了一个良好的开端。但是，让地方政府对车辆税拥有更多的决策权理论上可以获得更好的效果。这不仅可能抑制私人车辆使用，同时还能取得新的收入来弥补过多的车辆造成的外部成本。

中国的城市可以继续使用税收和收费政策来提高拥有和使用车辆相对于使用公共交通系统的成本，或者影响购房选址决策。地方政府可以按照私人汽车使用造成的全部环境和社会成本收费，如提高牌照费用、燃油税、通行费和停车费或者多种形式的拥堵费。依靠需求的价格弹性，地方政府可以由此取得可观的收入覆盖城镇化的部分支出。如何设计车辆税，让车辆的使用达到想要的影响要比我们这里讨论的复杂，而且这与房价、土地使用限制和基建投资模式相关。但至少可以认为地方政府对汽车的所有权和使用权征税会对环境产生良好的影响，同时取得大量的税收弥补城镇化带来的基础建设开支。

目前，中国的地方政府并未对汽车征收重税。车辆注册税产生的现金流很小，而汽车的燃油税又由中央政府征收。地方政府对停车费、通行费和拥堵费的征收处于摸索阶段，数额虽在增长，但总体仍未成为地方政府的主要收入来源。

像在大多数国家一样，对机动车注册的年度征税是以发动机功率

为基础。目前以此为基础的税收大约仅占增值税共享额的6%。车辆注册税确实满足作为一个优质地方税的条件。在现有的机动车数量及其增长速度下，车辆注册税具有税收潜力。尤其重要的是，税负完全由本地承担。地方政府可以负责该税收的管理，十分简单。提高车辆注册费用可能刺激避税行为，如在低收费地区进行注册。但这些避税行为可以通过注册要求、定期检查和严厉的处罚来进行控制。机动车所有权费用的增税潜力比目前的实际执行结果大得多，一旦地方政府决定对机动车所有权征以更高的税（如果地方政府被允许这么做），收入将会显著增加。

燃油税是一个更加有利可图的税种，能够更直接地对机动车的使用进行征税。问题是在中国的大城市这能否由地方政府进行管理。最理想的情况是在加油站征税。或者退一步，可以像现在这样在燃料出厂时征税，但货物的装运目的地可以被跟踪。这可能造成税率在不同的地方也有所不同。即便在目前中央政府的税率下，对燃油征税可以使地方政府的收入显著增加。

对大城市的燃油使用更高税率征税公平吗？中国的汽油价格已经高于美国和大多数发展中国家，但是低于欧洲国家的平均水平（世界银行发展研究中心，2014，pp. 439—535）。另一方面，中国的汽油价格并不高，无法覆盖燃油消费引起的外部成本。

提高中国大都市地区的燃油税税率是否有效？在边际上，这会造成生活成本的增加，影响移民决策。汽油价格提高与城市规划目标相一致，如减少车辆使用造成的拥堵和污染，以及增加城市扩张的成本等。然而，在所有这些当中，除非税率有很大的提高，不然我们并不清楚替代弹性是否高到可以达到目的。

拥堵和尾气排放可以通过管理需求来减少。上海、北京和广州已经开始对车辆的数目进行控制。这些城市对车辆的注册进行限制，新注册的牌照设有配额。车辆管理所通过多种手段分配限额，如牌照拍

卖（上海）、摇号（北京），以及两者的结合（广州）（世界银行发展研究中心，2014，pp. 439—535）。

世界银行（世界银行发展研究中心，2014，pp. 439—535）认为，对高密度城市地区的拥堵成本和空气污染征税的最直接手段是道路费和停车费。燃油税和牌照费也能达到目的，但针对性一般。道路费在中国的高速公路上很常见，有些城市地区甚至讨论过是否应当对道路重度使用者收费。停车费是对公路使用者的另一种征税手段。从实践来看，提高停车费十分有效。停车费和税收都是具有价格弹性的，有证据表明可以有效减少汽车拥堵，降低小汽车在交通工具中的使用占比（OECD，2010）。

像山东省这样的省政府会提高车辆注册税还是燃油税？不管哪种税，应当在一个统一的税率下征收，而非由各县市制定不同的税率。否则逃税情况会非常严重。但如果想对城市地区的机动车征收更高的差别税率，那么统一的税率达不到这一目的。

地方零售税[1]

如果将税基从源头（生产地）转向目的地（消费地），销售税可以成为地方政府资金来源的有效工具（Bird，2006）。以美国为例，地方政府的零售税在消费地征收。相反，假如以源头为税基，如中国的增值税，税收在产品生产和运输节点征税，则税收的一部分可能是由其他地区的消费者负担。例如，布宜诺斯艾利斯和波哥大对销售的总收入征税，尽管并非以目的地为税基，但收入仍然可观。长久以来，废除布宜诺斯艾利斯的这种流转税的呼声很高，然而缺乏有效的替代手段使改革不断延迟。

1 这部分主要来自 Bahl，Goh and Qiao，2014。

假如对目的地税基的管理能有效合理，以某些消费品为税基的销售税收入将会十分可观，成为优质的地方税种。对如高端珠宝、耐用品和进口奢侈品等类似的消费品来说，这是很有可能的。但对大部分消费品来说，零售税的执行会刺激逃税行为，消费的节点会转移向不容易被执法部门发现的地下交易。

向非正式经销商征税存在的问题也是为什么不能将生产型消费税的收入转为在城市地区征收高税率零售税的原因。否则，特别是啤酒、白酒和香烟将会是很有吸引力的税基。这是另外的一个选择：所有的这些消费税仍然按现阶段的安排征收，但收入可以通过一些公式计算后分配给城市。这实质是一种转移支付收入，但不会赋予地方政府任何改变税率的权利。实际上，这就是一种政府间收入共享的转移支付。

中国正处于“营改增”的进程之中，需要拓宽增值税税基。然而，改革的另一方向是将营业税转变为对生产要素成本征税的地方商业增值税。Bird（2013，p. 7）认为，从法国、意大利和日本的实践来看，基于产地的地方增值税也许不仅是让厂商为其所获取的当地服务支付成本的合理办法，而且还可以在合适的管理下不造成严重的经济成本。

正如我们所讨论的，针对消费的地方税具有政府间的影响。假如只在城市地区征税，会形成很大的避税空间。假如在全省实行统一税率，却可能产生均等化的问题。一个解决方法是在全省征税，将税收的一部分直接投入收入共享资金池，剩下的部分可以由地方保留。

附加税[1]

地方税收的一些管理问题可以通过采用“附加”的方式避免，亦

1 这部分主要来自 Bahl，Goh and Qiao，2014。

即允许地方政府为中央政府税基选择一个附加税率。附加的方式在工业化国家被广泛采用。瑞士地方政府收入的主要来源就是个人所得税附加；罗马征收由中央政府设定税基的所得税附加。美国许多州的地方政府在州政府征收的零售税税基上增加一个额外税率。至少有三个城市——曼谷、莫斯科、首尔——对增值税附带自己的额外税率（Martinez－Vazquez，2013）。

在中国，城市维护建设税和教育费附加作为一种附加税已实施多年。这两种税的税基是增值税、消费税和营业税的总额，作为附加税其收入全部归地方政府所有。税率却由中央政府设定。

附加税可以被看作一种受益收费，也即享受地方公共服务应当支付的费用。[1] 改革后，现有的城市维护建设税和教育费附加将被一种"城市服务税"替代。地方政府会拥有提高附加税税率的权利。在这里，山东省拥有一些增收潜力。目前，城市维护建设税和教育费附加约占 GDP 的 0.51%。如果附加费增加 100%，作为一种"城市服务税"，产生的收入约为 GDP 的 1.02%，由此增加的收入约占营业税 880 亿元收入净损失的三分之一。

个人所得税可以作为征收附加税的税种。山东省对个人所得税征收 50% 的附加税产生的收入足以覆盖营业税收入损失的 7%。而个人所得税的有效税率仅仅从 GDP 的 0.2% 上升到 0.3%。很多有力的观点认为应当更多地使用个人所得税，这样做税负转移的可能性很小。不幸的是，个人所得税的税基过窄，收入潜力有限。此外，对劳动力已有的高税率是主要的不利条件。除非社会保障缴款率降低，否则这可能不是一个可行的办法。

这种方式还存在其他的问题。附加税是以源头为基础的税收，部分税负可以被转嫁。另外，个人所得税收入受到中央政府税收政策——

1 关于收费的争论很敏感。因为地方公司和本地居民均享受地方政府提供的服务，但增值税和销售税是源头导向型，所以如果地方公司与其他地区有贸易往来，有部分税收负担会转嫁到其他地区。

如逐渐提高免征额和降低税率等——的影响很大。另一方面，按照国务院的规定，今后城市维护建设税和教育费附加并入公共财政预算之中，不再专款专用，因此这与国务院改革的精神是一致的。

由于税收可能会集中于个别区县，个人所得税附加可能将造成公平问题。执行个人所得税较高税率的地区在竞争中处于不利地位。即使税率是统一的，还有会让拥有企业的地方政府实现税收积累，却把给通勤的劳动力提供住所的地方政府排除在外的问题。一个解决方法是将其作为省级政府税收，然后投入共享资金池，用于均等化支出。另一种方法是将其视为使用城市公共服务的征税，允许地方政府在一定的基础上保留该收入，并在均等化转移支付分配体系中考虑这一因素。

政府间转移支付

中央政府可以通过增加一般转移支付的方法弥补“营改增”下地方政府的收入缺口，途径有两种：一是建立补偿性的补贴制度，二是增加对所有地方政府的垂直转移支付比例。实际上，如果目的仅为弥补营业税收入损失，以上两种途径都不会太奏效。

山东省在第一种途径下可能会做得更好，尽管第二种途径可能是更好的公共政策。我们以取消营业税为例进行说明。在 2014 年的预算中，山东省的收入净损失约为 880 亿元人民币。在补偿性的补贴制度下，中央政府会补贴给山东省同等数额的资金以覆盖损失。这相当于 2014 年专项转移支付和一般性转移支付的 70%。补偿性补贴制度在世界上有广泛的应用，目的是补偿地方政府由于中央政府的行为而受到的损失。但是这一制度的问题在于，对未来的收入通常没有安排。不管是南非还是巴基斯坦，重要的地方税被中央废除，但相应的补贴却

不随地方税增长率增长。结果是地方政府越来越依赖中央补贴，而这些补贴对税基却缺乏弹性。

第二种途径可能在山东省并不那么受欢迎，但却可能是一个好的公共政策。在这种情况下，中央政府需要按照全国营业税损失额增加一般性转移支付资金池中的资金数额。这部分资金会像其他无条件转移支付一样进行分配。由于山东省获得的人均转移支付低于其他省份，因此即使是在第一年，山东省也可能无法获得与营业税收入损失数额相等的转移支付。

第七章　结论及展望

山东省正在进行一场有魄力的财政改革。改革方案充分遵循了国务院的规定，直面该省遇到的问题，实现了国务院法规与地区实际情况的结合，具有完善财政制度的巨大潜力。

山东省政府对改革寄予很高的期望。省长郭树清如是评价：

“各级要进一步提高对公共财政职能的认识，强化公共财政理念，不断调整财政支出结构，增强政府公共服务能力，提高财政资金使用效率，全面推进财税制度改革，着力构建现代财政体系。[1]”

改革的一般性评价

山东省正努力推进财税管理体制的现代化，调整税收行为，完善政府间财政关系。改革举措大部分与国际上好的做法相一致，紧密遵循了国务院法规，立足于解决山东省目前在政府间财政安排方面存在的许多问题。在人民代表大会决议的指导下，改革涉及支出效率、收入安排，以及省内均等化等方面。

在改革派省长的领导下，山东省推出了一系列强有力的改革措施，一旦执行便可从三个亟待改革的方面显著提高公共财政能力。贯彻执行新预算法，可以有效地提高支出绩效；合理化征税手段和逐步取消

1　http：//www. sd. xinhuanet. com/ldhd/2013 – 06/22/c_ 116245333. htm

税收优惠，可以增加财政收入；省内政府间转移支付体系不断改进，可以更好地实现均等化目标。

改革方案有三个支撑点。第一，通过对无效率的支出行为、过度负债和腐败设立防范措施，使财税管理更加透明，从而实现财税管理的现代化。第二，通过税制改革进一步将政府和竞争性部门的职能分开。第三，完善和简化省级财政体系，进一步实现富裕和贫困地区之间的公平。

财税管理

新预算法的实施是财税管理最重要的举措。通过要求省和地方政府将与政府行为有关财务收支全部纳入预算，该法消除了预算外收支的可能性。此外，该法将地方政府的四个分预算整合在一起，极大地提高了预算的透明度。预算的重心也由控制性转向计划性，并引入跨年度预算。专项转移支付的取消将会增大计划支出规划的灵活性。这都是十分重要的改革。

计划于2017年完成的国库收付制度会成为预算法的补充，增强对资金的管理。此外，新法规将逐步取消大部分的专项资金，禁止增设预算项目。同时设立预算稳定基金平滑化短期内的财政盈亏，避免一般性预算中的大量资金结余。

债务框架的建立将会限制政府举债。所有地方债务的举借必须得到省政府的批准，并纳入预算。禁止利用融资平台进行融资，现存的（不合规定的）债务则会被“清理”。

山东省的改革中，假如财税管理部分实施成功，政府支出制度将会更有效。改革会使一些资金从劣后级项目中释放出来，转而投向基本服务项目。如果如我们所料，这会产生间接收入效应。

大多数呼吁全面改革的建议都存在问题。理清地方政府四类预算

之间的关系是前进的重要一步。但是，目前经常性预算和资本预算仍被忽略。关键在于资本投资规划和跨年度预算能否在没有资本预算的情况下有效执行。

第二个问题与坚持硬预算约束有关。改革方案呼吁对年度赤字进行紧急救助和当年支付补贴。如果问题是收入流不稳定，或者项目支出有延期，出现未能预期的经济波动时，这类方法是有效的。假如政府对预算稳定基金的收支平衡设有一个安全线，资金则可有效运转。但如果这种赤字是由结构问题（如超支或收入低增长）引起，允许年度预算列赤字可能变得有风险。对中国而言，设立防范措施十分重要，因为地方政府没有征税立法权来筹集额外资金用于经常性支出。当收入增速超过支出时，预算稳定基金对年度收支不平衡的熨平作用才会更明显。

在债务管理改革上，新增债务如何偿还这一点是不清晰的，我们也不清楚风险分析会如何进行。区县一级的政府除了土地出让收入外并没有其他独立的财政收入来源。但在政府性基金内，这一来源将被指定作为专项债的偿债资金源。那么一般公共预算内的借款偿债来源是什么？一种可能性是新债务可用转移支付偿还，但这样会模糊债务与转移支付之间的界限。

最后，改革的实施策略和时间表也存在问题。在山东省 140 个区县中，有的属于市区，对财政实务有着相对丰富的经验，有的属于地方县市，资源和能力有限，实行这些改革措施仍有困难。改革要顺利实施，离不开省政府强有力的领导，对地方政府持续进行监管并提供培训。当然，这也可能会进一步拖延改革的进行。

税收改革

第二方面的改革集中于如何进一步理顺公共部门和竞争部门的关

系。山东省的改革方案建议建立一套完备的纳税人信息系统，提高征收率，降低征收成本和纳税遵从成本。更重要的是，为企业提供补贴的做法将停止。在税收方面，除非经过国务院批准，企业的税收优惠均将废止。这些优惠现在可能包括免税和退税，也包括当政府税收目标完成时企业应缴但未交部分税收。

山东省的改革方案对政府收入问题提出了良好的建议，通过改进信息系统提高税收管理效率，取消可自行决定的税收优惠等。山东省税收缺乏努力可能是因为其管理薄弱，税收优惠过于慷慨，改革方案对此并未进行评估。在我们看来，方案指明的方向正确无误，然而最终能多大程度上解决税收短缺的问题仍未可知。一些非直接的证据表明，收入流失十分巨大。山东省的税收征收率（以税收相对于 GDP 衡量）比全国平均水平低了整 3 个百分点。但是在年度预算中，对收入潜力进行这样的非直接估算并不能成为对税式支出进行完全统计等正规做法的有效替代。

税收改革的实施肯定会遇到问题，需要足够多的时间来解决。税收优惠政策可能业已确立，不易撤销，政府甚至对此有文件规定。多年以来，政府利用这一政策支持地方产业，且认定税收优惠对过去的高速经济增长具有不可忽视的作用。间接促进经济发展的途径——提供良好服务——并未被重视，看起来也不那么令人满意。此外，当经济增速已然下滑时，要取消一直以来被视为能够有效刺激经济发展的优惠变得愈加困难重重。我们注意到，近期国务院新规似乎要求对取消税收优惠不能过于激进。限制税收优惠是好政策，对增收也有促进作用，但实施起来将会十分缓慢。

政府间财政关系

山东省目前的困扰有三个：一是支出责任与管理责任的划分可能

并不合理；二是省以下地方政府的收入分配可能并不充分均等；三是政府间转移支付制度的结构存在缺陷。

山东省的改革方案明确指出了困扰的关键所在，解决方案也遵循国际上的实践经验。第一，现有支出职能的责任划分将会依据减少责任模糊为原则进行复议。这会使得山东省的省、地市、区县三个层级的支出责任划分产生改变。改革要求重新划分责任，并于 2015 年在教育、卫生和交通方面进行试点。

改革正应从此着手。一定程度上，政府发现外部性和规模经济得到的重视不够，可能会转向更加集权一些的财政体制。在该体制中，县级政府的直接支出责任比现在小一些，更多的责任转移给了省级政府。

第二个需要解决的主要问题是地方政府间巨大的财政差异。省政府在改革中的目标是构建统一的收入分享机制，减少这种差异。尽管在 2013 年对该分享机制进行过改进，取得了显著的改善，但仍存在一些重大的问题。更重要的是，山东省需要确定最终要实现多大程度上的均等。具体的收入分享方案尚未成型，但从改革指出的方向看来，收入的分配将建立在确定规则的基础上。

第三，改革方案要求减少专项转移支付，增加一般性转移支付，取消资金配套要求，完善省与地方政府之间的转移支付结构。这将使系统简单化和透明化，赋予支出决策者更多的决策空间。对政府间转移支付体系的改革，方案目前并未涉及细节问题，但减少专项转移支付的想法与中央政策一致。对均等性转移支付系统的改革势在必行，但改革方案中尚未提及如何筹集这部分资金、与共享税税收相比资金规模有多大，以及实现均等的程度等问题。

山东财政改革的这一要点并不像其他两个那样深入，方案主要是描述了将采用什么样的方法。政府间财政改革方案呼吁省政府解决一些基本问题，包括是否应当将更多的政府治理决策权从县级政府收回

至上级政府，以及公共服务水平均等化与刺激经济增长之间如何权衡。

展　望

山东省在财政改革上付出了努力，制定了财税管理体制现代化的规划，在提高支出效率和增加财政收入的同时，减少浪费并解决一些腐败问题。山东省紧密地遵循了国务院的法规，吸取了许多有益的国际经验，将成为其他省份学习的榜样。然而，要发挥改革方案作为规划和指导工具的作用，则必须对方案的目标进行深化和细化，并根据目标和实施进程不断进行调整。

省政府的政策领导

中国的地方政府并不像工业化国家的地方政府那样在许多预算决策上拥有自主权，他们不具有开征税收的权力。实际上，公共财政预算的范围是中央政府设定的。但是，省和省以下政府在某些方面拥有自主权，能对财政施加影响。在下一个版本的改革中，省级政府可能会对其政府间财政政策的立场进行阐述，主要包括以下方面：

（1）山东省是中国政府治理结构最为分散的省份之一。收支分配的复杂性是否会引起省级层面治理的集中化？

（2）整个改革方案是否将促成政府部门与竞争性部门的分离？是否会大规模地取消企业补贴和税收优惠？新成立的产业升级基金是否会将政府拉回到一个与竞争性部门保持更紧密联系的位置上来？

（3）省与地方政府之间的转移支付是否会建立在明确的规则之上？还是仍然保持现有的体系，赋予省级政府或地级政府更多的自由裁量权，由其根据判断来分配资金？

（4）收入分享均等化资金合适的规模是多少？

（5）省向省以下地方政府的转移支付是否会朝着少一些专项转移支付，多一些一般性转移支付的方向改变？是否所有的资金配套要求都会被取消？

（6）在还本付息能力有限的情况下，省政府应当如何管理监督地方政府的一般责任性举债行为？

（7）在硬化地方政府预算约束上，省级政府将会采取多么强硬的态度？

（8）山东省是否会极力消除不正当激励以求实现改革目标？

改革方案的年度修订

为了保证按照改革方案对公共财政体制进行改进的持续性，方案不仅需要深化和细化，也需要定期修订。“一次性”的方案在指导公共财政改革上没有持久生命力。当前版本的改革方案所包含的以数值度量的条款甚少。例如，缺少现阶段税收优惠的数额、为支持经济发展直接补偿给企业的补贴数额，以及省与地方政府之间转移支付的数额等数据。

掌握切实的数据对改革方案进行年度修订将有利于：

（1）修正改革目标；

（2）规划预算；

（3）对不同地区地方政府和政府官员的改革进展进行排名和监督；

（4）识别困难和障碍，并制定解决策略。

实施的问题

山东省改革方案的主要问题在于是否能够及时有效地按计划实施。

有四个重要的方面需要注意。第一，清除一些根深蒂固但适得其反的做法，使改革更容易实施。将私人部门完全从公共部门剥离开不是一件容易的事。竞争性部门已经习惯了政府各种各样的补贴和税收优惠。要让地方政府官员撇开与竞争性部门的直接关系的困难程度，或者要将政府与私人部门完全划清界限需要多长时间，都尚未可知。跟进这方面的进展是一个优先任务。

第二，也是更困难的一方面，提高地方政府公务员的专业能力。从某种意义上讲，新预算法要求财税管理上的深刻改变，因此必须加大对培训和监管的投入。特别是在一些农村地区，即使没有新法的出台，公务员的知识水平仍有待提高。随着改革的推进，建立一个公务员专业能力培养体系十分重要，否则将成为阻碍改革推进的一个重要障碍。

第三，调查跟进财政制度中不正当激励的影响并制定调整政策解决这一问题十分重要。

最后，由于实施该方案的工作繁多，财政制度因此受到冲击的可能性也会增加，制定实施计划十分有必要[1]。省级政府可以根据计划来决定改革推进的顺序。

1 关于财政改革顺序的讨论，请参见 Bahl and Martinez - Vazquez（2006）。

附录1 图 表

表1 **山东省人口结构表**

年份	人口数（百万人）	全国排名	城镇人口比例（%）
2000	90. 0	2	26. 8
2001	90. 4	2	27. 8
2002	90. 8	2	29. 0
2003	91. 3	2	31. 1
2004	91. 8	2	32. 2
2005	92. 5	2	45. 0
2006	93. 1	3	46. 1
2007	93. 7	2	46. 8
2008	94. 2	3	47. 6
2009	94. 7	3	48. 3
2010	95. 9	2	49. 7
2011	96. 4	2	51. 0
2012	96. 8	2	52. 4
2013	97. 3	2	53. 8

数据来源：万德数据库、中国经济数据库。

表 2　　2013 年山东省公共服务水平

项　目	山东省	全国平均水平
医疗（每万人）		
医院床位数	50.32	45.5
医生人数	62	53
护士人数	25	20
环境（万吨）		
二氧化硫排放量	164.5	65.93
一氧化氮排放量	165.1	71.85
粉尘排放量	69.7	41.23
固体垃圾排放量	18 172	10 571
危险物排放量	509	105
人口		
0—14 岁人数（%）	15.48	16.4
25—64 岁人数（%）	73.54	73.9
65 岁以上人数（%）	10.98	9.68
婴儿死亡率（%）	2.42	2.69
行政在职人员供给系数[1]	30	27
教育		
每十万人小学生人数	6 463	6 913
小学师生比（%）	16.16	16.76
每十万人初中生人数	3 283	3 279
初中师生比（%）	12.08	12.76
每十万人高中生人数	3 213	3 227
高中师生比（%）	14.43	14.95
文盲率	4.97	4.88
交通（每百万人）		
铁路里程（公里）	44	75.81
公路里程（公里）	2 606	3 202.09
内河通航里程（公里）	11.52	92.57

数据来源：国家统计局。

1　行政在职人员供给系数 = 人口数/行政在职人员数。

表3 山东省国内生产总值情况

年份	GDP（亿元）	占中国GDP的比例（%）	排名	人均GDP（元）	排名	地市级人均GDP（元）	县级人均GDP（元）
2000	8 340	8	3	9 326	9	10 951	
2001	9 200	8	3	10 195	9	12 150	
2002	10 280	8	3	11 340	9	13 570	
2003	12 080	9	3	13 268	7	16 267	
2004	15 020	9	2	16 413	7	20 034	14 094
2005	18 520	10	3	19 934	7	24 027	17 295
2006	22 080	10	2	23 603	7	28 404	20 540
2007	25 970	10	3	27 604	7	33 526	24 492
2008	30 930	10	3	32 936	8	39 942	29 235
2009	33 900	10	3	35 894	8	42 269	32 371
2010	39 170	10	3	41 106	9	48 615	36 317
2011	45 360	9	3	47 335	10	55 259	
2012	50 010	9	3	51 768	10	57 791	
2013	55 230	9	3	56 323	10	62 461	
2014	59 430	9	3				

数据来源：万德数据库、中国经济数据库。

表 4　　山东省国内生产总值结构

年份	第一产业（%）		第二产业（%）		第三产业（%）	
	山东	全国	山东	全国	山东	全国
2000	15	15	50	45	35	40
2001	15	14	50	45	36	41
2002	14	13	50	44	36	42
2003	12	12	54	45	34	42
2004	12	13	56	46	32	41
2005	11	12	57	47	32	41
2006	10	11	57	47	33	42
2007	10	10	57	47	33	43
2008	10	10	57	47	33	43
2009	10	10	56	46	35	44
2010	9	10	54	46	37	44
2011	9	10	53	46	38	44
2012	9	10	51	45	40	46
2013	9	9	50	44	41	47
2014	8	9	48	43	43	48

数据来源：万德数据库、中国经济数据库。

注：

1. 第二产业包括工业和建筑业。

2. 第三产业包括：（1）交通运输、仓储和邮政业；（2）批发和零售业；（3）住宿和餐饮业；（4）银行和保险业；（5）房地产业；（6）国家机关、政党机关、社会团体。

表 5　　2013 年中国各省、市、自治区支出分级情况

地区	支出数（十亿元）				支出百分比（%）		
	总支出	省级	地市级	县级	省级	地市级	县级
北京市	417.4	170.2	230.3	16.9	40.8	55.2	4.0
天津市	254.9	104.1	135.8	15	40.8	53.3	5.9
河北省	441	71.5	84.2	285.2	16.2	19.1	64.7
山西省	303	61.9	58.3	182.9	20.4	19.2	60.4
内蒙古自治区	368.7	57.6	85	226	15.6	23.1	61.3
辽宁省	519.7	64.4	162	293.3	12.4	31.2	56.4
吉林省	274.5	60.4	76.3	137.8	22.0	27.8	50.2
黑龙江省	336.9	78.5	92	166.4	23.3	27.3	49.4
上海市	452.9	159.1	281.9	11.9	35.1	62.2	2.6
江苏省	779.8	87	175.1	517.8	11.2	22.5	66.4
浙江省	473	48.2	84.7	340.2	10.2	17.9	71.9
安徽省	435	59.6	125.2	250.1	13.7	28.8	57.5
福建省	306.9	42.1	75.3	189.4	13.7	24.5	61.7
江西省	347	54.5	54.4	238.1	15.7	15.7	68.6
山东省	**668.9**	**66.7**	**161.7**	**440.5**	**10.0**	**24.2**	**65.9**
河南省	558.2	79	134.5	344.7	14.2	24.1	61.8
湖北省	437.2	48.4	111.1	277.6	11.1	25.4	63.5
湖南省	469.1	80.8	103	285.3	17.2	22.0	60.8
广东省	841.1	118.6	319.3	403.1	14.1	38.0	47.9
广西壮族自治区	320.9	61.7	64.6	194.7	19.2	20.1	60.7
海南省	101.1	27	22.9	51.3	26.7	22.7	50.7
重庆市	306.2	96.3	135	74.9	31.5	44.1	24.5
四川省	622.1	84.2	114.9	423	13.5	18.5	68.0
贵州省	308.3	65	36.5	206.8	21.1	11.8	67.1
云南省	409.7	87.3	63.3	259.1	21.3	15.5	63.2
西藏自治区	101.4	49.5	20.3	31.6	48.8	20.0	31.2
陕西省	366.5	80.8	87.3	198.4	22.0	23.8	54.1
甘肃省	231	47.3	36.9	146.7	20.5	16.0	63.5
青海省	122.8	48.8	16.3	57.7	39.7	13.3	47.0
宁夏回族自治区	92.2	21.9	23.1	47.3	23.8	25.1	51.3
新疆维吾尔自治区	306.7	80.9	46.7	179.1	26.4	15.2	58.4

数据来源：《2013 年地方政府财政运行分析》，财政部预算司。

注：台湾省、香港特别行政区、澳门特别行政区数据未示出。

表 6　　2014 年全国及山东省财政运行情况

项　　目	山东省	全国平均水平
人均支出（元）		
人均一般公共预算支出	7 331	9 438
人均政府性基金预算支出	4 047	3 540
人均国有资本经营预算支出	27	42
人均社会保险基金预算支出	2 197	2 462
支出占 GDP 的比例（%）		
一般公共预算支出	12.08	20.28
政府性基金预算支出	6.67	7.61
国有资本经营预算支出	0.04	0.09
社会保险基金预算支出	3.62	5.29
人均财政收入（元）		
人均一般公共预算收入	5 135	5 546
人均政府性基金预算收入	4 059	3 655
人均国有资本经营预算收入	27	45
人均社会保险基金预算收入	2 470	2 865
财政收入占 GDP 的比例（%）		
一般公共预算收入	8.46	11.92
政府性基金预算收入	6.69	7.86
国有资本经营预算收入	0.98	0.10
社会保险基金预算收入	4.07	6.16
中央转移支付		
人均中央转移支付（元）	2 054	3 773
中央转移支付占 GDP 的比例（%）	3.4	8.1
截至 2013 年 6 月底政府性债务		
人均政府性债务（元）	7 261	17 040
政府性债务占 GDP 的比例（%）	11.96	28.11

数据来源：财政部官网；审计署官网；《2015 年 2 月山东财政预算公开专刊》。

表7　　2014年山东省一般公共预算收入

项　　目	预算执行数（百万元）	人均金额（元）	占GDP比例（%）
税收收入	396 564	4 051	6.7
增值税	59 696	610	1.0
营业税	113 592	1 160	1.9
企业所得税	48 289	493	0.8
个人所得税	11 518	118	0.2
资源税	11 957	122	0.2
城市维护建设税	23 133	236	0.4
房产税	12 249	125	0.2
印花税	6 056	62	0.1
城镇土地使用税	26 469	270	0.4
土地增值税	25 774	263	0.4
车船税	4 665	48	0.1
契税	27 367	280	0.5
其他税收收入	25 800	264	0.4
非税收入	106 107	1 084	1.8
专项收入	15 352	157	0.3
行政事业性收费收入	30 220	309	0.5
国有资源（资产）有偿使用收入	38 195	390	0.6
其他收入	22 340	228	0.4
本年收入合计	502 671	5 135	8.5
债务收入	16 200	165	0.3
地方政府债券收入	16 200	165	0.3
转移性收入	275 036	2 810	4.6
返还型收入	42 685	436	0.7
一般性转移支付收入	86 443	883	1.5
专项转移支付收入	71 942	735	1.2
调入资金	19 586	200	0.3
上年结转及结余收入	54 380	556	0.9
收入总计	793 907	8 110	13.4

数据来源：《2015年2月山东财政预算公开专刊》。

表 8　　山东省济南市市中区及商河县财政情况对比

项　目	市中区		商河县	
	金额（百万元）	比例（%）	金额（百万元）	比例（%）
税收收入	7 637	93.13	513	76.68
增值税	980		47	
营业税	2 628		198	
企业所得税	1 554		44	
非税收入	563	6.87	156	23.32
一般公共预算收入	8 200	100	669	100
一般公共预算支出	3 207		2 102	
转移支付	-4 993		1 433	
人均公共财政预算支出	6 286		3 681	

数据来源：市中区官网、商河县官网。

注：市中区的数据为 2014 年数据；商河县数据为 2013 年数据。

表 9　　2014 年山东省四本预算收支执行情况

项　目	金额（百万元）	人均金额（元）	占 GDP 比例（%）
一般公共预算			
一般公共预算收入	793 907	8 110	13.36
税收及非税收入	502 671	5 135	8.46
转移性收入	201 070	2 054	3.38
调入资金	19 586	200	0.33
上年结转及结余	54 379	555	0.92
债务收入	16 200	165	0.27
一般公共预算支出	793 907	8 110	13.36
本年支出	717 590	7 330	12.08
上解支出	8 333	85	0.14
债务支出	5 332	54	0.09
预算稳定调节基金	17 801	182	0.30
结转下年支出	44 283	452	0.75
累计净结余	567	6	0.01

续表

项 目	金额（百万元）	人均金额（元）	占 GDP 比例（%）
政府性基金预算			
收入总计	476 584	4 868	8.02
本年收入	397 366	4 059	6.69
上级补助收入	8 782	90	0.15
调入资金	2 879	29	0.05
上年结转及结余收入	67 556	690	1.14
支出总计	476 584	4 868	8.02
本年支出	396 171	4 047	6.67
上解上级支出	197	2	0.00
调出资金	7 602	78	0.13
累计结余	72 613	742	1.22
国有资本经营预算			
收入总计	3 050	31	0.05
本年收入	2 672	27	0.04
上年结转收入	378	4	0.01
支出总计	3 050	31	0.05
本年支出	2 631	27	0.04
结余	419	4	0.01
社会保障基金预算			
收入总计	241 778	2 470	4.07
本年收入	187 930	1 920	3.16
财政补贴收入	40 573	414	0.68
支出总计	215 068	2 197	3.62
支出	208 907	2 134	3.52

数据来源：《2015 年 2 月山东财政预算公开专刊》。

表 10　　山东省财政支出情况

年份	人均 GDP（元）	排名	人均财政收入[a)]（元）	排名	人均财政支出（元）	排名	人均转移支付[b)]（元）	排名	转移支付[b)]/GDP	排名
2000	9 326	9	515	9	681	21	212	31	2%	30
2001	10 195	9	634	9	834	21	231	31	2%	30
2002	11 340	9	672	9	948	22	311	31	3%	31
2003	13 268	7	782	9	1 108	21	361	31	3%	30
2004	16 413	7	902	9	1 296	21	450	31	3%	31
2005	19 934	7	1 160	10	1 585	22	497	31	2%	28
2006	23 603	7	1 457	10	1 970	22	620	29	3%	28
2007	27 604	7	1 789	10	2 415	22	727	29	3%	27
2008	32 936	8	2 078	11	2 872	24	892	28	3%	27
2009	35 894	8	2 322	11	3 451	28	1 205	28	3%	26
2010	41 106	9	2 868	12	4 323	27	1 382	28	3%	27
2011	47 335	10	3 586	13	5 190	29	1 783	28	4%	25
2012	51 768	10	4 191	14	6 097	29	2 007	28	4%	25
2013	56 323	10	4 685	15	6 872	28				

数据来源：万德数据库、中国经济数据库。

注：

a）财政收入包括税收收入及非税收入，不包括转移支付收入。

b）转移支付指中央政府转移支付。

表 11　　山东省地市级及县级财政经济情况差异

在地市级层面：

地市级人均 GDP（元）	2004 年	2005 年	2006 年	2007 年	2008 年	2009 年	2010 年	2011 年	2012 年
平均值	20 034	24 027	28 404	33 526	39 942	42 269	48 615	55 259	57 791
最高值	49 909	64 606	79 766	90 928	111 574	111 543	127 654	143 921	144 778
最低值	4 147	5 090	5 961	7 504	8 933	10 190	12 798	16 105	21 436
标准差	12 046	15 048	18 241	20 646	24 637	24 575	28 030	31 233	29 203
变异系数	60%	63%	64%	62%	62%	58%	58%	57%	51%

地市级人均财政支出（元）	2004 年	2005 年	2006 年	2007 年	2008 年	2009 年	2010 年	2011 年	2012 年
平均值	1 250	1 564	1 869	2 338	2 762	3 254	4 138	5 048	5 673
最高值	3 052	3 541	3 534	4 237	4 877	5 702	7 678	9 669	10 055
最低值	457	569	765	1 045	1 256	1 503	1 950	2 396	3 361
标准差	719	841	879	1 050	1 215	1 368	1 728	2 148	1 972
变异系数	57%	54%	47%	45%	44%	42%	42%	43%	35%

数据来源：万德数据库、中国经济数据库。

注：包括 17 个山东省地级市。

在县级层面：

县级人均 GDP（元）	2004 年	2005 年	2006 年	2007 年	2008 年	2009 年	2010 年
平均值	14 094	17 295	20 540	24 492	29 235	32 371	36 317
最高值	46 669	53 036	63 624	75 714	90 483	100 786	116 316
最低值	3 457	3 922	4 496	5 473	6 625	7 401	9 125
标准差	8 683	10 903	13 172	15 755	18 675	21 246	23 761
变异系数	62%	63%	64%	64%	64%	66%	65%

县级人均财政支出（元）	2004 年	2005 年	2006 年	2007 年	2008 年	2009 年	2010 年	2011 年	2012 年
平均值	777	958	1 209	1 518	1 808	2 106	2 680	3 335	4 066
最高值	2 668	3 436	3 489	4 566	6 346	7 062	8 970	9 901	11 108
最低值	307	370	505	670	849	1 075	1 102	1 556	2 030
标准差	426	548	649	781	982	1 101	1 366	1 684	1 964
变异系数	55%	57%	54%	51%	54%	52%	51%	50%	48%

数据来源：万德数据库、中国经济数据库。

注：包括 92 个县，不含市辖区。

表 12　　全国及山东省土地出让金情况

年份	全国		山东省	
	金额（十亿元）	占 GDP 比例（%）	金额（十亿元）	占 GDP 比例（%）
2010	2 710	6.6		
2011	3 150	6.5		
2012	2 889	5.4		
2013	4 125	7.0	286.5	5.2
2014	4 260	6.7	309.8	5.2

数据来源：国土资源部官网，山东预算报告。

表 13　　截至 2013 年 6 月全国及山东省地方政府性债务情况

债务类型	全国		山东省	
	金额（十亿元）	占 GDP 比例	金额（十亿元）	占 GDP 比例
负有偿还责任的债务	10 885.920	17%	449.913	8%
负有担保责任的债务	2 665.577	4%	121.868	2%
可能承担一定救助责任的债务	4 339.372	7%	138.999	3%
总计	17 890.870	28%	710.780	13%

数据来源：审计署。

表 14　补偿“营改增”税收损失的可能途径——基于 2014 年预算数据

项　目	途径	收入变化额（亿元）
营业税	废除	-1 130
“营改增” A 计划	不改变分享比例	250
“营改增” B 计划	50% 分享比例	1 100
城市维护建设税及教育费附加	增收 100%	300
个人所得税附加	增收 50%	60
四种房产税	将房产税征收额提高至 GDP 的 2%	160
提升税收监管水平	取消等额于 1% GDP 的税收优惠	590

数据来源：《2015 年 2 月山东财政预算公开专刊》。

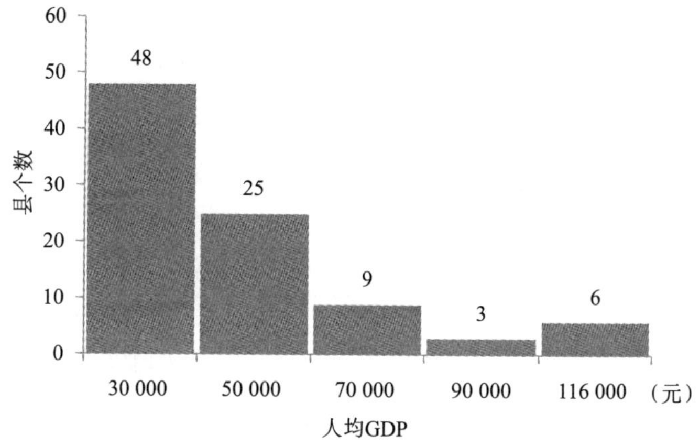

图 1　山东省人均 GDP 县级分布情况表

数据来源：万德数据库、中国经济数据库。

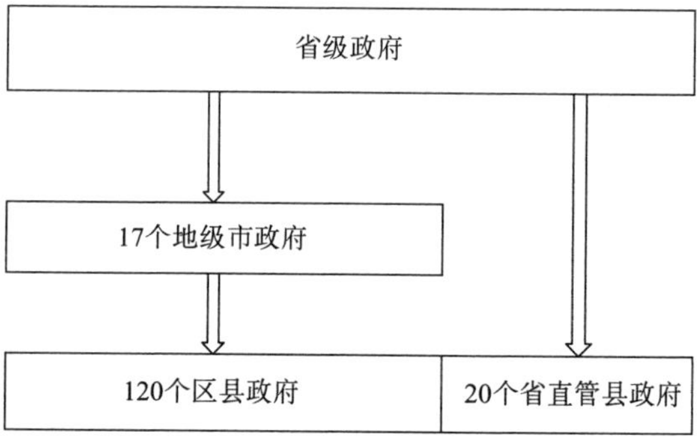

图 2　山东省的政府行政结构图

附录 2　回归分析

回归 A：计算山东省税收努力

通过回归分析计算山东省税收努力。征税能力（T/Y）通过外生变量（Xi）的回归函数得到。Ti = 第 i 个省的税收收入；Yi = 第 i 个省的 GDP；X_1 表示人均 GDP，用于衡量税基；X_2 表示第二产业占 GDP 的比例；X_3 表示第三产业占 GDP 的比例；X_4 表示城镇化率。

预期所有变量与征税能力之间呈正相关关系。通过三种不同测算方法得到的结果见表 A－1。我们发现影响征税能力的主要因素如下：

表 A－1　　测算征税能力回归结果

变量	税收占 GDP 的比重		
	(1)	(2)	(3)
X_1	0.00948 **	－0.0103 **	0.00662
	(0.00471)	(0.00429)	(0.00490)
X_2	0.0969 ***		0.0870 ***
	(0.0211)		(0.0219)
X_3	0.0939 ***		0.0974 ***
	(0.0148)		(0.0153)
X_4		0.00652	0.00724
		(0.00529)	(0.00524)
常数项	－0.0758 *	0.137 ***	－0.0539
	(0.0428)	(0.0351)	(0.0441)

续表

变量	税收占 GDP 的比重		
	(1)	(2)	(3)
观察值	537	524	524
R^2	0.755	0.725	0.753
省的个数	30	30	30

注：括号内为标准误：*** $p<0.01$，** $p<0.05$，* $p<0.1$

所有变量的值均取对数。

税收努力（E_i）的算式为：$E_i=(T/Y)_i/(\widehat{T/Y})_i$

通过三种方法测算得出山东省的税收努力情况如表 A－2：

表 A－2　　山东省税收努力情况

年份	方法一		方法二		方法三	
	税收努力	排名	税收努力	排名	税收努力	排名
1994	0.67	27	0.67	26	0.69	26
1995	0.67	27	0.68	25	0.68	25
1996	0.72	27	0.73	24	0.73	25
1997	0.80	25	0.80	22	0.82	22
1998	0.85	24	0.84	22	0.87	20
1999	0.89	20	0.87	18	0.91	18
2000	0.92	17	0.89	19	0.94	15
2001	0.94	15	0.92	13	0.96	14
2002	0.93	18	0.89	18	0.95	16
2003	0.94	16	0.89	18	0.96	15
2004	0.89	19	0.83	20	0.91	18
2005	0.86	22	0.82	20	0.87	22
2006	0.84	23	0.82	21	0.85	22
2007	0.80	23	0.80	22	0.81	23
2008	0.75	25	0.76	26	0.76	25
2009	0.75	25	0.74	25	0.76	25
2010	0.75	25	0.76	24	0.75	25
2011	0.73	28	0.74	26	0.73	28

回归 B：计算山东省转移支付缺口

我们简单计算了山东省人均转移支付缺口，通过人均 GDP、行政在职人员供给系数[1]、人口密度等变量建立回归方程，分别对总转移支付、一般转移支付和专项转移支付进行回归测算。

自变量包括：x_1 人均 GDP；x_2 行政在职人员供给系数；x_3 人口密度。

回归结果表明三个自变量均显著，且与预期一致，见表 B－1。

表 B－1　转移支付回归结果

变量	(1)	(2)	(3)
	总转移支付	一般转移支付	专项转移支付
人均 GDP	-0.6^{***}	-0.6^{***}	-0.6^{***}
	(0.16)	(0.15)	(0.18)
行政在职人员供给系数	-2.1^{***}	-2.1^{***}	-2.1^{***}
	(0.22)	(0.22)	(0.25)
人口密度	-0.3^{**}	-0.3^{**}	-0.3^{*}
	(0.14)	(0.13)	(0.16)
常数项	23.97^{***}	23.38^{***}	23.44^{***}
	(2.39)	(2.34)	(2.75)
观察值	30	30	30
R 方	0.82	0.82	0.79

注：括号内为标准误：*** $p<0.01$，** $p<0.05$，* $p<0.1$。所有变量值均取对数。

通过回归方程我们计算得到转移支付的期望值。我们发现转移支付的期望值与实际值之间有很大的差异，期望值较实际值高很多。人均总转移支付的期望值与实际值之间的缺口为 859 元，一般转移支付缺口为 562 元，专项转移支付缺口为 297 元，见表 B－2。

1　行政在职人员供给系数 = 人口数/行政在职人员数。

表 B－2　　山东省转移支付缺口

指标	(1)	(2)	(3)
	总转移支付	一般转移支付	专项转移支付
山东省			
期望值	2 888	1 818	1 070
真实值	2 029	1 256	773
缺口	859	562	297
全国			
平均值	5 232	3 236	1 996

注：以上表中总转移支付、一般转移支付和专项转移支付的值均为人均数。

回归 C：全国 30 个省、自治区、直辖市[1]人均财政支出的影响因素

我们通过 2000—2013 年的数据建立 OLS 模型，测算中国 30 个省（自治区、直辖市）人均财政支出的影响因素。模型一的自变量为人均 GDP；模型二的自变量为人均 GDP 和人口数。回归结果如下：

表 C－1　　人均财政支出回归结果

变量	(1)	(2)
	人均财政支出	人均财政支出
人均 GDP	0.64***	0.59***
	(0.03)	(0.019)
人口	—	-0.33***
	—	(0.012)
常数项	2.3***	8.55***
	(0.29)	(0.33)
观察值	420	420
R^2	0.88	0.96

括号内为标准误：*** $p<0.01$，** $p<0.05$，* $p<0.1$。所有变量值均取对数。

1　台湾省、西藏自治区、香港特别行政区、澳门特别行政区除外。

回归 D：计算山东省县级财政支出的收入弹性

我们通过一个固定效应模型分析山东省 91 个县县级财政支出的收入弹性。因变量为人均财政支出，自变量为人均 GDP。回归结果见表 D－1。

表 D－1　　山东省 91 个县人均财政支出回归结果

变量	县级人均财政支出
人均 GDP	0.70***
	(51.75)
常数项	－0.04
	(－0.32)
观察值	637
R^2	0.90

注：括号内为标准误：*** $p<0.01$，** $p<0.05$，* $p<0.1$。所有变量值均取对数。

参考文献

[1] Bahl, Roy (1971) "A Regression Approach to Tax Effort and Tax Ratio Analysis" International Monetary Fund Staff Papers, Vol 18. No. 3.

[2] Bahl, Roy (1999). Fiscal policy in China: Taxation and intergovernmental fiscal relations (San Francisco: 1990 Institute and University of Michigan Press).

[3] Bahl, Roy (2009) Property Tax Reform in Developing and Transition Countries (Washington D. C.: USAID).

[4] Bahl, Roy (2010). "Financing Metropolitan Areas" in Local Government finance: The challenges of the 21st Century, Second Global Report on decentralization and Local democracy (Cheltenham, UK: Edward Elgar).

[5] Bahl, R and Jorge Martinez – Vazquez (2006). "Sequencing Fiscal Decentralization". World Bank Policy Research Working Paper 3914, Public Sector Governance Group. Washington D. C.: World Bank.

[6] Bahl, Roy, and Jorge Martinez – Vazquez (2008). "The Property Tax in Developing Countries: Current Practice and Prospects" in Making the Property Tax Work: Experiences in Developing and Transitional Countries, ed. by Roy Bahl, Jorge Martinez – Vazquez and Joan Youngman (Cambridge: Lincoln Institute of Land Policy), pp. 35 – 57.

[7] Bahl, Roy, Chor – Ching Goh and Baoyun Qiao (2014). Reforming

the Public Finance System to Fit a More Urbanized China (Beijing: China Financial & Economic Publishing House).

[8] Bahl, Roy and Richard Bird (2008). "Subnational Taxes in Developing Countries: The Way Forward" Public Budgeting & Finance, Volume 28, Number 4, pp. 1 – 25.

[9] Bird, R. M. (2006) "Local and Regional Revenues: Realities and Prospects," in R. M. Bird and F. Vaillancourt, eds, Perspectives on Fiscal Federalism. WBI Learning Resources Series (Washington D. C.: World Bank), pp. 177 – 196.

[10] Bird, Richard (2013). "The VAT as a Local Business Tax" Tax Notes International, September 16, page 1 – 7.

[11] Bird, Richard and Enid Slack, editors (2004) International Handbook of Land and Property Taxation (Cheltenham, UK: Edward Elgar).

[12] Chen, Shiyi, and Jun Zhang (2008). The Efficiency of China Local Expenditure: 178 – 2005. China Social Science. 2008 (4) (in Chinese).

[13] De Cesare, Claudia (2010). "Overview of Property tax in Latin America". Working Paper WP10CD1 (Cambridge Ma: Lincoln Institute of Land policy).

[14] Gan, Li (2013, updated). "Findings from China Household Finance Survey" Powerpoint Presentation, (Texas A&M University).

[15] Hofman, Bert and Susana Cordeiro Guerra (2007). "Ensuring Inter-Regional Equity and Poverty Reduction" in Fiscal Equalization: Challenges in the Design of Intergovernmental Transfers edited by Jorge Martinez-Vazquez and Bob Searle (Springer) pp. 31 – 60.

[16] Hou, Yilin, Qiang Ren and Ping Zhang (2015). The Property tax in China: History, Pilots and Prospects (New York: Springer).

[17] Li, Junsheng, Baoyun Qiao, Lezheng Liu. (2014). "Building Sound Governance through Clearly Assigning Intergovernmental Resposibilities" [J]. Journal of Central University of Finance and Economics, 0 (03): 3 (in Chinese).

[18] Liu, Lili and Baoyun Qiao (2013). "Restructuring of Legacy Debt for Financing Rural Schools in China" in Until Debt Do Us Part: Subnational Debt, Insolvency, and Markets edited by Octaviano Canuto and Lili Liu (Washington D. C.: The World Bank), pp. 81 - 108.

[19] Lou, Jiwei. 2013. Rethinking of intergovernmental fiscal relations in China. Beijing: China Finance and Economics Press. [13] Lotz, Jorgen (2006). "Local Government Organization and Finance: Nordic Countries" in Local Government in Industrial Countries, ed. by Anwar Shah (Washington D. C.: World Bank) pp. 223 - 264.

[20] Lotz, Jorgen and Elliott Morss (1967). "Measuring Tax Effort in Developing Countries" International Monetary Fund Staff Papers. Volume 14, no. 3, pp. 478 - 499.

[21] Man, Joyce (2013). "Evaluation of Property Tax Reform and Experiments in China" Background paper prepared for world bank urbanization project, August 23, 2013.

[22] Martinez-Vazquez, Jorge (2013). "Local non - property tax revenues" in Financing Metropolitan Governments in Developing Countries edited by Roy Bahl, Johannes Linn and Deborah Wetzel, (Cambridge: Lincoln Institute of land Policy) pp. 183 - 212.

[23] Mathur, Om Prakash, Debdulal Thakur and NileshRajadhyasksha (2009). "Urban Property Tax Potential in India" (New Delhi: National Institute of Public Finance and Policy).

[24] McCluskey, W. J. and Riel Franzsen (2013). "Property taxes and Land Taxes" in Government Finance in Metropolitan Areas in Developing Countries edited by Roy Bahl, Johannes Linn and Deborah Wetzel (Cambridge: Lincoln Institute of land Policy).

[25] OECD (2006). "Stockholm, Sweden", OECD Territorial Reviews.

[26] OECD (2010). Governance in Guangdong, Territorial Reviews (Paris: OECD).

[27] Qiao, Baoyun and Lezheng Liu, 2013, Intergovernmental Fiscal Relationship and Risk-sharing Function: Background and Framework. Intergovernmental Fiscal Relationship and the Risk-sharing Function of Public Finance, edited by Baoyun Qiao and Lezheng Liu. China Financial and Economic Publishing House: Beijing.

[28] Qiao, Baoyun, Lezheng Liu, Yin Xundong, Guo Shen (2014). "A Comparative Study on Local Government Incentives" [J]. Economic Research, 2014 (10): 102 – 110 (in Chinese).

[29] Research on the Establishment of Modern Fiscal System in Shandong, Shandong Province March2, 2015.

[30] Smolka, Martim (2013) Implementing Value Capture in Latin America: Policies and Tools for Urban Development, Policy Focus Report (Cambridge: Mass, Lincoln Institute of land Policy).

[31] Wetzel, Deborah (2013). "Metropolitan Governance and Finance in Sao Paulo" in Government Finance in Metropolitan Areas in Developing Countries edited by Roy Bahl, Johannes Linn and Deborah Wetzel (Cambridge: Lincoln Institute of land Policy), pp. 309 – 338.

[32] Wong, Christine (2012). "Toward building Performance – Oriented Management in China: The Critical role of Monitoring and Evaluation

and the Long Road Ahead" ECD Working Paper no. 27 (Washington: World Bank).

[33] Wong, Christine (2013) "Paying for Urbanization in China: Challenges of China's Municipal Finance in the Twenty – First Century" in Government Finance in Metropolitan Areas in Developing Countries edited by Roy Bahl, Johannes Linn and Deborah Wetzel (Cambridge: Lincoln Institute of land Policy), pp. 273 – 308.

[34] Wong, Christine, Christopher Heady and Wing T. Woo (1995), Fiscal Management and Economics Reform in the People's Republic of China, Hong Kong: Oxford University Press.

[35] World Bank (2013). Beyond the Annual Budget: Global experience with Medium Term Expenditure Frameworks (Washington D. C.: The World Bank).

[36] World Bank (2015). "China Economic Update: Reform Priorities in China's Financial Sector" (World Bank, Beijing, June).

[37] World Bank and Development Research Center (2013). China 2030: Building a Modern, Harmonious, and Creative Society (Washington D. C.: World Bank).

[38] World Bank and Development Research Center (2014). Urban China: Toward Efficient, Inclusive and Sustainable Urbanization (Washington D. C.: The World Bank).